AESTHETICS OF EQUILIBRIUM

Purdue Studies in Romance Literatures

 volume 36

AESTHETICS OF EQUILIBRIUM

The Vanguard Poetics

of Vicente Huidobro

and Mário de Andrade

Bruce Dean Willis

Purdue University Press
West Lafayette, Indiana

∞ The paper used in this book meets the minimum requirements of American National Standard for Information Sciences—Permanence of Paper for Printed Library Materials, ANSI Z39.48-1992.

Printed in the United States of America
Design by Anita Noble

Library of Congress Cataloging-in-Publication Data
Willis, Bruce Dean, 1968–
   The vanguard poetics of Vicente Huidobro and Mário de Andrade / Bruce Dean Willis.
      p.   cm. — (Purdue studies in romance literatures ; v. 36)
   Includes bibliographical references and index.
   ISBN-13: 978-1-55753-422-4 (alk. paper)
   ISBN-10: 1-55753-422-5
      1. Huidobro, Vicente, 1893–1948—Criticism and interpretation. 2. Andrade, Mário de, 1893–1945—Criticism and interpretation. 3. Latin American Poetry—20th century—History and criticism. I. Title II. Series.
   PQ8097.H8Z955 2006
   861'.62—dc22   2006001192

Contents

Contents

List of Abbreviations

The following abbreviations have been used to refer to the works of Mário de Andrade.

PC
Poesias Completas

OI
Obra Imatura

"Prefácio"
"Prefácio" in PC

Paulicéia
Paulicéia Desvairada in PC

"Parábola"
"Parábola d'*A escrava que não é Isaura*" in OI

Escrava
A escrava que não é Isaura in OI

Preface

The Latin American Avant-Garde

Context for Vicente Huidobro's
and Mário de Andrade's Poetics

Generally defined as the era between the world wars, the avant-garde or vanguard period was a time of unprecedented urban and industrial growth and consequent struggles to define the young republics of Latin America.[1] These artistic acts of self-definition, mindful of the European vanguard movements' disparaging treatments of Western tradition and revered awe for so-called "primitive" cultures, revolutionized Latin American literary, musical, and plastic art expressions. Although the vanguard movements can be thought of as united by their European heritage, pertaining to formal and thematic innovations that were part of a general, ongoing process of artistic change, they can also stand apart, each related to the particular aesthetic and social issues that served as its national or regional foci. Brazilian *modernistas,* for example, revolutionized literary expression in Brazilian (as opposed to Continental) Portuguese, while Mexican *estridentistas* rhetoricized the social progress of the Mexican Revolution, yet artists in both movements were influenced by Italian futurism. In classifications of the avant-garde, Vicente Huidobro (1893–1948) is inevitably associated with his movement, *creacionismo* (creationism, sometimes called literary cubism), and Mário de Andrade (1893–1945) with Brazilian *modernismo* (he was an acknowledged leader and received the informal title of "Pope of Modernism"), in the same way that Manuel Maples Arce represents *estridentismo* or the early Borges *ultraísmo.*[2] These classifications are meaningful in that they help to comprehend the varying strategies of the vanguard movements, yet the classified movements may also be seen as different means to the same end. The common goal of all the movements is the writing of literature, especially poetry, as an original, subjective, and subversive act. These avant-garde context terms—original, subjective, subversive— set the parameters for dynamic creative acts that challenge artistic traditions. Each individual artist explains his or her own vision, although all the artists break with the rules and standards of the past while desiring a new, modern, simultaneous, and total (and thus universal) mode of expression.

In spite of regional differences, most analysts defend the universality of the Latin American movements as parts of one avant-garde linked to Europe and North America.[3] The generally Eurocentric orientation of the Latin American vanguard movements, in fact, meant that a Peruvian vanguard writer, for instance, would probably be more familiar with what was being written in Paris, Madrid, or Berlin than in Buenos Aires, Santiago, or São Paulo. When this paradoxical state of affairs became obvious to those Latin American artists who had traveled in Europe and been asked about their fellow Latin American artists, the returning travelers published Panamerican anthologies, included more works by fellow Latin Americans in their little magazines, and strengthened contacts with other Latin Americans met in Europe. Such attempts often did not move beyond mere catalogues of names and, with few exceptions, did not foment transnational movements or cooperation; moreover, almost all of these fleeting inter-Latin American contacts were among fellow Spanish Americans to the exclusion of Brazilians. Notable exceptions include writer/philosopher Alfonso Reyes's influential stay in Brazil as Mexican ambassador, Chilean poet Gabriela Mistral's visit to Brazil, and Mário de Andrade's newspaper reviews of Borges, Girondo, Güiraldes, and the Buenos Aires literary scene.

Current scholars of the vanguard period have more aggressively developed Spanish American / Brazilian comparative studies. Beyond the excellent resources in the separate Brazilian and Spanish American fields, the paramount resources that unite the two fields comparatively include Merlin H. Forster and K. David Jackson's landmark *Vanguardism in Latin American Literature* (1990), Jorge Schwartz's annotated compilation *Las vanguardias latinoamericanas* (1991) and Mihai Grünfeld's *Antología de la poesía latinoamericana de vanguardia* (1995). The development of such resources has been paralleled by book-length comparative studies of Latin American poetry, for example Gordon Brotherston's book (1975) and the collaborative effort of Mike González and David Treece (1992). As far as the vanguard period is concerned, the culmination of these comparative efforts and a standard for the next generation is Vicky Unruh's *Latin American Vanguards: The Art of Contentious Encounters* (1994), covering a half-dozen major themes each represented by four or five pithy analyses of the works of vanguardists from all over the continent.

A survey of Forster and Jackson's extensive bibliography and *Las literaturas hispánicas de vanguardia* by Harald Wentzlaff-Eggebert confirms the favored holistic approach to the Latin American vanguards while revealing that the majority of critical studies of this period focus on poetic strategies either within one work, among the poems of one author, or among the poems of one movement. Attention has been given to the analysis and classification of the various literary magazines that were of paramount importance at the time, such as *Amauta, Contemporáneos, Klaxon, Martín Fierro,* and *Revista de Avance,* and to comparisons of Latin American with European avant-garde expressions. Several scholars have compiled manifestos and related prose works into anthologies with explanatory introductions, some opting to organize the texts according to literary and social issues, with chapter headings such as *creacionismo, criollismo, indigenismo,* and *negrismo* (Schwartz, Gloria Videla de Rivero), while other compilers and bibliographers have conformed to political geography (Forster and Jackson, Nelson Osorio, Schwartz, Hugo Verani, Wentzlaff-Eggebert). A recent and innovative compilation of critical articles is *¡Agítese bien! A New Look at the Hispanic Avant-Gardes* (including analysis of Brazilian works), addressing "texts which engaged extra-literary cultural manifestations" such as fashion, sport, and jazz (Pao and Hernández-Rodríguez xvii).

The present analysis breaks new ground by focusing thoroughly on the writings on poetics of Huidobro and Mário as two of the most influential Latin Americans of the vanguard period.[4] Although they represented different movements, nations, and linguistic traditions within the avant-garde, they shared similar poetic ideas and, more importantly, expressed those ideas in similar ways. Specifically, I trace the development and use of the writers' concept of equilibrium as a polysemantic metaphor (allegory, parable, leitmotif) and as a rhetorical device (aphorism, discourse, example) for expressing aesthetic ideas in prose about the process of creating poetry. Existing literary studies of Mário's and Huidobro's texts have focused almost exclusively on their poems, novels, and dramatic works. Few anthologists of their essays and related theoretical prose have provided studies of these texts as literary works, overlooking in large part the need for literary analysis of the metaphorical and rhetorical relationships within and among these texts. Additionally, the present study's focus on the essay or theoretical prose genre complements the critical attention that these kinds of texts by vanguard writers such as Mariátegui, Vasconcelos, and Pedro Henríquez Ureña have received. Thinking about avant-garde literature as an original, subjective, and subversive act provides a fertile environment for the comparative study of these texts. The extent to which each writer's prose works on aesthetics can be understood to represent avant-garde aesthetics in a universal sense will be explored and challenged within the particular geopolitical context, social circumstances, and literary influences of each.

• The Historical Context of the Avant-Garde

The avant-garde expresses common goals of originality, subjectivity, and subversion because it has always been associated with pushing the limits of style or developing a new aesthetic, in every way moving on past tradition, even past itself, to modernity. The very selection and use of the term *avant-garde,* as explored by Matei Calinescu in *Five Faces of Modernity,* attempted to define the modern moment:

> The obvious military implications of the concept point quite aptly toward some attitudes and trends for which the avant-garde is directly indebted to the broader consciousness of modernity—a sharp sense of militancy, praise of nonconformism, courageous precursory exploration, and, on a more general plane, confidence in the final victory of *time* and immanence over traditions that try to appear as eternal, immutable, and transcendentally determined. (95; original emphasis)

Indeed, this victory of time over tradition is the same that Octavio Paz identifies as a tradition in itself, "la tradición de la ruptura" which is *the* modern tradition: "es la expresión de la condición dramática de nuestra civilización que busca su fundamento, no en el pasado ni en ningún principio inconmovible, sino en el cambio" (*Los hijos del limo* 24). The artistic mission of the avant-garde becomes, therefore, the establishment of the tradition of change.

Such a mission is fundamentally paradoxical. Calinescu notes that as early as the 1860s, when the term was just beginning to be used in an artistic context (and long before cubism and futurism), Baudelaire had already recognized the inherent paradox of an "advance guard" in the guise of the disciplined conformity that the military metaphor connotes (110). This insight proved to be a prophecy fulfilled in the constant splintering and congealing of avant-garde groups, the often abortive attempts to produce definitive manifestos and literary magazines, and the race to label and support promising, independent young artists. The members of the avant-garde reacted against the very practice of establishing schools of artistic expression, instead placing supreme value on the unique and individual expression of each artist. Yet they constantly developed new movements, groups or "ismos" and spent much effort on proselytizing. René de Costa has summarized this contradiction: "Everyone in the avant-garde wanted to be original and yet belong to a movement" (*Vicente Huidobro: The Careers of a Poet* 47). Paz's "tradición de la ruptura" is thus present in the struggle to define how much change (nonconformism) can be accommodated by tradition, or how much tradition (conformity) can be tolerated in an ever-changing artistic environment.

Even in their haste to break free from the bonds of the past, the vanguardists displayed, and to a lesser extent acknowledged, both earlier and contemporary literary influences. Most important of the earlier influences were the French symbolists, who were themselves seen as iconoclasts; it was easy for the vanguardists to assimilate them as representatives of a visionary tradition, worthy of much praise for their ideals and inspiring some emulation of their techniques. The intensified suggestiveness of metaphor as the unconscious unit of expression, which the Symbolists found in their precursor

Baudelaire, became, in turn, the Symbolists' greatest legacy to the vanguard poets. Regarding Huidobro's inheritance of Symbolist tendencies, Frank Paul Rutter describes his technical and thematic affinities with Baudelaire's otherworldly images in *Fleurs du mal,* Verlaine's typography and rhythm, Rimbaud's verbal precision, and Mallarmé's themes of emptiness and absence, though Rutter stresses Huidobro's indirect assimilation of these traits (61–108). Videla de Rivero also alludes to the importance of Baudelaire, Rimbaud, and Mallarmé; Rimbaud especially influenced Huidobro's *creacionismo* through the idea of the poet as a visionary or mystic who can sense and express what the ordinary person cannot perceive, a concept itself derivative of the Romantic conception of the poet as seer (36). In Mário's case, Gilberto Mendonça Teles recognizes the influence of the Symbolists (and their immediate precursors) in Brazil, stressing particularly Baudelaire's synesthesia, Rimbaud's challenging of the conventionality of signifiers in "Alchimie du verbe," the musical composition elements of Verlaine and Mallarmé, and the idea of the collective soul in Jules Romains's *unanimismo.* Teles claims that this latter movement, which developed an antagonism to the Symbolists, influenced the composition of Mário's *Paulicéia Desvairada* (*Vanguarda* 19–54).

Contemporary literary influence upon the Latin American avant-garde came primarily from European avant-garde writers and, to a very reduced extent, from other avant-garde writers of the Americas. In general terms, Videla de Rivero highlights *cosmopolitismo* as an important unifying tendency of the vanguard on both sides of the Atlantic (5–17). To be cosmopolitan essentially meant to be well-read and up-to-date on the latest literary tendencies, no matter whether one was writing about rural areas and themes (Ricardo Güiraldes's 1926 *Don Segundo Sombra,* for example) or about the city itself (Maples Arce's 1924 *Urbe).* In this way, the general ideas of Marinetti, Edschmid, Apollinaire, Tzara, Breton, and others were rapidly assimilated and heatedly discussed. Specific connections among Huidobro or Mário with their contemporaries in Europe and the Americas will arise in context in later chapters; at this point the results of general comparative studies will be summarized, keeping in mind that most of the influential artists associated with Huidobro were his acquaintances, whereas almost all of those associated with Mário, except his fellow Brazilians, were known to him only in print.

Rutter develops Huidobro's stylistic similarities with members of the *Nord-Sud* magazine group in Paris—Apollinaire, Blaise Cendrars, and Pierre Reverdy; the latter disputed with Huidobro the originality of the *creacionista* style, a debate that gave rise to numerous critical analyses and that was finally settled (129–81). Mireya Camurati highlights the sources of *creacionismo* in Emerson, Gabriel Alomar, and Armando Vasseur; both Camurati and especially Susana Benko explore Huidobro's links to the cubists in Paris—most notably Picasso, Gris, and Delaunay—regarding simultaneity and the visual impact of poems. A large and still-growing bibliography exists concerning Huidobro's relationships with the founding members of the Spanish and Argentine *ultraísta* groups; likewise there is much anecdotal material detailing Huidobro's quarrels with Neruda, Pablo de Rohka, and other artistic personalities. The main sources for all of this latter material are David Bary, Jaime Concha, and de Costa.

Teles identifies Apollinaire as an important source for Mário's writings on aesthetics. Apollinaire was well known to Mário not only through his literary treatise *L'esprit nouveau et les poètes* but also, posthumously, through the Parisian journal founded in 1920 and named, in honor of his book, *L'Esprit Nouveau (Vanguarda* 83, 163–64). Charles Russell's description of Apollinaire's attempts to translate pictorial simultaneity into a poetic style (81–86) reflects what would become Mário's main theoretical interest in polyphonics/simultaneity. Maria Helena Grembecki bases her study of Mário's influences on his reception of the ideas of the *L'Esprit Nouveau* contributors, especially Paul Dermée, Jean Epstein, and Huidobro himself; the reader notes in *A escrava que não é Isaura* that Mário was also quite familiar with the Italian futurists, French surrealists, German expressionists, and other vanguard writers in Russia, Spain, the Netherlands, and the United States, not to mention Brazil. Nites Therezinha Feres also studies Mário's vast readings (and his analytical notes in the margin) of French authors, while Haroldo de Campos highlights Mário's familiarity with the German vanguard, especially August Stramm.

• Personas and Ouevres

The literary and cultural accomplishments of Huidobro and Mário exemplify their status as cosmopolitan paragons.[5] Huidobro traveled to Europe and back seven times in his life, sometimes staying there several years at a time. His contacts with the avant-garde in Paris and Madrid were numerous and fruitful. Though mostly unsuccessful in promoting his *creacionismo* movement, he was instrumental in sparking interest in the general avant-garde period in Spain, Argentina, and Chile (and to a lesser extent in Latin American nations he did not visit, such as Cuba, Mexico, and the Dominican Republic). This was a direct result of the impact of five books showcasing the primacy of the shocking image, all published in Madrid in 1918—*Hallali, Tour Eiffel, Poemas Articos, Ecuatorial,* and a second edition of *El espejo de agua.* His success was also, to some extent, the result of his scandalous personality. Beyond the consideration of his many petty grudges against other artists and writers, some of his more notorious acts included his clandestine elopement with Ximena Amunátegui, the daughter of a well-off Santiago family, and the subsequent abandonment of his wife and children; the staging of his own kidnapping in Europe, supposedly in retaliation for the anti-imperialist dogma of his *Finis Britannia;* an unsuccessful campaign for the presidency of Chile, marred by the detonation of a bomb in front of his house; and an eventually fatal head wound received while a correspondent in Germany at the end of World War II—he claimed Hitler's personal telephone as his trophy. His mature expression in *Altazor* and *Temblor de cielo,* his innovative style in *Mío Cid Campeador* and *Cagliostro,* and his experimental staging in *En la luna* have earned those works a place of fundamental importance in the development of poetic, narrative, and performance strategies in twentieth-century Latin America. His manifestos, though less known, are essential to understanding Huidobro's thought regarding the ideal practice of poetics.

Mário traveled outside Brazil just once, and although he made a few trips to different areas of the Brazilian interior and lived in Rio de Janeiro for a few years, he only infrequently left his beloved city of São Paulo. Active in both the musical and literary milieux of that city, he was propelled to fame by his leadership in the February 1922 Modern Art Week and his publication of *Paulicéia Desvairada* that same year. His poetic and narrative works and his critical essays on music, literature, linguistics, folklore, dance, and cinema fill some dozen volumes of his *Obras completas*. In addition, his prolific correspondence has been published over the years since his death in another dozen or so volumes. During his lifetime he held numerous cultural offices, including director of São Paulo's Departamento de Cultura, professor of philosophy and art history at the Universidade do Distrito Federal, and founder of São Paulo's Sociedade de Etnografia e Folclore. He was an enthusiastic promoter of the founding of the Universidade de São Paulo. His interest in ethnography led him to make the excursions to the interior and to the northeastern regions of Brazil; this interest reached its artistic apogee in his narrative masterpiece, *Macunaíma*. This heteroglossic "rapsódia" [rhapsody] exemplifies Mário's desire to celebrate a pan-Brazilian cultural tradition and idiom, especially evident in the syncretism of dialects and in linguistic experimentation, as also in his poetry collection *Clã do Jaboti*. As the acknowledged "Pope" of the *modernista* movement, Mário wrote the treatise *A escrava que não é Isaura*. This work and the "Prefácio Interessantíssimo" of *Paulicéia Desvairada* are the essential texts for understanding the aesthetic orientation of *modernismo* both as a national movement and as a part of the international vanguard. Though not widely known abroad at the time, these texts were very influential in Brazil.

As can be surmised from their extra-literary activities, Huidobro and Mário were men of very different lifestyles and priorities. Yet as far as their literary trajectories, both writers moved from producing conservative juvenilia (*Ecos del alma* [1911] and *Há uma gota de sangue em cada poema* [1917]) to masterpieces of vanguard expression in poetry and prose (*Altazor* [1931], *Mío Cid Campeador* [1929] and *Paulicéia Desvairada* [1922], *Macunaíma* [1928]). Both struggled to differentiate their ideas from already existing or concurrent movements: Huidobro especially from surrealism and Mário mostly from futurism. Both had works translated into English during their lifetimes; *Mío Cid Campeador* (1929) and *Cagliostro* (1934) were published as *Portrait of a Paladin* (1931) and

Mirror of a Mage (1931), and Mário's novel *Amar, verbo intransitivo* (1927) was translated into English with the title *Fraulein* (1933). Most importantly for the concerns of this analysis, both authors wrote significant theoretical prose works dedicated to the definition and expression of avant-garde poetics.

• Comparative Studies of Huidobro and Mário

Existing comparative studies of Huidobro and Mário outline trajectories as above or briefly note salient comparisons. Ana Pizarro's *Sobre Huidobro y las vanguardias*, besides mentioning Huidobro's similarities with the Brazilian *antropofagia* movement and impact on the Brazilian *concretistas,* offers the comparison of Huidobro's *Mío Cid Campeador* and Mário's *Macunaíma* as narrative models. The texts were published within a year of each other, both can loosely be classified as experimental novels, and both are "un común hurgar en los orígenes, la necesidad de afincar y afincarse en una tradición" (67).[6] In "Huidobro e o Brasil" José Santiago Naud sets up a concise series of correspondences between Huidobro's poetics and Brazilian *modernismo.* For Naud, Huidobro and Mário converge "na crítica à situação da América Latina, que padece da falta de um centro cultural e sofre pressões de dependência" [in criticism of the Latin American situation, which suffers from the lack of a cultural center and from the pressure of dependency] (29).[7] Comparing fragments from *Altazor* and *Paulicéia Desvairada,* Naud tellingly affirms: "Neles a impulsão lírica (Poética) e a reflexão crítica (Retórica) consolidam uma entidade em equilíbrio; o belo natural e o belo artístico completam-se" [In them the lyric impulse (Poetry) and critical reflection (Rhetoric) consolidate an entity in equilibrium; natural beauty and artistic beauty make each other whole] (30–31). Focusing on music as a metaphor for the characteristically vanguard use of heteroglossia, Unruh links Mário's "concept of poetic polyphony using a simultaneous overlay of disconnected phrases" in his "Prefácio Interessantíssimo" with Huidobro's "comparable weaving together of voices through the words that have been 'enemies since the beginning of the world'" in his manifesto "La poesía" (243–44).

In an outstanding comparative analysis chapter of *Na Ilha de Marapatá,* Raúl Antelo explores Huidobro's influence, through his publications in French in *L'Esprit Nouveau* (especially "La création pure"), on Mário, a relationship he labels "um dos primeiros e mais férteis vínculos do Modernismo com a poesia de vanguarda latino-americana" [one of the first and most fertile links of *modernismo* to Latin American vanguardist poetry] (6). Antelo develops major aesthetic parallels and discordances between them, comparing their senses of the poet's fluctuating relationship with the bourgeosie, for example, or the epic tones of *Altazor* and Mário's "Eu sou trezentos." Antelo's insightful conclusion differentiates Huidobro's inherent and ultimately isolating authoritarianism from Mário's greater emotional need to connect to popular culture.

The first comparative article focusing exclusively on the two writers was Leonilda Ambrozio's 1982 "Mário de Andrade e Vicente Huidobro: Identidades." Although Ambrozio bases her brief article on some of the same theoretical texts to be considered in the present analysis, she limits her conclusions to a few points of agreement and disagreement between the authors, for example: "Portanto, tanto Huidobro como Mário acreditam na necessidade do esforço consciente do poeta" [Thus, both Huidobro and Mário believe in the necessity of the poet's conscious force] (110) and "Quanto à métrica, Mário é menos radical" [As far as meter, Mário is less radical] (111). She is right to bemoan the persistent lack of communication between Brazilian and Spanish American literature as a lamentable reality, a circumstance that limited what could have been a much greater contact between the Brazilian *modernistas* and Spanish American vanguard artists. In general, her conclusions are undeniable, yet they are only the tip of the iceberg. What Ambrozio left out of her brief quotations from diverse texts is the thrust of the present study: the analysis of these theoretical texts as literary works in their own right, with characteristic techniques, images, and structures that lend force to the expression of a new poetics.

Such a literary analysis of these poetics texts is my intent here, and not a comparison of the stated poetics with poetry by the same writers. Besides the fact that the latter approach is the more common (and there already exist such studies on

Huidobro and Mário which will be mentioned in later contexts), it is also the more inexact, mixing ideas from both sources in a sometimes rushed desire to achieve a total exegesis. Poetics and poetry are often thought of as demarcating a relationship not unlike that of Saussure's *langue* and *parole,* in which poetics represents the range of ideal possibilities, while a poem can be only one concrete actualization of those possibilities. Hence a necessary distance exists between the two kinds of texts, even within the critical evaluation of the same author. Baudelaire provides a classic example of this distinction in his ironic remark about Poe: "Behold a poet who pretends that his poetry was composed according to his own poetics" (qtd. in Poggioli 165). A poetics expresses an idealized aesthetic desire that an individual poem or even a collection of poems may not manage to encompass entirely.

- ## An Aesthetics of Equilibrium: Theme and Variations

I propose to demonstrate that an aesthetics of equilibrium became the central concept in Mário's and Huidobro's poetics, and that the ways in which both writers appropriated the applications of such a concept support a more concrete understanding of key questions they sought to address: What is the role of the unconscious in artistic creation? Should conscious expression be abandoned, as Breton and the surrealists claimed? Is an inspired poet ruled by the heart or by the mind? How can a poet more directly engage a larger public? How does a Latin American artist reconcile European and autochthonous influences? Such a concept of equilibrium did already exist in European vanguard parlance before either Huidobro or Mário used the term in an aesthetic context. Mário's explicit references to European writers leave no doubt about the term's origin, and although Huidobro had intuited the concept in his early writings, his use of the term dates from after his collaboration with *L'Esprit Nouveau* and other European magazines. *L'Esprit Nouveau* was an important source, with which both writers were familiar, for the idea and image of equilibrium in an aesthetic context, in other words in the context of theorizing and prescribing new norms for considerations on taste and beauty in art. In several issues of the magazine, the concept of equilibrium describes a desired or pleasing style. For example, the font and centering of the large-print title of the essay "Science et esthétique: Équilibre" by Paul Recht draws the reader's eye to the term *équilibre*. Recht's essay promotes equilibrium as a dynamic and harmonic life essence, in addition to linking aesthetics to scientific discourse, a popular tendency that both Mário and Huidobro would follow:

> L'équilibre n'est pas l'inertie, tout au contraire. Sa plénitude vivante n'est atteinte que par le maximum de déséquilibres élémentaires qui se compensent, s'annulent, s'adaptent et finalement se cohèrent, si bien que la *sensation* d'équilibre en résulte. [. . .] *L'équilibre est harmonieux ipso facto.* [. . .] Le sens de la vie, je veux dire son orientation, se révèle toujours par un changement d'équilibre. (483–85; original emphasis)

Metabolism, the orbits of the planets, and Brownian motion are all invoked as natural examples of equilibrium, although Recht also develops the concept on an aesthetic level when he notes that artistic genius means producing a balanced order in the midst of disorder. Renowned French architect Le Corbusier offers a more elemental and schematic approach to the concept of equilibrium in "Le sentiment déborde":

> Il est naturel que l'homme cherchant le bonheur s'efforce vers un sentiment d'équilibre. Équilibre = calme, maîtrise des moyens, lecture claire, ordonnance, satisfaction de l'esprit, mesure, proportion, —en vérité: création. Le déséquilibre témoigne d'un état de lutte, d'inquiétude, de difficultés non résolvés, d'asservissement, de recherches, stade inférieure et antérieur, préparatoire. Déséquilibre: état de fatigue. Équilibre: état de bien-être.

Le Corbusier's style exemplifies the vanguard desires to list, define, and equate. Strikingly, he equates equilibrium with creation, an important notion that Huidobro and Mário develop much more thoroughly. Le Corbusier's use of an equation with the equals sign (=) (evoking Marinetti's prescription to use mathematical and musical signs in his 1912 "technical" futurist manifesto), and Recht's specification of a *maximum* quantity, are linguistic and graphic traits that appear in the poetics of both Latin American writers, especially Mário's.

I begin this analysis with a detailed comparative study of two parables, one by each author, which opens a theoretical framework for exploring the techniques and goals of the authors' poetics of equilibrium (Introduction). Huidobro's first manifesto, "Non serviam," and Mário's "Parábola," which opens his poetic treatise *A escrava que não é Isaura,* define the desire for equilibrium in poetic creation through a rich thematic cluster, common to both texts, of biblical references, the slave-and-master paradigm, gender roles, and revolutionary rhetoric. Individual chapters (in parts 1 and 2) devoted to the main theoretical texts of Huidobro and Mário follow the opening analysis. The chapters consider the formal and thematic characteristics of each text separately before offering collective analyses of Huidobro's *Manifiestos* and Mário's "Prefácio Interessantíssimo" and *A escrava que não é Isaura,* with references to additional key poems, essays, and interviews or correspondence by each writer. The conclusion, after a brief comparative summary of the two writers' ideas and techniques in light of the descriptive and prescriptive functions of a poetics, probes the stabilizing role of a poetics of equilibrium within the temporal constraints of the avant-garde as understood by theorists such as Paz, Renato Poggioli, Charles Russell, Unruh, and John Weightman.

Acknowledgments

The initial stage of this project was conceived as my dissertation at the University of Virginia, where the Department of Spanish, Italian, and Portuguese cultivated a supportive environment for my independent study comparing the Spanish American and Brazilian vanguards. I especially acknowledge David T. Haberly and Donald L. Shaw, my advisors, for their inspiration and patience. Dr. Shaw's quick and insightful comments on my drafts, and his critical guidance in the comprehensive planning and structure of my research, were most appreciated. Dr. Haberly's encyclopedic knowledge and contagious enthusiasm for all things Luso-Brazilian have been a solid foundation for me since the beginning of my research into the Brazilian vanguard; his very helpful and honest support continued in his thorough readings of my drafts. Other readers who provided lucid feedback, suggestions, and support in the initial stages of this project include Gustavo Pellón, Karen Rauch, E. C. Graf, and Jeff Bersett. Special thanks also to Keith Mason and Cathy Cuppett for moral support and for help with technical aspects of beginning and completing the project.

The opportunity to build on my previous research became possible during my time at the University of South Alabama. While at the university, Lawrence R. Schehr aided me in bringing out theoretical aspects of some of my readings and, with Bernard Quinn and Calvin Jones, helped me develop the potential of such a research opportunity. The University of South Alabama Research Council, in conjunction with the College of Arts and Sciences and the Department of Foreign Languages and Literatures, funded my travel to Brazil and Chile in July and August 2000, enabling me to carry out archival research at the Instituto de Estudos Brasileiros (IEB) on the campus of the Universidade de São Paulo, and at the Fundación Vicente Huidobro (FVH) and Biblioteca Nacional in Santiago. This research led to the strengthening of my conclusions regarding the thematic importance of equilibrium in the works of both writers and in the cultural context of the times. I gratefully acknowledge the support of the IEB staff, particularly Murillo Marx and Maria Teresa Joia, and also time spent in consultation with Telê Porto Ancona Lopez at the IEB. In

Santiago the FVH executive secretary, Liliana Rosa Beraterrechea, graciously facilitated my research at that archive.

Some of the material in this book has appeared in earlier versions. The Introduction was published as "A Desire for Equilibrium in Avant-Garde Poetics: Vicente Huidobro's 'Non serviam' and Mário de Andrade's 'Parábola d'*A escrava que não é Isaura*'" in *Chasqui* 26.2 (1997): 56–71. Approximately the first half of the material in Chapter 5, "At the Dock and on the Street," appeared as "Necessary Losses: Purity and Solidarity in Mário de Andrade's Dockside Poetics" in *Hispania* 81 (1998): 217–24. Chapter 2, "Orientation and Trajectory," is a revised and translated version of "Orientación y trayectoria de Huidobro en 'Aviso a los turistas' y 'Manifiesto tal vez,'" *Hispanófila* 134 (2002): 75–90. I thank these journals' editorial boards and reviewers for their comments and suggestions.

I extend thanks to my colleagues in the Department of Languages at the University of Tulsa for their steady confidence in and support for my research, and my gratitude to two anonymous readers for the Purdue Studies in Romance Literatures series for their remarks and recommendations. Many thanks to PSRL's production editor, Susan Y. Clawson, for her wisdom and patience. Finally, the support of my family has been paramount to me throughout this project. I thank my wife, Blanca, and daughters, Giselle and Juliette, for their patience and understanding, and my father and mother, Drs. Craig D. and Marilyn E. Willis, for their encouragement, enthusiasm, and empathy.

A Note on Translation and Orthography

Text cited in Spanish and French appears without translation, as per PSRL policy. Text in Portuguese is followed by a bracketed English translation. Longer translations, located in the Appendix, are keyed to the text by the number in brackets. All translations are my own unless otherwise indicated. Because of changes in Portuguese orthography rules, and also because of the Brazilian Modernists' desire to distinguish written Brazilian Portuguese from European standards, the spelling in Mário de Andrade's texts sometimes differs from the current norms. I have cited his texts, from the sources I list, without altering his spelling.

Introduction

A Desire for Equilibrium in Avant-Garde Poetics

The Parables "Non serviam"
and "Parabola d'*A escrava que não é Isaura*"

Among the manifestos, prologues, declarations, and other proclamatory texts characteristic of the avant-garde period's various movements, the expression of a new poetics dominates the subject matter and tends to exemplify itself in the very format of these texts. Employing a variety of styles, the texts are sometimes allegorical; those few texts that are strictly allegorical tend to be well represented in anthologies but too often overlooked in critical analyses. In fact, these allegorical works constitute not just theoretical but also narrative sources for beliefs about poetics, and as such they are particularly rich in language, symbol, and structure. I wish to identify Huidobro's "Non serviam" and Mário's "Parábola d'*A escrava que não é Isaura*" specifically as parables. The parable is a kind of allegory that

> illustrates a moral attitude, a doctrine, a standard of conduct, or a religious principle [. . .] The simple narratives of parables give them a mysterious, suggestive tone and make them especially useful for the teaching of moral and spiritual truths. ("Parable")

Another kind of truth, intrinsic to these vanguard parables, can be added to the definition: artistic truth. Since the parable as a genre has a well-known biblical context, both authors' use of the parable format likens their expressions of artistic truth to the spiritual insights imparted by Christ; this relationship has special relevance in interpreting the poet's prophetic role. Furthermore, the parable genre's "suggestive tone" stimulates the exploration of symbolic identities such as feminine and masculine images and, in the present case, the roles of slave and

1

master. I make the generic designation of parable exclusively for the purpose of the present study; Huidobro makes no mention of the word *parable* in his text, and Mário, although he gives his text the title of "Parábola," vacillates between the terms *história* and *quase parábola* in its opening paragraph.

The sparse critical attention devoted to these separate parables mixes them, in the case of each author, with that author's other theoretical works; the tendency has been to pursue a theme or idea monolithically, quoting as needed from different manifestos or other texts and contexts. José Quiroga's detailed look at "Non serviam" constitutes a worthy exception and will be addressed below. The comparative studies of Huidobro's and Mário's works or literary trajectories mentioned in the Preface do not engage a direct comparison of the two parables. In contrast, the aim of this introduction is the comparative literary analysis of these specific poetics texts, without, at this point, drawing any relationship to other poetics texts or to poetry by the same writers.

Huidobro claimed that he read "Non serviam" as a conference presentation in the Ateneo of Santiago in 1914.[1] Allegorically, the text defines a new poetics in the form of the confrontation between a rebellious poet slave and his mistress, Mother Nature.[2] Anthologized as the first of Huidobro's manifestos, the text can be divided into three sections: the third-person narrative, the poet's address to his fellow poets, and the poet's words to Mother Nature. Juan Larrea reveals that the title of Huidobro's parable comes from "Futurismo," a 1904 text (before Marinetti's futurist manifesto) in which the author, Gabriel Alomar, portrays Adam as "el primer indómito, el primer protervo, que ha lanzado el *non serviam* representando la protesta de la humanidad" (qtd. in Larrea 227). This leads to the discovery of a key similarity between Huidobro's and Mário's parables through the character of Adam; Huidobro's unnamed poet is a metamorphosis of Alomar's Adam.[3] The casting of Huidobro's "Non serviam" protagonist as an Adam figure can indeed be intuited from the parable text alone, but the knowledge of Alomar's proclamation makes it clearer and, moreover, links it definitively to Huidobro's 1916 *Adán*, his first free-verse poetry. The parable's unnamed protagonist thus prefigures Huidobro's all-encompassing Protagonist; as

Quiroga argues, "All of Huidobro's heroes, from *Altazor* to *Mío Cid Campeador,* are descendants (or we should say substitutions) of Adam" (520).

Mário's parable forms the introduction to his theoretical treatise, *A escrava que não é Isaura,* written between 1922 and 1924 and published in 1925.[4] The treatise forms a sequel to the "Prefácio Interessantíssimo" of his *Paulicéia Desvairada.* He had written the "Prefácio," after producing the poems that form the body of *Paulicéia,* as a conciliatory explanation of his poetry's aesthetic context. Before publication, *Pauliceia* had been labeled *futurista* by the vanguard leader Oswald de Andrade, provoking a spate of conservative fervor in São Paulo newspapers. "Parábola," which deals with the creation, corruption, and rediscovery of poetic language, forms the structural foundation of the treatise, both as its textual beginning and as a constant point of reference throughout. In the parable, Poetry is Eve's rival, a slave created by Adam. She is costumed by the passage of civilizations over time but then restored to her original nudity, in a dramatic revelation, by Rimbaud as the modern poet. The third-person narrative of the parable is framed by an opening paragraph in the first person and an appended explanatory note that continues the opening paragraph.

The allegorical creation of poetry is the theme that unites these parables; Huidobro's poet-protagonist wishes to make his own trees, mountains, rivers, and seas as poetic creations, while Mário's Adam draws from himself the very personification of Poetry. In both parables, this allegory is characterized by a fourfold thematic cluster: (1) biblical subtexts, (2) a slave and master relationship, (3) a distinct relegation of gender roles, and (4) the idea of a poetic revolution. All of these fundamental characteristics, and their related theoretical underpinnings, must be analyzed both in their specific contexts and within the general theme of poetic creation.

• Biblical Subtexts: The Sacred Word

The rich biblical background of both parables serves to reinforce the schismatic nature of the new poetics while at the same time lending the authority of Holy Writ to these texts. Mário's parable starts with Genesis, while Huidobro's makes reference to Revelation. Genesis not only tells the story of an initial creation, but also of a punitive destruction by flood and a second flourishing of life; similarly, Revelation is not just the story of the Earth's ultimate demise but also of the subsequent revelation of the divine, ideal existence. Not surprisingly then, Mário's Genesis-based parable implies an apocalypse, while Huidobro's Revelation-based text invokes a new Eden. It is this duality of creation and destruction, inarguably basic in folk and religious cosmologies, that characterizes the mission of a new poetry in the writings of these two avant-garde leaders.

The biblical subtext of Huidobro's parable is not readily apparent. He directs his poetic revolution against Mother Nature, a decidedly unbiblical figure, who is rather like a Greek goddess, interacting freely with her mortal subjects. In the beginning, the poet finds it necessary to appease the wrath of "la madre Natura," so that she does not strike him with a lightning bolt, yet afterwards he can politely admonish her as a futile believer in her own antiquated ideas: "Ya no podrás aplastar a nadie con tus pretensiones exageradas de vieja chocha y regalona. Ya nos escapamos de tu trampa. Adiós, viejecita encantadora" (715). She is also the feminine face of the Creator, notably aged and bitter: "Hemos cantado a la Naturaleza (cosa que a ella bien poco le importa). Nunca hemos creado realidades propias, como ella lo hace o lo hizo en tiempos pasados, cuando era joven y llena de impulsos creadores" (715). The poet states that a change is necessary, and that he and his generation are the ones who should implement it; they will make their own world, which should have no basis for comparison with the existing world.

Thus far, the background of the parable is ostensibly pagan—the revolt of some audacious mortal against the divine mother. Huidobro has decided not to follow Alomar too closely; he does not name his protagonist "Adam" and thus does not strengthen the presence of a Genesis subtext. Yet Huidobro makes a paramount, though subtle, biblical reference in the last paragraph: "Una nueva era comienza. Al abrir sus puertas de jaspe, hinco una rodilla en tierra y te saludo muy respetuosamente" (716). These jasper doors are similar to the wall of the New Jerusalem as described in Revelation 21.18–19: "The wall was made of jasper, and the city itself was made of pure gold, as clear as glass. The foundation stones of the

4

city wall were adorned with all kinds of precious stones. The first foundation stone was jasper, the second sapphire [...]." The troublesome fact arises that it was the *walls* of the city that were made of jasper, not the doors, or gates, which were made of pearl, according to Revelation 21.21. Nevertheless, in the context of the commencement of Huidobro's "nueva era," this somewhat inexact New Jerusalem is the metaphor for a new world. Implicitly divine, it recalls Huidobro's well-known declaration, "el poeta es un pequeño Dios." The poet is not God, of course, but *a* god, endowed with supernatural creative powers.

Why is it that Huidobro cannot resist this biblical allusion, which does not seem either obvious or necessary? The symbolic opening of the doors of a new era would suffice to deliver his basic message. The use of jasper, then, gives weight to Huidobro's revolution by invoking that most final of revolutions, the apocalypse, and by providing a sacred context for his new poetry that could not have been implied from the revolt against Mother Nature. The poet, clearly on the winning side, reveals the revolutionary world that, by implication, is perfect and holy. The result, no matter how subtle or unconscious, is that Huidobro's parable portrays the poet's rupture with the past as an act tantamount to the apocalypse, and his new poetry as the promised revelation of divine grace and beauty.

Inevitably, the initial act of the poet's revolt must also be compared to Lucifer's rebellion, effectively casting the protagonist in a Miltonian role as Harold Bloom's paradigm of the modern poet. However, the consequences of that initial rebellion—which involve an implicitly divine new creation—and the facts relating the textual background to Alomar's futurism, more convincingly support the view of the poet as Adam.[5] Furthermore, the connection between the poet/self as Adam and as Christ is a very fluid one, appearing as much in Huidobro's parable as in Mário's in the context of the individual expression of artistic truth. In the end, the main idea is that the poet is an Other, separate from the godhead, who constitutes a part of the divine manifestation in the natural world but who seeks to create his own explicitly human, implicitly divine manifestation through art.

In contrast to "Non serviam," the biblical background of Mário's "Parábola" is both obvious and necessary. It is also more complex, since it is made doubly manifest: on one level, the idea and plot of the parable are derived from Genesis, while on another level, the opening paragraph of the text and the appended explanatory note offer a commentary on the nature of the expression of individual and universal truths, making reference to Jesus' use of parables. Thus the Old Testament references support the narrative structure of the parable, whereas the New Testament reference provides a meta-narrative frame.

In Mário's opening sentences, he hesitantly defines the text to follow first as a "história" and then as a "Quase parábola," affirming the latter with the declaration: "Gosto de falar com parábolas como Cristo . . ." [I like speaking in parables like Christ . . .] (OI 201). To defend contextually this strongly authoritative statement, Mário distinguishes Christ's divine "Verdade" from his own, humble "minha verdade," setting up the New Testament frame. Continuing in a religious vein, he denies any association of official dogma with his informal title of "the Pope of (Brazilian) Modernism" ("É mentira dizer-se que existe em S. Paulo um igrejó literário em que pontifico" [It's a lie to say there's some big church in S. Paulo where I pontificate]) and concludes, in reference to the contemporary São Paulo literary scene, that everyone has his or her own tendencies, ideas, and truths: "Isso não quer dizer que haja discípulos pois cada um de nós é o deus de sua própria religião" [That doesn't mean there are disciples, because each of us is the god of his own religion] (OI 201). This is an unequivocal confirmation of Huidobro's "pequeño dios" slogan, effectively enshrining Mário in the pagan poetic pantheon. It is also a surprising statement, leaning towards blasphemy, given Mário's avowed Catholicism; perhaps for this reason he inserts a letter "(A)" after "religião" in order to direct the reader to endnote A in the appendix of *A escrava que não é Isaura*. He finishes the paragraph, once more vacillating curiously on textual definition, with the enthusiastic "Vamos à história!" (OI 201).

It is appropriate at this point to consider endnote A. The tone is not openly apologetic, although Mário concedes that the "religião" sentence is "vaidosa" [vain]. Instead, Mário defends the necessary presence of the individual in religion, giving the example of five monks worshipping God in a monastery; they can never really be five monks but rather "1, 1, 1, 1, e 1 monges. Cada 1 adora Deus a seu modo" [Each one worships

God in his own way] (OI 279). He further points out that in art, the individual personality has existed throughout the ages, but that only now, with the new poetry's stress on the "subconsciência," has that individualism been balanced.[6] The individual personality can be altered by the force of the unconscious because "a subconsciência é fundamentalmente ingênua, geral, sem preconceitos, pura, fundamentalmente humana. Ela entra com seu coeficiente de universalidade para a outra concha da balança. Equilíbrio" [the unconscious is fundamentally ingenuous, vague, without prejudice, pure, fundamentally human. She brings her coefficient of universality to the other scale of the balance. Equilibrium] (OI 279). Mário's quirky love of equilibrium and balance concretizes his analogy of religion and art, which serves to unify and support the essence of his pseudo-biblical parable. While God, or the divine, exists as part of the collective unconscious that unites all humans, the ways in which He is worshipped vary greatly; likewise, in art, the individuality of each artist or work should balance, and not impede, the expression of a universal unconscious. The definition of this unconscious is not given, but its characteristics are to be found in the adjectives Mário uses to describe it: "ingênua," "geral," "pura," and "humana."

Not surprisingly, Mário employs this same lexicon on three other key occasions in the parable. First, he describes his truth, as opposed to Christ's truth: "humana, estética e tranzitória" (OI 201). Later he characterizes Poetry, Adam's newly created slave: "Humana, cósmica e bela" (OI 201). Finally, he reprises Poetry's unaltered essence in the moment of her unveiling: "nua, angustiada, ignara, falando por sons musicais, desconhecendo as novas línguas, selvagem, áspera, livre, ingênua, sincera" [nude, anguished, innocent, speaking in musical sounds, not recognizing the new languages, savage, crude, free, ingenuous, sincere] (OI 202). Mário's truth and (the new) Poetry are therefore lexically equated with the unconscious and the universal. The only difference is that Mário humbly recognizes his own truth as "tranzitória," whereas Poetry, "cósmica," seems more permanent. Not so the overly adorned, superficial poetry of Mário's (and Rimbaud's) predecessors, symbolized by the myriad garments with which the various civilizations insist on dressing the slave; in such case poetic beauty is not augmented but rather obstructed because—following Mário's balance—an excess of individualism sabotages the expression of the universal. To return, then, to the parable's New Testament frame, it can be concluded that Mário goes one step further than Jesus' custom in his practice of telling parables; he not only tells the parable, but he also explains it. He not only shows his hand by revealing, in the end, the identities of Adam's slave and the ingenious vagabond, but also he provides, in the opening paragraph and in the appended note, the literary historical background of his psychological assertions about modern poetry.

Mário's Old Testament references shape the parable's narrative and cleverly mirror the dialectic of individual and universal truths established in the parable's frame. Adam's creation of Poetry, described as a plagiarism of God's creation of Eve, arranges a narrative parallel of Mário's modest "minha verdade" in relation to Christ's eternal "Verdade"; Poetry is humankind's attempt to express Truth. The fig leaf, a manifest consequence of the original sin, begins the cascade of clothing that eventually buries Poetry. Cain's lambskin garment, like Adam's fig leaf, is only possible as the consequence of sin; his guilt, caused by the murder of Abel, indirectly blots out the Truth of innocent Poetry. The parade of generations and civilizations bearing stockings, hats, boots, jewelry, fans, etc. replicates a procession of pilgrims bringing offerings to a holy site in atonement for their sins.[7] It is left up to that ingenious vagabond Arthur Rimbaud, an intriguing Christ figure, to change the focus of worship from the ostentation of the Pharisees to the humble innocence of naked Poetry. In the aesthetic frame of reference, Rimbaud restores contact with the unconscious by clearing away the excessive clutter of individualism to expose the universal; Rimbaud, like Christ, is the bringer of Truth. The strength of both authors' biblical subtexts lies in the way that they support the revolutionary aspect of avant-garde poetry. Huidobro hints that the force of the apocalypse resides in the consciously non-imitative intent of the new poets to create poetry, which shall be the New Jerusalem, the New Eden, or heaven itself. Mário starts with Genesis to create an explanatory myth of how poetry was born and evolved to its pre-

Rimbaud state, and how Rimbaud's revelation rescued and restored it, unveiling the divine Truth.

Even so, albeit to varying degrees, not one of the poetic protagonists escapes the trap of mimesis. Huidobro's poet seemingly breaks away from nature, yet even though he says "Yo te responderé que mis cielos y mis árboles son los míos y no los tuyos y que no tienen por qué parecerse" (715), he still must call them "cielos" and "árboles"; he cannot surpass the limits of already established referents. Similarly, Adam desires to create but can only copy, while Rimbaud's innovation is shown to be retroactive; he only rediscovers (uncovers) the original Poetry. The incomplete essence of their poetic creation must be reconciled with the fact that poets cannot truly be gods; they cannot create from nothing. The most far-flung fantasy has some kind of anchor in reality, even if it is only words or images. Ironically, both Mário and Huidobro recognize and struggle against the existence of that anchor, which is the very referentiality of language. Mário's Poetry, when she is exposed by Rimbaud, is "falando por sons musicais" (OI 202); her mode of expression recalls the disarticulated vocalizations that conclude Huidobro's *Altazor.*

• Slaves, Masters, and the Identity of the Self

A lexical reading demonstrates the existence and importance of the slave and master relationship in the two parables. In "Non serviam," the word *esclavo* is used twice, *esclavitud* once, *amo* [master] once, *servicio* once, and forms of the verb *servir*, including the Latin *serviam*, eight times. Numerically, Mário's "Parábola" lags behind, with only three instances of the word *escrava*; however, the parables are on equal footing in that they both show words from this lexicon in their titles: *serviam* and *escrava*. The poet's role as slave or master changes from Huidobro's text to Mário's; in "Non serviam," the poet-slave has been dominated by Mother Nature, while in "Parábola," the poet-master creates his slave, Poetry, who is later liberated by another poet. Nevertheless, the role reversal does not hide the essential metaphor: poetic expression is enslaved. In one case the servile, sterile adulation of nature impedes poetic expression; in the other, the gradual eclipse of Truth, motivated by sin and guilt, conceals it. However, the imbalance inherent in a slave and master relationship leaves room to evolve from the initial oppression of poetic creativity to its eventual freedom.

The slave and master relationship embodies an elementary philosophical axis: the self and the other. Hegel's re-creation of the original self-other relationship is that of "lordship and bondage"; the first two individuals were equal until, in the struggle of each to establish his role as the essential self, one bested the other and became his master. As Hegel explains, the struggle grew out of the natural disunity of self-awareness:

> Self-consciousness is faced by another self-consciousness; it has come *out of itself*. This has a twofold significance: first, it has lost itself, for it finds itself as an *other* being; secondly, in doing so it has superseded the other, for it does not see the other as an essential being, but in the other sees its own self. (111; original emphasis)

In the resulting hierarchy, the slave depends on his master in terms of power and service, but, paradoxically, the master depends on his slave for an idea of the certainty of his self. The slave, however, gradually realizes his independent consciousness through the two key moments of work and fear. In sum, the oppression of the slave develops his independent consciousness while it diminishes the master's.

"Non serviam" lends itself to interpretation on the basis of Hegel's ideas. The parable's first paragraph alludes to the slave's developing self-consciousness, after years of servitude: "Y he aquí que una buena mañana, después de una noche de preciosos sueños y delicadas pesadillas, el poeta se levanta y grita a la madre Natura: *Non serviam*" (715). That the text begins with the conjunction "y" suggests that it continues some earlier narration or action, and there is indeed a background given to the "one fine morning" phrase: the poet's dreams and nightmares. Dreaming, always a manifestation of the unconscious, signals the slave's developing consciousness and independence. Furthermore, the poet-slave's nocturnal meditations are presented as the natural and immediate precursor of his getting up and yelling at his mistress, "Non serviam!" The dreams echo the direct cause of the poet's actions, as stated by the narrator: "No era un grito caprichoso, no era un acto de rebeldía superficial. Era el resultado de toda una evolución, la suma de múltiples experiencias" (715). Other references to the past, such as the poet's use of the present-perfect tense in his address to his fellow poets, and the phrase "pero ya tengo edad para andar solo por estos mundos" (716), establish that the poet has indeed been a slave for some time. He even decries his past acceptance, "sin mayor reflexión" (715), of the servile relationship; only now has he thoroughly experienced Hegel's critical moments of work and fear to realize his own independent consciousness.

Furthermore, in the poet's vocal moment of self-actualization, his cry is repeated *and translated* by a supposedly natural phenomenon, the echo: "Con toda la fuerza de sus pulmones, un eco traductor y optimista repite en las lejanías: «No te serviré.»" (715). Quiroga rightly clarifies that the echo "does not arise from nature or from the poet, but out of pure textual desire—a shadowed voice corporealized by the synecdoque [*sic*] of its lungs" (518). In fact the magic echo, beyond translating the Latin, embellishes it by adding the second-person-singular direct-object pronoun "te." This distinct voice, which functions as a creative speech act rather than the merely repetitive echo of the natural world, is a prolepsis of the poet's creation of an alternate world, expressed in the later phrase, "Yo tendré mis árboles que no serán como los tuyos, tendré mis montañas . . ." (715). The echo mediates the poet's self in words, significantly shifting from Latin, a "dead" language, to the vibrantly creative tongue of the poet's rebellion. Indeed, the poet in contemplation of his self is a Narcissus figure, and with the reinforcement of his Echo he is led to still greater self-awareness.

In the last section of the parable the poet speaks directly to Mother Nature, boasting that he will become her master ("seré tu amo") but settling for a kind of relationship of equals: "Te servirás de mí; está bien. No quiero y no puedo evitarlo; pero yo también me serviré de ti" (715). The poet's proposal therefore resembles not so much a role reversal as the uneven passage to Hegel's potential relationship of equals in synthesis. Following through, the poet clearly separates his actions from hers: "Yo tendré mis árboles que no serán como los tuyos, tendré mis montañas . . ." (715); he recognizes the limits of his own self. Even the poet's surprising praise of his "años de esclavitud a tu servicio" (716) supports the idea that the fruit of all his labor is precisely the step of self-awareness that he can now take. Mother Nature ends up as a "viejecita encantadora," though still honored by the poet as he reveals his new era: "hinco una rodilla en tierra y te saludo muy respetuosamente" (716). The poet and his former mistress are now equals, and sometimes rivals, in the newly separated realms of art and nature.

Mário's "Parábola" presents a chain of slave and master relationships. Adam, although perhaps not the slave of God, of course reveres Him as his master. Adam is in turn the master of Poetry, since she is after all the "escrava" of the title, although she does not appear to serve him. Ultimately, Rimbaud, like the legions of Greeks, Persians, Chinese, etc., is an implied slave of Poetry's beauty and truth; but he is also her liberator, the chosen one who arrives after generations of servitude.

In the beginning, Adam's *plágio* [plagiary] unlike Huidobro's poet's "nueva era," does not arise from years of meditation in work and fear. Instead, it springs spontaneously from greed and cunning mimicry: "Invejoso e macaco o primeiro homem resolveu criar também" [Envious and apelike the first man resolved to create too] (OI 201). The slave's only duty is to serve as "exemplo das gerações futuras" [example for future generations] (OI 201). All the peoples of the ancient world become her admirers; she is in this sense not their slave but rather their mistress. According to Hegel, the slave's (Poetry's) rebellion can only happen after many years of service, in which the individual consciousness has matured to the point of expression. For that reason, just as Huidobro's revolutionary poet stands out among his brother poets, Rimbaud distinguishes himself from his fellow pilgrims to Mount Ararat by breaking the monotonous cycle of their activity. The pilgrims' clutter of clothing was interpreted, in the parallel context of Mário's meta-narrative commentary, as produced by an excess of individualism. To counteract this excess (to achieve equilibrium), Mário states that the unconscious must also be present; this is the same equilibrium implied by Hegel's synthesis. Yet

Rimbaud, rather than restoring equilibrium, suddenly tips the balance to the unconscious side by revealing Poetry, "escandalosamente nua" [scandalously nude] in the face of modern values. She is a dreamlike image; her naked body and musical vocalizations shock the uptight, overdressed passersby that one can imagine on the busy São Paulo thoroughfare of "a sociedade educadíssima, vestida e policiada da época actual" [the extremely well-heeled, well-dressed and repressed society of current times] (OI 202).

Poetry becomes a new mistress; she is now worshipped by "os poetas modernistas," freed from the guilt of Adam and Cain. Her resurrection has been the culmination of years of consciousness-forming, and her role is to provide the link with the unconscious, mirrored in "Non serviam" by the poet's dreams. The new poetry therefore springs from the collective unconscious, but also must espouse the poet's individual expression. Both authors insist on the desire for a balance of these elements (although Mário more clearly than Huidobro, by virtue of his narrative frame). For that reason, Huidobro's poet cannot truly become Mother Nature's master, since she represents the universal; rather, he concedes that he will continue to respect her because he has learned from her as a model. Mário's liberated Poetry is exactly that, a model on a pedestal, that the modern poets "se puseram a adorar" [dedicated themselves to worshipping] (OI 202).

The figure of Adam as representative of the self is an idea shared by both authors that springs from the collective unconscious; in *Mysterium Coniunctionis,* Jung concludes that Adam symbolizes the self because of his habitual fourfold nature in alchemy, as incorporating the four elements, the four cardinal points, etc.[8] In this sense of the self, Huidobro's poet (even without the knowledge of Alomar's precedent) is as much of an Adam figure as Mário's Adam. After the original sin, the biblical Adam is conscious of nature (his nature or his self) and attempts to dominate it by wearing the fig leaf; in Mário's parable, he also places one on his slave. Rimbaud reverses Adam's initial action by uncovering nature to probe the unconscious. In contrast, Huidobro's poet, like Hegel's slave, becomes aware of his self as opposed to his mistress, Mother Nature; his rebellion is his original sin. Differing from Mário's Adam,

Huidobro's poet already possesses a link to the unconscious through his "preciosos sueños y delicadas pesadillas" (715). Both authors cast Adam in the dynamics of a slave and master relationship to show the interplay of the conscious and unconscious elements of the creative act, leading to the possible reconciliation of the self with the other.

• Gender Roles and Duality

Another dimension of the self-other dialectic can be scrutinized in the relegation of gender roles. In "Non serviam" the woman is the mistress and the man is the slave, whereas in "Parábola" the initial relationship is the opposite: a male master and a female slave. The later development of Poetry as the idol/mistress of her male worshippers returns to the same arrangement of gender roles as "Non serviam." It is therefore necessary to explore both of the opposite sex pairings: mistress and male slave, master and female slave. Todorov has questioned the implication inherent in Hegel's paradigm of "lordship and bondage" that the quest for the recognition of the self is a struggle.[9] While agreeing that the nature of the self requires an other, Todorov proposes that the initial self-defining dichotomy was not the relationship of master and slave, but rather of mother and child. The child is born with an incomplete sense of self that can only be fulfilled by the mother; for this reason, the child wants to catch his mother's gaze, to recognize himself in the mirror of the eyes of the other. This is not a struggle—the child wants nothing more complicated than the mother's presence—although Todorov does identify a different battle, at a later stage, among the child and his peers for adult recognition.

If Huidobro's protagonist is seen as the child of "la *madre* Natura" (my emphasis), in addition to being her slave, then it is easy to extrapolate his dissatisfaction with the one-way status of their relationship. Her self exists completely, but he needs her recognition to be complete. Like a desperate toddler, he initially grabs her attention by making her angry. She is about to chastise him with a lightning bolt when he quickly ingratiates himself by complimenting her. He has succeeded in obtaining her attention, and thus her recognition, with little trouble. However, because Hegel's slave and master relationship exists alongside the mother and son relationship, the atmosphere of struggle intensifies. Furthermore, the second struggle that Todorov postulates may be foreshadowed in the poet's address to his fellow poets; in the presence of the adult, he tries to establish authority over his equals. After his presumably successful revolt, the poet disparages Mother Nature's matronly role: "adiós, madre y madrastra" (716). Through the use of *madrastra*, the poet diminishes his relationship with her, bringing into doubt any genetic or hereditary connection, while associating her with a traditional villainess archetype, the Wicked Stepmother. If he were to vanquish the false mother (stepmother or witch), Huidobro's poet would join the heroic ranks of fairy-tale figures such as Cinderella or Hansel and Gretel. Yet he cannot truly defeat her, as has been shown, since more than a mere witch or stepmother, Mother Nature represents the original and divine forces of the universe. She is the Great Mother of the collective unconscious—an essential link to the unconscious elements of poetic creation.[10]

In "Parábola," on her perch atop Mount Ararat, Poetry can also be identified with the Great Mother, in her manifestation as the Earth Mother. When Rimbaud passed by the mountain, wanting to see it, he "admirou-se de, em vez do Ararat de terra, encontrar um Guarisancar de sedas, setins, chapeus, jóias, botinas, máscaras, espartilhos . . . que sei lá!" [marveled at finding, instead of Mount Ararat, a Mount Guarisancar of silks, satins, hats, jewelry, boots, masks, girdles . . . and who knows what else!] (OI 202). He does not recognize the "Ararat de terra," nor can he know, in that moment, that Poetry waits beneath the clutter of costumes. Expecting to see Mother Earth, he jumps into the pile, clearing it all away, and finds in her place a different mother, Poetry. It is important to note the noun that Mário uses for Rimbaud in this moment of discovery: "E o menino descobriu a mulher nua" [And the boy discovered the nude woman] (OI 202); Rimbaud, the ingenious vagabond who wrote all of his poetry between the ages of sixteen and nineteen, is here a "menino," or boy, before Poetry. Furthermore, he is a child at the mother's breast; Mount Ararat is symbolically a breast of the earth, a poetic source. It is also the cradle of post-diluvial civilization, as the fertile ground where the womblike ark was opened and Noah and his family were finally returned to the nourishing earth. Poetry's geographical location is therefore richly symbolic of a return to the Great Mother.

Standing revealed, Poetry meets Rimbaud's gaze. In this moment of mutual recognition, Mário appropriately chooses to reveal to the reader the identities of the slave and the vagabond. Although Poetry may acknowledge her liberator in this audacious youth, she does not understand Rimbaud's tongue; on the contrary, she is described as "desconhecendo as novas línguas" (OI 202). Rimbaud, however, as the influential Symbolist and author of "Alchimie du verbe," is most suited to appreciating her way of "falando por sons musicais" (OI 202). Rimbaud's physical struggle was limited to getting to the bottom of the mountain of clothes, but, as in "Non serviam," the foreseen possibility of Todorov's struggle among equals is suggested in the presence of a group of poets in the last paragraph. Again, there will be a contest for authority among peers, a situation that in fact proved to be characteristic of the avant-garde movements in general. Therefore, the fighting among equals represents the poet's search for leadership and acceptance in the artistic milieu, while the mother and child relationship symbolizes the poet's struggle to know himself, and thus create poetry.

The opposite duo, of master and female slave, suggests the father and daughter relationship. Such a relationship, in the context of the master and slave hierarchy, has been shown by Sandra Gilbert and Susan Gubar to be typically mythological:

> Like the metaphor of literary paternity itself, this corollary notion that the chief creature man has generated is woman has a long and complex history. From Eve, Minerva, Sophia, and Galatea onward, after all, patriarchal mythology defines women as created by, from, and for men, the children of male brains, ribs, and ingenuity. (12)

Mário's Adam produces Poetry from his tongue, a birth which, on the psychological level of language production, is more like Athena's birth from Zeus's headache than Eve's birth from Adam's rib. Athena, from the head of the most powerful of the gods, is the goddess of wisdom; Adam's creation, from the tongue of the first man, is Poetry. Such a uniquely masculine birth reflects the Romantics' striving for unilateral creation; Dr. Frankenstein, like Mário's Adam, engenders new life at the cost of repressing the maternal role.[11]

16

Jacques Derrida examines the paternal nature of language in "Plato's Pharmacy." Though the written word comes to naught, the spoken word, as the father's seed, brings new life: "[. . .] living speech makes its capital bear fruit and does not divert its seminal potency toward indulgence in pleasures without paternity" (152). In "Parábola," Adam's act of creation, from his tongue (and not his rib), is a symbolic description of language. His speech act literally creates Poetry as offspring. The effortless simplicity of this act cannot be doubted in the Edenic context: "E como não soubesse ainda cirugia para uma operação tão interna quanto extraordinária tirou da língua um outro ser" [And since he didn't know yet the surgery necessary for such an internal and extraordinary operation, he drew from his tongue another being] (OI 201). This act extends Adam's role as the paradigm of poets, being the original namer of animals, plants, and other natural entities. All are creatures of God, but Adam is the father of language; indeed, Adam's word creates reality as does the Word of God. His tongue is the phallus that disseminates the spoken symbols, both defining and limiting his environment; spoken language defines the other through exclusion, thereby limiting the self by process of elimination.

Does this father-daughter relationship exhibit the same dynamics as the mother-son relationship? The son, as a child, needs his mother's presence in order to feel complete, and the older son rebels against his kind to promote himself. Yet these needs are ignored in the father-daughter relationship of Adam and Poetry, since there is no mother involved and the daughter is born fully adult; there exists no childhood phase of recognition and self-awareness, nor any need for Adam's acknowledgment. Instead, as has already been seen, the dynamic interchange in Mário's parable is displaced from this initial, spontaneous relationship of Adam and his slave to the culminating, reciprocal recognition between Rimbaud and Poetry.

The gender roles in both parables go beyond the elaboration of the fundamental dialectic of the self and the other by serving, additionally, to differentiate the masculine and feminine essences of poetic creation. In both cases, the slave's rebellion, or the desire to link individual expression with the collective unconscious, is expressed in terms of an agent and a recipient; the agent is the masculine force of language and the recipient is the feminine force of nature. This description emphasizes the dual nature of poetic creation, not unlike the Taoist concept of yin and yang, and conveys the idea that the revolution aims not to change from one side to the other, but rather to restore the balance between them. The yin and yang are thus respectively feminine and masculine, passive and active, recipient and agent, nature and language, universal and individual, unconscious and conscious, other and self. Furthermore, this essential duality reflects not only the Gnostic division of the spiritual and the physical, but also, and with greater relevance, the sexual imagery of the Kabbalah. This body of mystical teachings exerted great influence on the Hispanic *modernistas* and other vanguard predecessors, and was therefore familiar to the vanguardists. In *Vientos contrarios* Huidobro himself notes his many hours of study devoted to "la Astrología, a la Alquimia, a la Cábala antigua y al ocultismo en general" (*Obras completas* 794). The Kabbalah holds that Adam's sin caused the exile of the feminine aspect of divinity. Kabbalistic sexual imagery therefore represents the desire for the reunion of the feminine and masculine entities of the godhead (immanence and transcendence, respectively), expressed as a universal harmony (Schaya 131). The similar characterizations of these opposing sexual forces in Huidobro's and Mário's parables—beyond foregrounding, once again, the role of Adam—work toward the same ideal goal of harmony in creation.

The gender pairings therefore shed new light on what the poetic revolution sets out to accomplish. The two parables' revolutions seemingly contradict one another; Huidobro's male protagonist rebels against Mother Nature, or the unconscious, in his moment of self-illumination, while by contrast Rimbaud's revolt is essentially seen as a return, in which he rediscovers the feminine unconscious to thwart an excess of individualism. Yet, with this dualistic understanding of the revolutionary relationship, these two ostensibly opposite revolutions can be reconciled to describe the same moment in the Latin American (and Western) history of literature and art: the definition of the avant-garde as a desire to restore equilibrium.

• Creating a Revolutionary Rhetoric

The goal of the poetic revolution is now clear: it is to reestablish the dual character of poetic creation, which is the same as

Mário's precious "Equilíbrio." But the question remains: what are the events and conditions that have led up to the necessity for a radical shift? Both authors supply a negative historical background, isolating a kind of developmental flaw that justifies the poetic revolution. In "Non serviam" this flaw is mimesis, while in "Parábola" it is poetic adornment or ornamentalism; as mentioned earlier, these flaws can be seen as an upsetting of the equilibrium—in the first case, there is too much focus on nature, in the other, too much on language. The required remedy, both a break with the past and a new creation, will be provided by the unnamed poet (Huidobro himself?) and by Rimbaud.

The historical context of "Non serviam" is presented in its second section, in which the poet summarizes to his fellow poets the reason for their dearth of accomplishment: "Hasta ahora no hemos hecho otra cosa que imitar al mundo en sus aspectos, no hemos creado nada. ¿Qué ha salido de nosotros que no estuviera antes parado ante nosotros, rodeando nuestros ojos, desafiando nuestros pies o nuestras manos?" (715). The poet condemns this exclusive mimesis and, in the act of calling for a new world, recognizes the role of his self: "[. . .] y no hemos pensado que nosotros también podemos crear realidades en un mundo nuestro, en un mundo que espera su fauna y flora propias. Flora y fauna que sólo el poeta puede crear, por ese don especial que le dio la misma madre Naturaleza a él y únicamente a él" (715). The moment of self-recognition, offered simultaneously with the cry for revolution, also defines the moment of establishing authority, in the context of the repeated first-person-plural present-perfect "hemos."[12] Ironically, this new role of the poet's self had long ago been conceded to him by his mistress, Mother Nature, though only now has the poet realized it. Again, the poet's dreams and nightmares—his link to the unconscious—are important as precursors to this day of uprising; Quiroga interprets them symbolically as *literary* precursors: "The 'preciosos sueños' and 'delicadas pesadillas' obviously allude to *modernista* nightmares that have become codified, literary and unreal" (517).

Moreover, the revolutionary day is set apart as a specific event to contrast with the vague and imitative past. In the first line the day is presented rather nondescriptly: "una buena mañana." However, a few lines later, the poet's cry "quedó grabado en una mañana de la historia del mundo" (715); the context has not become much more specific, but definitely more portentous. To continue this idea, Huidobro specifies the importance of the cry "Non serviam": "No era un grito caprichoso, no era un acto de rebeldía superficial. Era el resultado de toda una evolución, la suma de múltiples experiencias" (715). The poet's act clearly represents the culmination of a varied, though still vague, trajectory. Finally: "El poeta, en plena conciencia de su pasado y de su futuro, lanzaba al mundo la declaración de su independencia frente a la Naturaleza" (715). The use of the imperfect tense in these sentences ("era" and "lanzaba") should be noted, since it implies the continued nature of the actions, and, arguably, their lasting import, as opposed to the finality of the preterite "fue" and "lanzó." More importantly, the poet is described as being "en plena conciencia de su pasado y de su futuro"; he has attained a new mental or psychic state of consciousness, like an apotheosis, as a result of his contact with the unconscious and his years of servitude in the development of his self-awareness. As noted above, his cry vocalizes the moment of equilibrium, but not just of the conscious and unconscious or the individual and the universal; it is also the summation of the past and the future into the present—a revolutionary rhetoric.

Mário's strategy for the presentation of poetic history is remarkably similar to Huidobro's, although Mário's is more colorful and complete through the inclusion of a symbolic wardrobe for Poetry. More detailed than the varied but vague "múltiples experiencias" of Huidobro's poet, Mário's multicultural fashion show is "eterogênea" [heterogeneous] and parodies the ornamental, exotic style of his poetic predecessors, the Parnassians: "Os gregos enfim deram-lhe o coturno. Os romanos o peplo. Qual lhe dava um colar, qual uma axorca. Os indianos, pérolas; os persas, rosas; os chins, ventarolas" [The Greeks ended up giving her the buskin. The Romans, the peplum. Somebody gave her a necklace, somebody else an arm ring. The Indians, pearls; the Persians, roses; the Chinese, fans] (OI 202). The layers of clothing pile up over the centuries to a stifling excess, symbolizing the decadence of previous poetry. Moreover, just as Huidobro contrasts a general historical background with the definite "una mañana de la historia del mundo," Mário suddenly specifies a key day:

> E os séculos depois dos séculos . . .
> Um vagabundo genial nascido a 20 de Outubro de 1854
> passou uma vez junto do monte. (OI 202 [1])

Interestingly, it is not the date on which Rimbaud goes to the mountain and unveils Poetry that is given; on the contrary, the specific day that breaks the monotony of the centuries, symbolizing the revolutionary moment, is Rimbaud's birthday. His life, from its first minute, is the poetic revolution.

Julia Kristeva's *Revolution in Poetic Language* illuminates the importance of Rimbaud and the Symbolist generation. Kristeva sees the self as a simultaneous stasis and pulsion of semiotic drives called the chora. Although these internal urges are semiotic, their moment of articulation (the thetic moment, the speech act) is of necessity symbolic. The self is therefore limited in its ability to express its needs or desires. Poetry, however, can sometimes allow some of the semiotic nature to break out; this is a phenomenon that Kristeva equates with Mallarmé's "The Mystery in Literature," an interior, feminine realm of expression:

> Indifferent to language, enigmatic and feminine, this space underlying the written is rhythmic, unfettered, irreducible to its intelligible verbal translation; it is musical, anterior to judgement, but restrained by a single guarantee: syntax. (97)

Interior space, literary mystery, semiotic urges, musical expression: the inherently feminine description applies equally to Mário's Poetry. It is a natural utterance restricted by syntax; Poetry's *symbolic* garments govern and restrain the expression of the *semiotic*. Once again, the act of writing poetry, of communicating poetically, is seen as the interplay of two diametrically opposed forces: feminine and masculine, universal and individual, semiotic and symbolic. Mário's admiration for Rimbaud is thus clarified by Kristeva's explanation of the Symbolist generation's prominence in giving reign to this inner poetic voice.

Kristeva further illuminates the function of poetry by comparing it with fetishism, which is a denial of the symbolic and a return to the semiotic realm as the mother's womb. Kristeva asks:

> In short, isn't art the fetish *par excellence,* one that badly camouflages its archaeology? At its base, isn't there a belief, ultimately maintained, that the mother is phallic, that the ego—never precisely identified—will never separate from her, and that no symbol is strong enough to sever this dependence? In this symbiosis with the supposedly phallic mother, what can the subject do but occupy her place, thus navigating the path from fetishism to auto-eroticism? (115)

Mário's poetic symbolism of the phallic mother conforms to these ideas, since Poetry is a mother whom Rimbaud undresses; the unveiling of the phallus is the revelation of language's power. Rimbaud, as Poetry's liberator, can enjoy the inspiration of the semiotic force of language, even if such contact is fleeting and periodic instead of a truly lasting union. Huidobro's poet, in contrast, challenges the phallic mother figure of Mother Nature, who is indeed endowed with the graphically symbolic phallus of the lightning bolt, a weapon more often wielded by male deities like Zeus and Thor. The rebel poet desires literally to "occupy her place," more of a poetic coup than a symbiosis.

The difference lies in the degree of fetishism. While Mário advocates contact with the semiotic (the semiotic is revolutionary in the context of the symbolic), or an attempt to evoke the creative womb, Huidobro propagates a direct assimilation of the semiotic force of creativity. Again it must be stressed that Huidobro's poet can never completely defeat Mother Nature; his years of servitude have been "la más preciosa enseñanza" (716), but he is now ready to move on. In fact, those same years as a slave to mimesis were a kind of fetishism, and so the change now is that he is, in Kristeva's words, "navigating the path from fetishism to auto-eroticism"; his expression, or his self, becomes the phallus of his own language.

Mário's and Huidobro's use of allegory conveys the desire for union with the chora in a colorful and emblematic way for a variety of reasons: to define, precisely and dramatically, the goal of art (and poetry) as they see it for their generation; to spur on their fellow artists to create from within and explore new contexts of meaning; to challenge conventions, such as mimesis (realism), ornamentalism (Parnassianism), and fixed poetic forms. Additionally, through allegory, the act of tapping into the semiotic chora's revolutionary power can be shown to temporarily abolish the parables' hierarchies: the slave is freed, the sexes are on equal ground, the end is the beginning. Therefore the ideal of poetic creation in the avant-garde moment is conceived as a potential union; as a new era and also a return to the beginning; as a reconciliation of opposites, an equilibrium. The idea that the avant-garde moment should be defined by a desire for equilibrium, and not excess, may perhaps seem incongruous. Yet any revolution arises from a perceived imbalance, and so the revolutionary rhetoric calls for a restoration of order. However, as is so often the case with revolutions, success does not fulfill political promises; the avant-garde is more often associated with excess for good reasons, which are illustrated by aspects of the works of Satie, Miró, Jarry, Aleixandre, Dalí, Girondo, Rivera, et al., including Huidobro and Mário. Therefore, the avant-garde's revolutionary rhetoric fascinates because its failure is both predictable, given the revolutionary cycle, and overwhelming, manifesting the avant-garde's famously hyperbolic excess, inevitably leading to exhaustion.

Huidobro and Mário both create allegories of this revolutionary rhetoric, surprisingly similar in form, theme, and symbol. Revolution is central to the plot of each parable, bolstered by biblical allusions that develop a sacred or mystical context, and by the slave and master relationship, which adds further complexities to the battle by implying the reconciliation of the self and the other, and, reinforced by gender pairings, the idea of a central duality or equilibrium. The most important difference between the two strategies is that Huidobro leans toward an expression of the conscious, individual, symbolic side of the scale, while Mário, in contrast, prefers to stress the unconscious, the universal, and the semiotic. The struggle of both authors to further characterize a poetics of equilibrium, without tipping the balance, continues in their manifestos, treatises, and other vanguard texts on poetics.

Part One

Poetry as Orientation of the Creative Self

Vicente Huidobro

In twentieth-century Latin American letters, Huidobro's works have proved fertile ground.[1] In addition to the supremacy of his masterpiece *Altazor,* fragments of which are inevitably included in Spanish American and Latin American literature or poetry anthologies, Huidobro has gained recognition for the originality of his poems, novels, and dramatic works. However, in spite of the fact that the importance of his writings on poetics, specifically his manifestos, is conceded, previous criticism of these texts has not generally focused on any literary orientation that could strengthen the ubiquitous theoretical readings. The literary qualities of the integral poetics texts, themselves, need to be taken into account.

For example, the rich variety of Huidobro's manifestos frequently escapes notice in critical analyses, because the tendency has been to pursue a theme or idea monolithically, quoting as needed from different manifestos or other texts and contexts.[2] Studies of the individual manifestos, or as an organic group, seem either dismissive or incomplete. De Costa's summarized evaluation, "an attack on Breton's Surrealism" (*Vicente Huidobro: The Careers of a Poet* 3), applies to some of the manifestos but not all, and it does not address the range of formats and images. Peter G. Earle describes the manifestos broadly: "valen más como autobiografía literaria y como testimonio de una problemática que como una teoría de vanguardia" (166). Without exploring the texts' literary qualities or their dialogue with other poetics, Earle argues that the manifestos reveal Huidobro's alleged aesthetic isolation and are therefore only "una contabilidad de gustos y disgustos" (171) and "una serie de tanteos" (174). Alicia Rivero-Potter and María Rosaria Alfani cite deftly from the manifestos in order to support the topics of their studies—the relationship between author and reader in Huidobro's novels, and the cinematic montage of *Ecuatorial,* respectively. Cedomil Goic's treatment of the manifestos in the "La teoría creacionista" section of *La poesía de Vicente Huidobro,* although perspicacious as far as Huidobro's theoretical resonance with his contemporaries, does not cover all the manifestos and is only somewhat analytical in a literary sense. Luisa Marina Perdigó's thorough analysis of the key *creacionista* texts inevitably schematizes the manifestos but does not explore their imagery in detail. Similarly, the analyses of Mireya Camurati and Guillermo Sucre, the best of those studies that cite as needed from several texts in order to reveal general tendencies, do not analyze in context, although they mention and cite, the images from the manifestos.

Ricardo Gutiérrez Mouat examines the tone of the manifestos en masse, concluding that unlike Darío and in spite of frequent scorn for his public, Huidobro needs the public for his posturing somewhere between "maestro" and "mistagogo" (120). For José Alberto de la Fuente, in his short summary of the manifestos, the texts express "un mundo en gerundio, en devenir, mágico, inaugurativo e imaginario" (62). Luis Navarrete Orta gives the manifestos more weight by including distinct sections devoted to six of them in his comparative study of Huidobro's poetry and poetics, although he characterizes the rest of them in a few lines, noting only vaguely the use of "recursos poéticos" (153). Conceptually insightful, his analysis exposes the time lag between Huidobro's affirmation of aesthetic ideas and his actual use of them in his poetry. Navarrete Orta begins, especially in the case of the manifesto "Total," the labor of a series of detailed, individual analyses of each text, permitting the comparison of themes, ideas, and images in a developmental context.

The manifestos comprise those texts that appear in the section *Manifiestos* as printed in Montes's edition of the *Obras completas*. Most of these texts were first published as a group in 1925, in French, with the title *Manifestes*.[3] De Costa describes the contents:

> The book contains ten manifesto-like essays, some of which had been published before, and is almost as interesting for what it does not reprint as for what it does. Uncollected, for example, is the 1921 *L'Esprit nouveau* piece on "La Création pure," which had once served as the basis for his promotional lectures in Madrid and Paris, as well as providing the preface for *Saisons choisies* (Paris: La Cible, 1921), a showcase anthology of his Creationist work. (*Vicente Huidobro: The Careers of a Poet* 77)

The missing manifesto, translated as "La creación pura," reappears in Montes's *Obras completas* version, along with three other pieces that were absent from the French edition ("Non serviam," "La poesía," and "Total"), to make a total of fourteen texts.[4] After the first piece—"Non serviam" (which was analyzed in the Introduction)—the remaining thirteen manifestos will be analyzed in the order in which they are printed in Montes's edition, which approximates a definitive chronological order; Huidobro's habit of predating his texts thwarts the establishment of such a chronology.[5]

Huidobro's written essays in French, and to an extent his exclusive use of the peninsular second-person-plural subject pronoun *vosotros* in Spanish, are related phenomena expressing his profound desire to be accepted in Europe. Contrary to the pattern of exiled Latin American authors who often continue writing about their native countries, Huidobro, whose "exile" was never forced, wrote about European identities, monuments, and problems. Living in the Parisian avant-garde milieu, he intensified his participation by writing some of his works directly in French. One can only wonder if, when in Madrid, he adopted Castilian pronunciation along with his use of *vosotros*. His tactics probably did gain him more acceptance in Europe, but they also cost him some renown in Latin America, where about half of his published work was delayed by translation.[6]

I base my decision to study the manifestos exclusively on the fact that they are the best and most concentrated of the author's poetics texts. The majority of Huidobro's other prose texts *(Finis Britannia, Vientos contrarios, Artículos,* his novels) do not concern themselves directly with a theoretical expression of his poetics. His articles on Menéndez y Pelayo, Benavente, Nervo, Darío, and Chocano in *Pasando y pasando* suggest Huidobro's artistic leanings and preferences but do not discuss his own theoretical ideas. I will bring into consideration other prose texts that do address his poetics, including the prefaces to *Adán* and *Altazor* (although the latter is a much more integral part of its full work than the former) and sections of *Pasando y pasando,* when appropriate. The aim of studying the manifestos exclusively also involves leaving aside related poems; however, these will be mentioned briefly when pertinent to theme and chronology.

The *Manifiestos* figure among Huidobro's more unique texts. Some of them are cast in the traditional mold of a manifesto or speech, in which the speaker cites established authorities and pertinent examples of poetry in order to refute them, following with his own statement of authority and poetic examples. These texts fulfill the characteristics of the manifesto as described by Jorge Luis Castillo: "la distintiva apariencia gráfica, (enumeraciones, frases en mayúsculas, espacios en blanco, elipsis) y el tono impersonal, histriónico, irreverente e iconoclasta" (151). Such is the model of the more openly theoretical manifestos, which occupy the middle half of the collection: "La creación pura," "Manifiesto de manifiestos," "El creacionismo," "Yo encuentro . . . ," "Futurismo y maquinismo," "La poesía de los locos," and "Necesidad de una estética poética compuesta por los poetas." These manifestos tend to rely more on the denunciation of other avant-garde and traditional poetics, and on pseudoscientific vocabulary that lends the appearance of rationality and logic. In contrast, the earliest and last manifestos show a wider range of structure and style, from a greater concentration of poetic images within the expression of the poetics itself ("La poesía," "Época de creación," "Manifiesto tal vez," and "Total") to highly original forms and themes that expose the psyche of the poetic mystique as myth ("Non serviam," "Aviso a los turistas," and "Las siete palabras del poeta"). Consequently, references to the poet as oracle, the ubiquitous poetic orientation of the *aleph,* and the power of creative language (in the secrets of the Tree of Knowledge and the elevation to atmospheric heights), along with biblical allusions that articulate the eschatological backbone of Huidobro's mystique, prove more abundant in the latter group of manifestos.[7]

Yet the common thread of the binary struggle for balance in poetic composition weaves through all of the manifestos, culminating in Huidobro's challenge in "Total": "¿No podéis dar un hombre, todo un hombre, un hombre entero?" (756). The bias seen initially in "Non serviam" toward the rational, conscious effort of artistic expression continues, especially in "El creacionismo" and in the critiques of surrealism in "Manifiesto de manifiestos" and "Yo encuentro . . ." In fact, the bias serves to characterize Huidobro's entire poetics; the self is the most important element in the creative act—the rebel poet, the center of the chart, the *aleph* tree, the middle of the whirling universe, the union with the divine, the independent totality. Huidobro does not cease to stress the harmony of the conscious self with the collective unconscious, but it is the self that must act to achieve this harmony. For this reason, Huidobro interprets poetic creation fundamentally as the poet's action of uniting, in equal proportion or potency, his or her rational mind with the collective unconscious as the semiotic source of language.

The major themes and ideas of "Non serviam" as explored in the Introduction will now be extended and developed. The most important of these are: a biblical background and scope; an attack on mimesis; the struggle of conscious and unconscious elements of poetic creation; the power of creative language, frequently concentrated in the image of the tree; and the mystical role of the poet as seer. Some new stylistic developments not present in "Non serviam" include pseudoscientific discourse, frequently based on a lexicon of energy and electricity; the power of poetry related to high, aerial spaces and vertigo, obviously related to *Altazor;* and images of direction or spatial orientation, such as paths, horizons, the cardinal points, and the earth's poles, which develop a dialectic of the specific direction of poetic composition in opposition to the poet's all-encompassing, *aleph*-like vision. All of these ideas highlight Huidobro's central preoccupation: the need to express poetry as the original production of the creatively aware self.

Poetic Engineering

Creating the Poetic Realm
in Huidobro's Early Manifestos

Huidobro's early manifestos display a combination of mystical and didactic approaches. Along with "Non serviam," "La poesía" builds Huidobro's poetic mystique while showing a more intrinsically creative and metaphorical textual construction. In contrast, the more traditional manifestos—"La creación pura," "Manifiesto de manifiestos," "El creacionismo," "Yo encuentro . . . ," "Futurismo y maquinismo," "La poesía de los locos," and "Necesidad de una estética poética compuesta por los poetas"—didactically expound and exemplify the principles of creacionismo. Not completely bereft of metaphor, the imagery of these latter texts sometimes supports Huidobro's mystique while maintaining his authoritarian tone. The brief "Época de creación" begins a transition back to more intrinsically creative texts—the final manifestos analyzed in chapters two and three.

• The Pierced Tongue

The inherent magic of words dominates the fundamental manifesto "La poesía (Fragmento de una conferencia leída en el Ateneo de Madrid, el año 1921)."[1] Bary notes that Larrea and Gerardo Diego, Huidobro's Spanish disciples, met their master for the first time at that 1921 conference in which Huidobro read this text. Larrea later summarized the piece as Huidobro's "eco de la doctrina mallarmeana de la palabra poética como lenguaje del paraíso y del juicio final" (Bary, *Nuevos estudios* 13); Larrea confirms the importance of these two biblical extremes in Huidobro's poetic vision. In a series of imaginative aphorisms and definitions, Huidobro elaborates his poetic mystique by restoring a kind of supernatural power to verbal expression, and then, by extension, to poets, or to those who would recognize and exercise this power of words. In both cases this act is facilitated by images that are implicitly or explicitly biblical and recall the dawn of civilization. Poetry is "el vocablo virgen de todo prejuicio; el verbo creado y creador, la palabra recién nacida. Ella se desarrolla en el alba primera del mundo. Su precisión no consiste en denominar las cosas, sino en no alejarse del alba" (716). The comparison to "el verbo" recalls the opening verses of the Gospel of John, lending poetry a divine nature. Its "precisión" lies not in denomination, as in the traditionally masculine role of Adam, but rather in maintaining the virginal, original qualities of the first dawn. Poetry is thus a feminine essence, as the womb or the source, while the masculine act of naming is relegated to the poet.

Huidobro emphasizes poetry's divine state through atemporality: "Para ella no hay pasado ni futuro" (716). Similarly, poetry represents alpha and omega: "La Poesía está antes del principio del hombre y después del fin del hombre. Ella es el lenguaje del Paraíso y el lenguaje del Juicio Final, ella ordeña las ubres de la eternidad, ella es intangible como el tabú del cielo" (716). The image of the eternal udders reinforces poetry's feminine essence.[2] In addition, the divinity of poetry becomes sanctified in ritual; Huidobro here depicts an almost personified poetry in terms of clothing and nudity, like Mário's Poetry of the "Parábola": "El lenguaje se convierte en un ceremonial de conjuro y se presenta en la luminosidad de su desnudez inicial ajena a todo vestuario convencional fijado de antemano" (717). Moreover, poetry's otherworldly essence is reminiscent of the neutralizing power of Mário's "equilíbrio"; it is "el último horizonte, que es, a su vez, la arista en donde los extremos se tocan, en donde no hay contradicción ni duda" (717).

Only the poet can understand and wield these grandiose powers of poetry. Accordingly, he assumes a cosmic identity: "Las células del poeta están amasadas en el primer dolor y guardan el ritmo del primer espasmo. En la garganta del poeta el universo busca su voz, una voz inmortal" (717). The poet, an Adam figure, primally experiences pain and ecstasy. The sexual connotations of "ritmo" and "espasmo" represent the artistic creative act as natural and reproductive, in fact comparing artistic expression to the first instance of procreation ("del primer espasmo"). Moreover, the poet's "garganta" and universal "voz" will become privileged corporeal synecdoches, calling attention to his verbal magic.

The poet's Adam-like nature bestows upon him his special skill; he subverts, by destroying and creating anew, the symbolic relation of signifier and signified:

> El poeta conoce los ecos de los llamados de las cosas a las palabras, ve los lazos sutiles que se tienden las cosas entre sí, oye las voces secretas que se lanzan unas a otras palabras separadas por distancias inconmensurables. Hace darse la mano a vocablos enemigos desde el principio del mundo, los agrupa y los obliga a marchar en su rebaño por rebeldes que sean, descubre las alusiones más misteriosas del verbo y las condensa en un plano superior, las entreteje en su discurso, en donde lo arbitrario pasa a tomar un rol encantatorio. (717)

Huidobro envisions the poet's magical ability to transform his readers: "Allí coge ese temblor ardiente de la palabra interna que abre el cerebro del lector y le da alas y lo transporta a un plano superior, lo eleva de rango" (717). Here, Huidobro's punctuation enhances the magical effect; he ingeniously eliminates commas from the clause "y le da alas" as if to imply that the gift of wings is a natural and immediate consequence of the poet's actions, bursting forth spontaneously in a spiritual spurt of growth ("y lo transporta a un plano superior").

The poet's role confirms his relationship with Mother Nature in "Non serviam." His world is composed of the same elements as the natural world, but the poet rearranges them drastically:

> El poeta hace cambiar de vida a las cosas de la Naturaleza, saca con su red todo aquello que se mueve en el caos de lo innombrado, tiende hilos eléctricos entre las palabras y alumbra de repente rincones desconocidos, y todo ese mundo estalla en fantasmas inesperados. (716)

Since the poet has a special illuminating power with words, he can access the semiotic: "él siempre vuelve a la fuente" (717); he can therefore challenge and reinterpret the symbolic expression (in language) of the semiotic. The image of the fountain, as Goic has shown exhaustively, further connects the poet's power to the biblical creation of Genesis (79–82).

This challenging of the symbolic is expressed in terms of the poet setting up his own world. Its frontier is poetry, "el último horizonte": "Al llegar a ese lindero final el encadenamiento habitual de los fenómenos rompe su lógica, y al otro lado, en donde empiezan las tierras del poeta, la cadena se rehace en una lógica nueva" (717). A manifestation of this "looking glass" world's altered phenomena appeared in "Non serviam" in the form of the "eco traductor y optimista." It is a world of reconciliation, represented by the dissolution of a series of opposites: "más allá de lo verdadero y lo falso, más allá de la vida y de la muerte, más allá del espacio y del tiempo, más allá de la razón y la fantasía, más allá del espíritu y la materia" (717).

As the manifesto's conclusion, the description of the poet in this creative and liminal realm illuminates one of Huidobro's key symbols—the tree—as the ultimate signifier:

> Allí ha plantado el árbol de sus ojos y desde allí contempla el mundo, desde allí os habla y os descubre los secretos del mundo.
> Hay en su garganta un incendio inextinguible.
> Hay además ese balanceo de mar entre dos estrellas.
> Y hay ese *Fiat Lux* que lleva clavado en su lengua. (717)[3]

The tree, planted by the poet, is an extension of his self; it becomes the seeing phallus that observes the "secretos del mundo." The tree manifests Jacques Lacan's observation that the phallus is "a signifier whose function in the intrasubjective economy of analysis might lift the veil from that which it served in the mysteries" (79–80). Lacan stresses the *possibility* of such a revelation, whereas Huidobro implies that it is an unconditional consequence of the poet's contact with his creative powers. Lacan explains the requirement for truly achieving this revelation:

> If the phallus is a signifier then it is in the place of the Other that the subject gains access to it. But in that the signifier is only there veiled and as the ratio of the Other's desire, so it is this desire of the Other as such which the subject has to

recognise, meaning, the Other as itself a subject divided by
the signifying *Spaltung* [splitting]. (83)

In Huidobro's context of poetic creation, the reconciliation of
opposites that he indicates must be seen to include the recognition of the self (or the subject) in the Other, a theme that he
explores more fully in "Aviso a los turistas."

Moreover, the archetypal image of the tree, as explored by
Jung, further develops the poet's act of creation in the context
of the exploration of the self's boundaries. Jung lists the tree's
symbolic contexts:

> Taken on average, the commonest associations to its mean-
> ing are growth, life, unfolding of form in a physical and
> spiritual sense, development, growth from below upwards
> and from above downwards, the maternal aspect (protection,
> shade, shelter, nourishing fruits, source of life, solidity, per-
> manence, firm-rootedness, but also being "rooted to the
> spot"), old age, personality, and finally death and rebirth.
> (*Alchemical Studies* 272)

Thus Huidobro's tree is not only the archetypal Tree of Knowledge, in that it is a privileged place for viewing "los secretos
del mundo"; the tree also symbolizes, in its "maternal aspect,"
the poet's return to the phallic mother as the semiotic source,
where it is possible to challenge the symbolic expression of language. The maternal and phallic tree encompasses the process
of life, death, and rebirth, the very acts of destruction and creation that characterize the avant-garde period's break with the
past.

Consequently, the poet undergoes a physical transformation
once he is in (or becomes) the tree: his throat and tongue, organs of language production, are burned and penetrated
("clavado") by fire and light. The sea balanced between two
stars—perhaps a metaphor for the poet's mind between his
eyes—reflects Mário's "equilíbrio," although the "balanceo" is
more fantastic than Mário's recognition of the role of the unconscious in modern poetry. Even so, the "balanceo," in the
context of the series of "más allá" pairings, continues the idea
of poetry as harmony or reconciliation. The presence of the four
alchemical elements also suggests universal harmony as a sense

of completeness or totality: earth (implied by the presence of the tree and indicated expressly in the phrase "las tierras del poeta"), fire ("incendio"), water ("mar") and air (implied with "estrellas"). The quaternary union of elements traces a mandala—a circular image that represents and centers the self. Such self-representation more profoundly resembles Adam, as Jung points out in *Mysterium Coniunctionis:*

> The circular arrangement of the elements in the world and in man is symbolized by the mandala and its quaternary structure. Adam would then be a quaternarius, as he was composed of red, black, white and green dust from the four corners of the earth, and his stature reached from one end of the world to the other. (388)

In Huidobro's context, the poet's self is buoyed or balanced in the center of the universe, in the tree that is both *axis mundi* and mother's womb, and thus implicitly analogized with Adam as the first poet.

Larrea has explored Huidobro's use of the tree as the center, as much the center of the world and of the self as of the mandala, in the exclusive context of Huidobro's poetry (241–44). Citing Mircea Eliade's *Images et symboles,* Larrea interprets the tree as the kinetic ascension to a higher truth or reality, specifically with reference to *Las pagodas ocultas* ("¡Oh, árbol milagroso!"), *Adán* ("¡Oh padre Adán! Arbol frondoso / Arbol de maravillas y prodigios"), *Horizon carré* ("Hacer un poema como la naturaleza hace un árbol"), and *Altazor* ("Silencio, la tierra va a dar a luz un árbol"). The tree's paramount symbolism thus elaborates Huidobro's idea of the poet's orientation, because the tree becomes a *path* of ascension and, simultaneously, the *place* of ascension—the center, the *aleph.* Furthermore, the tree image shares the symbolism of the cross in later manifestos; here such an overlap is implied by the word "clavado," suggesting the nails in Christ's hands and feet. Consideration of the tree's appearance in "La poesía" and in other manifestos, where the movement of ascending to a sublime truth encompasses the act of fulfillment in poetic creation, unquestionably enriches the context of this image in Huidobro's entire oeuvre.

The fantastic context of the poet and his tree in "La poesía" exposes the illusory nature of the poet's vision. In fact, Huidobro does little in this manifesto to explain how the poet can truly achieve such an exalted state of knowledge, or even how one goes about becoming a poet. The interest of the text lies purely in the mythification of his poetics, in his insistence on the divinity of the poet. However, the final affirmation of godlike creativity, the poet's "Let there be light," does not imply the ability to create from nothing; rather, the poet's creativity resides in his challenge to linguistic convention (symbolic discourse). As a case in point, the illuminating phrase mentioned above—"El poeta [. . .] tiende hilos eléctricos entre las palabras y alumbra de repente rincones desconocidos" (716)—anticipates the light-diffusing function of this same "Let there be light." Thus the radiance from the poet's pierced tongue is an invented (and not natural) light, modern and shocking when paired with classical Latin; the poet's illumination is an electric *Fiat Lux*.[4]

• Balance and Flow

"La creación pura: *Ensayo de estética*," is Huidobro's attempt to arrange and defend his aesthetic system. It was first published as "La création pure: Essai d'esthétique" in the April 1921 edition of *L'Esprit Nouveau* and then reappeared the same year as the prologue to the anthology *Saisons choisies*.[5] The text includes his classification of three types of artistic production and their evolution, and also his chart depicting the creative process. The main ideas in the analysis of this manifesto are the further definition of the artist's non-mimetic creative role, supported by a pseudoscientific discourse and mechanistic presentation of poetic composition, and the binary harmonies that Huidobro recommends in order to strengthen the artist's creative potential.

Huidobro begins by categorically rejecting previous aesthetic theories in order to dramatize the need for his new ones. His evolutionary system of *Arte reproductivo, Arte de adaptación,* and *Arte creativo* expands his earlier observation, referred to in context, that "toda la historia del arte no es sino la historia de la evolución del Hombre-Espejo hacia el Hombre-Dios"

(719). Even though he refers to the primitive origins of reproductive art (the art of the Mirror-Man), he admits that the idea for the creative art of the God-Man was originally expressed to him by an Andean indigenous poet, whom many would consider to be "primitive":

> Esta idea de artista como creador absoluto, del Artista-Dios, me la sugirió un viejo poeta indígena de Sudamérica (aimará) que dijo: "El poeta es un dios; no cantes a la lluvia, poeta, haz llover." A pesar de que el autor de estos versos cayó en el error de confundir al poeta con el mago y creer que el artista para aparecer como un creador debe cambiar las leyes del mundo, cuando lo que ha de hacer consiste en crear su propio mundo, paralelo e independiente de la Naturaleza. (719)

Larrea shows that the Aymara origin of this phrase is in doubt, first because the Aymaran's identity is never disclosed by Huidobro and, more importantly, because the phrase is very similar to one cited by Huidobro's friend Maurice Raynal in the "Avant le cubisme" chapter of his 1953 book *Peinture moderne,* referring to the period of 1906–08. Larrea quotes Raynal: "Los artistas han visto abiertos sus horizontes a través de este verso de un antiguo poeta hindú: 'Oh, poète, ne nous parle de la pluie, fait pleuvoir plutôt'" (229). Larrea suggests that Huidobro changed the origin of the phrase in order to promote his native continent, but concludes that the true origin may never be known. However, in a different context Bary mentions Larrea's apropos discovery, based on the Old Testament book of I Kings, that the verb *to rain* in Hebrew can also mean "to disseminate the word of God" (*Nuevos estudios* 53)— the poet who makes rain is divine. Regardless of where the idea came from, it is only slightly modified ("to rain" > "to bloom") as the subject of Huidobro's famous verses from "Arte poética": "Por qué cantáis la rosa, ¡oh, Poetas! / Hacedla florecer en el poema" and "El poeta es un pequeño Dios" (219).

Yet in the shadow of the "viejo poeta indígena," Huidobro feels the need to differ from his source by focusing on the creation of a parallel, independent world, rather than the transformation of the existing world's natural laws. The reason for this subtle distinction may be to distance Huidobro's views from the precedent identified by Raynal, or perhaps to explain away the paradox of a so-called "primitive" poet being the source of the theory of *Arte creativo* as the most advanced stage in the author's system, or simply to satisfy the whims of egocentrism. In any case, Huidobro clarifies this distinction by repeating the rebellion motif, only to show that if the artist is casting off the imitation of Nature's creative manifestations, it is in order to embrace the imitation of Nature's creative powers:

> El Hombre sacude su yugo, se rebela contra la naturaleza como antaño se rebelara Lucifer contra Dios, a pesar de que esta rebelión sólo es aparente, pues *el hombre nunca estuvo más cerca de la Naturaleza que ahora que ya no busca imitarla en sus apariencias, sino hacer lo mismo que ella, imitándola en el plano de sus leyes constructivas,* en la realización de un todo, en el mecanismo de la producción de nuevas formas. (720; original emphasis)

Huidobro immediately applies the idea of a "mecanismo de la producción" to the theory of artistic creation by means of a symmetrically designed box flow chart (see fig. 1). The mechanism's input is the natural world ("tal como una planta, un pájaro, un astro o un fruto" [720]), filtered by the artist's "Sistema," which is essentially his perception and selection of its phenomena. The filtered input is then transformed by the artist's "Técnica," or his study and choice of which artistic modes of expression to use, into the output (the poem), described as a "Regreso al mundo objetivo bajo forma de hecho nuevo creado por el artista." Thus the poet himself, in the

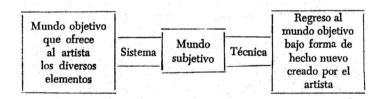

Mundo objetivo que ofrece al artista los diversos elementos	Sistema	Mundo subjetivo	Técnica	Regreso al mundo objetivo bajo forma de hecho nuevo creado por el artista

Fig. 1. Mecanismo de producción. From Vicente Huidobro, "La creación pura," in his *Obras completas,* ed. Hugo Montes (Santiago: Andrés Bello, 1976), 1: 721. Reproduced with permission of the Fundación Vicente Huidobro, Santiago, Chile.

"Mundo subjetivo," occupies the center of this process. As seen in "La poesía," the poet's personal world lies beyond the borders of the "último horizonte," an unconscious zone where the poet can contemplate all the world's mysteries; the "Mundo subjetivo" seems to assume these qualities as the place of poetic creation, to which the poet retires and from which he returns with poems. The poet's circular journey and the interplay of conscious and unconscious realms support a comparison with Joseph Campbell's cycle of the hero in *The Hero with a Thousand Faces* (245). The hero's goal is to bring back to the conscious world what he has experienced or learned in the mythical unconscious zone, just as the poet shares his otherworldly insights in poems.

Yet Huidobro does not take up any mythological underpinnings in this essay, stressing rather the scientific, industrial parallel inherent in his phrase "mecanismo de producción."[6] The tone established at the beginning of the manifesto, in which he warns, "Por ello debemos alejarnos lo más posible de la metafísica y aproximarnos cada vez más a la filosofía científica" (718), intends to appropriate scientific discourse as a legitimizing technique. Hence his depiction of the evolution of the Mirror-Man into the God-Man as analogous to that of prehistoric equines into the modern horse (719). After the flow chart presentation, this pseudoscientific discourse justifies Huidobro's defense of what he perceives as the poet's creative license threatened by "estos científicos," "los sabios modernos" (721). The relationship with science emphasizes not just the inevitability of humankind's place in Nature but also the creative powers inherent in both:

> El Hombre empieza por ver, luego oye, después habla y por último piensa. En sus creaciones, el hombre siguió este mismo orden que le ha sido impuesto. Primero inventó la fotografía [. . .] Luego el teléfono [. . .] Después el gramófono [. . .] y por último, el cine, que es el pensamiento mecánico. (721–22)

Although this miniature summary of scientific history is rather selective, and does not follow exactly the order it claims to mimic, it nonetheless validates the distinction that Huidobro tries to make between the sterility of outright mimesis and the

41

fecundity of humankind's natural creative or interpretive abilities: "No se trata de imitar la Naturaleza, sino que hacer como ella; no imitar sus exteriorizaciones sino su poder exteriorizador" (720).

The key to harnessing this "poder exteriorizador" lies within the flow chart's central position, the "Mundo subjetivo." By manipulating the manifesto's sets of variables, one can discover that the optimal conditions for the "Mundo subjetivo" in the creative process are expressed by the concept of harmony. Huidobro states that the "apogeo" of an artistic period is the middle stage of his evolution of "sensibilidad" and "inteligencia," the stage he designates as the "Armonía" of these two ideas (718). He bases his legitimizing scientific examples on a comparison with unspecified works of art that, like the inventions he lists, are "obedeciendo siempre las mismas leyes de *adaptación* al medio" (722; my emphasis); the *Arte de adaptación* period, in his first scheme, is also the period in which the idea of harmony unifies: "Arte en armonía con el medio" (718). Finally, Huidobro describes the attainment of an authentic artistic style as a harmony: "La armonía perfecta entre el Sistema y la Técnica es la que hace el Estilo [. . .] Diremos, pues, que un artista tiene estilo cuando los medios que emplea para realizar su obra están en perfecta armonía con los elementos que escogió en el mundo objetivo" (721). An imbalance of these elements means that the artist "no logrará jamás un estilo, sólo tendrá una manera" (721); unfortunately, no clear explanation reveals exactly how the harmony of style differs from the imbalance of the lesser "manera."

Nevertheless, this fascination with the symmetry of "sensibilidad" and "inteligencia," "arte" and "medio," and "Sistema" and "Técnica" subtly reveals again the need for balancing the conscious and the unconscious. For example, in describing the artists of the decadent, ending phase of his cycle, the phase that follows the "apogeo," Huidobro states: "Ellos ejecutan las obras por pura sensibilidad, y hasta se puede decir que maquinalmente, pues el hábito hace pasar del consciente al inconsciente" (718–19). This condemnation of submission to the unconscious previews Huidobro's quarrel with surrealism in "Manifiesto de manifiestos"; more importantly, it implies that if Huidobro thinks of the decadent (third) artistic phase as dominated by the unconscious, then the "apogeo" (second) phase must be a balance of the two, while the beginning (first) phase is dominated by the conscious. This observation roughly equates the conscious with "inteligencia" and the unconscious with "sensibilidad" in the cycle. As stated, this is an implicit, perhaps accidental, reference to the balance of the conscious and the unconscious, but not for that reason does it cease to be important in the establishment of Huidobro's harmony.

Finally, after stressing the importance of balance in the "Mundo subjetivo," Huidobro ends by referring to the balance of the artistic work itself, inspired by the laws of physics: "'[. . .] debe tener, como los astros, una atmósfera propia y una fuerza centrípeta y otra centrífuga. Fuerzas que le dan un *equilibrio perfecto* y la arrojan fuera del centro productor'" (722; my emphasis). The apparent balance of the natural world as input must match the equilibrium of the artist's work as output. The interpretation of the "centro productor" in this context glosses all of its previous associations; in the "mecanismo de producción," the center is the "Mundo subjetivo" or the self which, as seen in "La poesía," implies the connection to the tree and to the semiotic source, or the chora.

Although a balance of the conscious and the unconscious ideally maximizes the strength of the "Mundo subjetivo," Huidobro's tendency, as in "Non serviam," is to favor conscious aspects of poetic creation. This predilection subtly resurfaces in his interpretation of a quote on truth from Friedrich Schleiermacher's *Aesthétik,* shortly before he presents the chart:

> "la poesía no busca la verdad o, más bien, ella busca una verdad que nada tiene en común con la verdad objetiva."
> "El arte y la poesía sólo expresan la verdad de la conciencia singular."
> Es preciso hacer notar esta diferencia entre la verdad de la vida y la verdad del arte; una que existe antes del artista, y otra que le es posterior, que es producida por éste. (720)

The singular or unique consciousness is the source of poetic truth, according to Schleiermacher; Huidobro's wording that poetic truth is "producida" by the artist would seem to equate the "conciencia singular" with his "Mundo subjetivo," effectively foregrounding the role of the poet's conscious.

As Navarrete Orta notes, this passage somewhat complicates Huidobro's binary system by presenting a further dichotomy of artistic (poetic) truth and life's (natural) truth (150). However, in his series of binary harmonies Huidobro implicitly associates the poet's conscious self (and therefore poetic truth) with a link to the unconscious and the semiotic; moreover, this link seems to be something that only the true poet or artist possesses. He astutely promotes this link because the surrealists, advocating automatic writing, "parecían así liquidar la tradición romántica/simbolista de la cual Huidobro extraía su mito del poeta aristocrático dotado del don creador que le era negado al resto de los mortales" (Gutiérrez Mouat 122). For that reason, Huidobro's slighting of the unconscious in this manifesto and in his next piece, "Manifiesto de manifiestos," never seeks to eliminate its importance in maintaining a balance. Instead, in order to distinguish his poetics from theirs, he accuses the surrealists of a fixation on the unconscious while he focuses on and justifies the need for conscious aspects of poetic creation.

• Delirium and the Superconscious

"Manifiesto de manifiestos" first appeared as the opening piece in *Manifestes,* with the title "Manifeste manifestes." In either language the title implies a sort of pompous finality or supremacy, as in "The King of Kings," but it also refers to the content of this manifesto, dealing as it does with Huidobro's critique of other manifestos and subsequent defense of his own ideas. The compared texts are Tzara's dadaist manifestos and three surrealist manifestos. Significantly, Huidobro is no longer the young innovator in this context, but rather the defender of already established ideas: "Después de lanzados los últimos manifiestos acerca de la poesía, acabo de leer los míos y, más que nunca, me afirmo en mis antiguas teorías" (722). In a personal context, his claim of seniority reveals that the avant-garde, despite appearances to the contrary, cannot escape the trap of tradition.

Asterisks divide the manifesto into three sections. The first section contains an introduction, in which Huidobro makes the observation that all the compared manifestos share an anti-mimetic orientation, and then a quick dispatch of Tzara's manifestos: "fueron tan comentados a su hora que no vale la pena volver sobre ellos. Además, son mucho más surrealistas—al menos en su forma—que los manifiestos surrealistas" (722). Primarily, the first section presents a critique of automatic writing that dovetails into the promotion of Huidobro's alternative, "el delirio." In the second section, Huidobro subverts the novelty that the surrealists claim in their interpretation of "la imaginación." The final section reaffirms the poem as an incorporation of "lo inhabitual."

Huidobro begins his attack on surrealism by citing Breton's definition of the movement: "'Automatismo psíquico puro mediante el cual uno se propone expresar el verdadero funcionamiento del pensar. Dictado del pensar ajeno a cualquier control de la razón'" (722). He argues that the definition is a non sequitur, since the very act of thinking implies reason, and could not exist without it: "no podéis apartar la razón de las demás facultades del intelecto, salvo en el caso de una lesión orgánica, estado patológico imposible de producir voluntariamente" (723). The "lesión orgánica" signals more legitimizing pseudoscientific discourse in Huidobro's defensive stance, as in the following conclusion based on Newton's laws: "El automatismo psíquico puro—es decir, la espontaneidad completa—no existe. Pues todo movimiento, como lo dice la ciencia, es transformación de un movimiento anterior" (723). Huidobro's ostensible embrace of science in the defense of reason reveals a nascent conservative stance compared to dadaism's and surrealism's increasing anarchy within the avant-garde.

Concerning the concept of reason, Huidobro cites Vico, Bergson, and Plato as apparently agreeing with the surrealists that the poet should espouse fantasy and inspiration instead of reason; however, Huidobro differentiates: "Lejos del poeta la *fría razón;* pero hay otra razón que no es fría, que mientras el poeta trabaja se halla al unísono con el calor de su alma" (723). This faculty of reason holds Huidobro's real interest: "Para qué dar tanta importancia a esta semipersonalidad (pues el automatismo sólo reside en los centros corticales inferiores) y no dársela a nuestra personalidad total y verdadera. / ¿Acaso creéis que un hombre dormido es más hombre—o menos interesante—que uno despierto?" (723). Since the unconscious subject is only a "semipersonalidad," Huidobro again stresses the need for balance by contrasting with "nuestra personalidad total y verdadera."

Both sides are necessary for balance; therefore, Huidobro admits the role of dreams and inspiration, but always tempered by the conscious:

> La característica del sueño consiste en la anulación de la voluntad. Esto no impide, desde luego, el que persistan otras actividades psíquicas. Pero, desde el instante en que queráis expresarlas por escrito, la conciencia entra instantáneamente en el juego. No hay modo de evitar esto, y lo que escribáis no habrá nacido de un automatismo psíquico puro. (724)

For this reason, Huidobro focuses on the moment of inspiration, the poetic "delirio." This he describes variously as "el juego completo del ensamble de las palabras," "el momento maravilloso de la mirada abierta desmesuradamente hasta llenar el universo y absorberlo como una bomba" and "esta partida de ajedrez contra el infinito," all indicating a kind of cosmic dialogue or identification with the universe, without which the poet sees no reason for living: "yo me suicidaría" (724). He emphasizes:

> Por tanto, si vuestro surrealismo pretende hacernos escribir como un médium, automáticamente, a la velocidad de un lápiz en la pista de las motocicletas y sin el juego profundo de todas nuestras facultades puestas bajo presión, jamás aceptaremos vuestras fórmulas. (724)

Of course Huidobro's threats are exaggerated and his use of the first-person plural is wishful thinking. Nonetheless, he manages to posit successfully the case for the inclusion of poetic creation's conscious element.

Huidobro goes on to characterize automatic writing as "banal" in contrast to the writing inspired by poetic "delirio." This latter concept becomes more important as he equates it with a state he calls the "superconciencia" and develops it, with more pseudoscientific lingo based on Marconian radio technology, as a part of his poetic mystique. The "superconciencia" is a step beyond downplaying the unconscious attributes celebrated by surrealism; it is not just the conscious but rather the superconscious. In this way Huidobro distances himself even more from surrealist associations. At the same time, he surprisingly equates the strange bedfellows delirium and superconscious as if to emphasize two diverse aspects balanced in the same phenomenon, perhaps because the former can connote an abandonment of reason while the latter seems to imply the restricting control of Freud's superego. The "superconciencia" springs from what seems to be a scientifically measureable condition:

> [. . .] cuando nuestras facultades intelectuales adquieren una intensidad vibratoria superior, una longitud de onda, una calidad de onda, infinitamente más poderosa que de ordinario. En el poeta, este estado puede producirse, puede desencadenarse mediante algún hecho insignificante e invisible, a veces, para el propio poeta. [. . .] La posibilidad de ponerse en ese estado sólo *pertenece* a los poetas, y no hay nada más falso que aquel refrán que dice: "De poeta y loco todos tenemos un poco." (725; original emphasis)

To develop the idea of the poets' monopoly on delirium, Huidobro further contrasts it with the weaker "ensueño," seemingly using conclusions from the anatomy laboratory: "El ensueño poético nace generalmente de un estado de debilidad cerebral; en cambio la superconciencia, el delirio poético, nace de una corteza cerebral rica y bien alimentada" (725). In a footnote to this sentence, the author supports the view that Breton's fasting caused his poetic revelations; Huidobro thus distinguishes his mystique further by having it appear to be as natural as eating when hungry. Automatic poetry, he implies, is the product of a malnourished, imbalanced brain. Furthermore, in contrast to the "ensueño," the "delirio" does not abandon reason: "Paralelamente a la imaginación, en el delirio la razón sube hasta las grandes alturas en que la atmósfera terrestre se rarifica y se necesitan pulmones especiales para respirarla, pues si ambas no se hallan de acuerdo la razón se ahogará" (725). Once more, in a kind of high-elevation frontier zone, the poet recognizes a need for agreement or balance ("acuerdo"); this time the balance is between reason and imagination. Finally, lest anyone confuse "ensueño" with "delirio," he differentiates them emphatically: *"Y mientras que el ensueño pertenece a todo el mundo, el delirio sólo pertenece a los poetas"* (725).

Although he rejects the mechanical notion of automatic writing, the author concludes this first section by referring again to poetic production as a "mecanismo" and a "máquina," as with the chart in "La creación pura." In the avant-garde contest to appropriate scientific discourse, Huidobro's strategy is to promote the paradox of a natural machine, one that incorporates telluric phenomena. In this context, the machine's force surges, "cargada de millones de calorías, de esas calorías químicas que transforman el carbón en diamante, pues la poesía es la transmutación de todas las cosas en piedras preciosas" (726). His "calorías" contrast again with Breton's starved inspirations, through the association energy = fuel = food. Only the well-nourished, energetic poet can achieve the state of delirium and its implied balance of conscious and unconscious, reason and imagination.

The second section of the manifesto begins with the debunking of the surrealists' presumedly original definition of imagination as "la facultad mediante la cual el hombre puede reunir dos realidades distintas" (726). Huidobro claims it is the same definition he had used in *Pasando y pasando,* and that it is also offered by Voltaire and Abel Rey; thus, ostensibly, Huidobro and the surrealists agree. However, he focuses on his own ideas regarding the importance of the poet's role:

> Yo agregaba entonces, y lo repito ahora, que el poeta es aquel que sorprende la relación oculta que existe entre las cosas más lejanas, los ocultos hilos que las unen. Hay que pulsar aquellos hilos como las cuerdas de un arpa, y producir una resonancia que ponga en movimiento las dos realidades lejanas. (726)

This passage, which echoes "La poesía," again depicts the poet as the center, the unifier of two distinct realities. The power of the image provides the poet with his ability to connect such distant entities through "la alegría de la revelación"; the image shines as "el broche que las une, el broche de luz" (726).

Huidobro follows up by providing examples of images, taking advantage of the moment to censure two examples from Breton's manifesto in favor of two examples from his own works, *Horizon carré* and *Adán,* which he promotes as more original. However, he clarifies that his examples are in no way representative of spontaneous inspiration; on the contrary, he claims that reason helped shape them, although no one can ever truly know how reason controls the images that our senses gather. He vaguely explains:

> Pues en nuestro alambique espiritual, en constante ebulli-
> ción, existen los que Loeb y Bohn llaman "fenómenos
> asociativos y sensibilidad diferencial" y la razón, a cada ins-
> tante, mete su cuchara en este alambique de asociación y
> contrastes; y tal vez cuando proclamáis lo fortuito y lo arbi-
> trario estáis como nunca lejos de ambos. (728)

Within this discussion of images, the image of the alembic—a kind of distilling flask—seeks to represent scientific authority but instead, in its pairing with "espiritual," furnishes the imprecise, hocus-pocus notion of science and alchemy left over from Romanticism. In contrast, the author does mention J. Loeb and G. Bohn, biologists popularly renowned for work on animal instinct and the physiology of the brain; Huidobro again mixes his aesthetic and scientific discourses in order to legitimize the modern moment.

The remainder of this second section attempts to prove the following anti-surrealist statement:

> No creo que las páginas más hermosas de la literatura hayan
> sido producidas bajo un dictado automático. Estoy conven-
> cido, incluso, de que las que parecen más locas provienen,
> por el contrario, de momentos en que nuestra conciencia se
> halla plenamente despierta. (728)

He gives an example from Ben Jonson's *Volpone; or, The Foxe* and an extensive fragment of Rabelais's *Pantagruel.* His conclusion—"es lo insólito, lo sorpresivo, lo que nos conmueve y disloca" (730)—does not explicitly condemn surrealism but does seem to confirm his declaration regarding the importance of reason in the development of the original image.

The final section of "Manifiesto de manifiestos" builds on the idea of the poem which, although it should affect the reader by its representation of "lo inhabitual," must be constructed of everyday things; the poem that is "construido a base de elementos inhabituales" will only produce astonishment, which

Huidobro claims is not the same thing as enthusiasm and its effect of carrying the spirit "hasta las alturas del vértigo consciente" (730). He extends his preference for electrical imagery in mechanical creation: "La vida de un poema depende de la duración de su carga eléctrica"; "hay que ser poeta para enhebrar las palabras cotidianas en un filamento Osram incandescente"; "El poeta es un motor de alta frecuencia espiritual"; "Ser poeta consiste en tener una dosis tal de particular humanidad, que pueda conferírsele a todo lo que pase a través del organismo cierta electricidad atómica profunda" (730). Gutiérrez Mouat views this reliance on electrical imagery as "el riesgo que corre una poética de la sorpresa [. . .] El poema creacionista se sabe un objeto efímero que debe recargarse de energía" (135).

Yet Huidobro's conclusion defends its claims by grounding them in tradition. He cites the predecessor-poet Saint-Pol Roux, "uno de los pocos artistas que quisieron dar al poeta todo el prestigio que entraña este vocablo mágico," exalting the power of poetry as a science in itself, with each poet espousing different rules, but all rules deriving from "una ley primordial, la ley de los dioses" (731).[7] Such inclusiveness in the manifesto's conclusion reflects the overall tone of the manifesto that, in spite of enumerating Huidobro's differences with surrealism, nonetheless has offered the surrealists a tentative welcome:

> En los manifiestos surrealistas hay muchas cosas bien dichas, y si los surrealistas producen obras que denoten un momento de gran altura del cerebro humano, serán dignos de todas las alabanzas.
>
> Debemos darles crédito, aunque no aceptemos su camino y no creamos en la exactitud de su teoría. (727)

In summary, this manifesto is a vehicle in which Huidobro defends the uniqueness of his own theories while criticizing surrealism without condemning it outright. Continuing his characteristic style and the development of his mystique, he offers a new context, through the relationship of reason and imagination in "el delirio" or "la superconciencia," for the important idea of balance. Both reason and imagination, he argues, are necessary for the creation of the unusual, strikingly original image.

• Wind in the Flute

In the opening sentence of the tripartite manifesto "El creacionismo," Huidobro defines his signature movement in general terms:

> El creacionismo no es una escuela que yo haya querido imponer a alguien; el creacionismo es una teoría estética general que empecé a elaborar hacia 1912, y cuyos tanteos y primeros pasos los hallaréis en mis libros y artículos escritos mucho antes de mi primer viaje a París. (731–32)

The statement has two objectives: first, to resist any association with artistic schools, against which the avant-garde rebelled, in theory, because such schools connoted strict rules and conformity; and second, to downplay the influence of Huidobro's relationship with the avant-garde in France by stressing his initial ideas in Chile, nonetheless strongly shaped by European thought. Such defensive objectives are not surprising, given de Costa's discovery that this manifesto is in fact a diluted version of an angry letter Huidobro wrote to Enrique Gómez Carrillo, after the latter had published an article questioning Huidobro's purported role as the founder of *creacionismo*. The letter was so abrasive (it ended with the poet obliquely challenging Gómez Carrillo to a duel) that no one would publish it until five years later when, after drastic revision and translation, it became "Le créationnisme" in *Manifestes* (73–77). By that time, the text was overdue. De Costa explains that "Whatever [Huidobro's] conception of the avant-garde and his seminal role in its development may once have been, by 1925 he knew he had no followers. Creationism belonged to history" (*Vicente Huidobro: The Careers of a Poet* 79). "El creacionismo" remains a foundational text for tracing the development of Huidobro's poetics.

The next four paragraphs of the manifesto continue the superficial history of *creacionismo,* culminating in June of 1916 in the Ateneo of Buenos Aires: "Fue allí donde se me bautizó

como creacionista por haber dicho en mi conferencia que la
primera condición del poeta es crear; la segunda, crear, y la
tercera, crear" (732). Huidobro begins a defense of *creacionismo* against the opinion, expressed by several critics in
different contexts, that the *creacionista* poem is "irrealizable."
A technique Huidobro used often—quoting his own words on
a previous and specific occasion—serves here to give continuity and uniformity to his theoretical stances over the years; at
the same time, it seeks to solidify his position as an already
established authority:

> Respondo ahora con las mismas frases con que acabé mi
> conferencia dada ante el grupo de Estudios Filosóficos y
> Científicos del doctor Allendy, en París, en enero de 1922:
> *Si el hombre ha sometido para sí a los tres reinos de la*
> *naturaleza, el reino mineral, el vegetal y el animal, ¿por*
> *qué razón no podrá agregar a los reinos del universo su pro-*
> *pio reino, el reino de sus creaciones?* (732)

In this last kingdom, Huidobro establishes again the parallel
between mechanical and poetic creations: "El hombre ya ha
inventado toda una fauna nueva que anda, vuela, nada, y llena
la tierra, el espacio y los mares con sus galopes desenfrenados,
con sus gritos y sus gemidos. / Lo realizado en la mecánica
también se ha hecho en la poesía" (732–33). In other words,
Huidobro places the critics' word "irrealizable" into the context of those doubters who responded in the same way when
offered predictions of technological innovations that have since
become realities. The mechanical marvels' parallel poetic innovation is the "poema creado," an independent phenomenon:
"se hace realidad a sí mismo" (733). Its independence com-
poses its beauty:

> Y no es hermoso porque recuerde algo, no es hermoso por-
> que nos recuerde cosas vistas, a su vez hermosas, ni porque
> describa hermosas cosas que podamos llegar a ver. Es her-
> moso en sí y no admite términos de comparación. (733)

Significantly, Huidobro's use of the subjunctive in this passage
denies the ontology of descriptive or "reproductive" poems, in
contrast to the affirmation of the "poema creado" as a self-con-
tained fact.

Huidobro also examines the poet's role: "Dicho poema es algo que no puede existir sino en la cabeza del poeta" (733); the uniqueness of the poet's vision gives each poem its own real and extraordinary existence. The remainder of this manifesto's first section seeks to consecrate this role, through examples of creative images conceived or selected by Huidobro. Starting with his own "El pájaro anida en el arco iris," he gives two pages of examples by Tzara, Francis Picabia, Georges Ribémont Dessaignes, Paul Eluard, Diego, and Larrea. Huidobro offers the last example, one of his own—"Night comes from others [*sic*] eyes"—in French, Spanish, and English to support the global context that he presents in concluding this section: "La poesía creacionista adquiere proporciones internacionales, pasa a ser la Poesía, y se hace accesible a todos los pueblos y razas, como la pintura, la música o la escultura" (736). This declaration echoes his opening proposition that *creacionismo* is not a school; indeed, he idealistically asserts that it transcends itself to become the capitalized Poetry, universal in contrast to the regional and temporal confines of a school.

The second section of "El creacionismo" encapsulates one of Huidobro's most important statements concerning the struggle for balance in artistic expression. He identifies an inherent duality in humankind that, although it can be frustratingly irresolvable, must be embraced by the poet in order to create. Huidobro initially describes the two parts of the duality as electric currents, but then he develops them into masculine and feminine forces, centrifugal and centripetal forces, innate and acquired personalities, and finally the opposition sensibility/imagination. Thus, the concept of duality envelops a wide range of opposed pairings—a layering that enriches understanding by offering a gamut of possibilities. Initially, this dichotomy is all-encompassing, even life-giving: "Hay en el hombre una dualidad que se manifiesta en todos sus actos, dos corrientes paralelas en las que se engendran todos los fenómenos de la vida" (736). Yet it immediately results in frustration and differentiation:

> Todo ser humano es un hermafrodita frustrado. Tenemos un principio o una fuerza de expansión, que es femenina, y una fuerza de concentración, que es masculina.

> En ciertos hombres domina una en detrimento de la otra.
> En muy pocos aparecen ambas en perfecto equilibrio. (736)

The denomination of expansion as feminine, and of concentration or contraction as masculine, serves to connect a gender-based context of semantic oppositions with a physical or material context, defined more precisely when he states that we all possess both centripetal and centrifugal forces.

Huidobro expounds this reunion of opposing physical forces, seen previously at the end of "La creación pura," in what proves to be a clarification of the meanings of "Sistema" and "Técnica" from the chart in that same manifesto:

> Poseemos vías centrípetas, vías que nos traen como antenas los hechos que ocurren a sus alrededores (audición, visión, sensibilidad general), y poseemos vías centrífugas, que semejan aparatos de emisiones y nos sirven para emitir nuestras ondas, para proyectar el mundo subjetivo en el mundo objetivo (escritura, palabra, movimiento). (736)

The double interaction with the "mundo objetivo" appears here as a relay of radio broadcasts. The central focus on duality has thus changed slightly from an explanation of the dual nature of humankind to the description of how humans interact artistically with their environment.

However, Huidobro shifts back to human nature itself. Now, instead of two forces or genders, the focus shifts to complementary personalities: "El poeta, como todos los hombres, tiene dos personalidades, que no son, hablando con propiedad, dos personalidades, sino por el contrario la personalidad en singular, la única verdadera" (737). Here Huidobro refers to the innate and acquired personalities that compose the "personalidad total," supposedly in the proportion of three quarters to one quarter respectively. He claims that the former is what Henri Bergson calls the "yo fundamental" and the latter the "yo superficial," or Etienne Condillac's "yo pensante" and "yo autómota" (737). Although the personalities are identified as separate components, their reconciliation as a whole is the poet's goal:

> En el creacionismo proclamamos la personalidad total.
> Nada de parcelas de poetas.

El infinito entero en el poeta, el poeta íntegro en el instante de proyectarse. (737)

These affirmations are prolepses of "Total," the last text included in *Manifiestos,* and they again highlight the incorporation of various contrasting elements, in this case the poet's prerequisite of encompassing the total personality.

The last sentences of this second section once again change the focus of duality. Up to this point, Huidobro has addressed, although not very explicitly and somewhat randomly, both the dualities of the poet himself and of his interaction with the world. Now he concentrates on artistic production through the following "dualidad paralela: la sensibilidad, que es el elemento afectivo, y la imaginación, que es el elemento intelectual" (737). As seen in "La creación pura," these elements, presented similarly but designated "sensibilidad" and "inteligencia," either dominated one another or were in harmony during the three stages of evolution within each phase of artistic production. Along these lines, Huidobro here reprises his critique of surrealism, insisting that in automatic writing these two elements are unequally weighted in favor of "la sensibilidad." In contrast, his "poesía creada" displays the opposite imbalance, violently portrayed: "la imaginación arrasa con la simple sensibilidad" (737). Given that the imagination is the intellectual property of the self or the poet ("Mundo subjetivo"), Huidobro's context again favors the poet's conscious behavior over unconscious sensory stimuli.

The intense variety of binary oppositions presented in the nineteen brief sentences of this section is remarkable in *Manifiestos,* surpassed in intensity, if not in variety, only by "Total." The fact that Huidobro offers this kaleidoscoping duality, unconditionally and without organizational commentary, in the explanation of three distinct facets of the poetic process (the poet, his relationship with the world, and his creation) strongly confirms his dichotomous vision. However, only two of these three facets resolve themselves in equilibrium: the poet ("la personalidad total") and his relationship with the world ("vías centrípetas" and "vías centrífugas"). The emphasis given to the intellectual, conscious role in the third facet—the act of creation—characteristically tips the balance to reveal Huidobro's bias.

The third and final section of "El creacionismo," mainly a valorization of the aesthetic principles emblazoned in *Horizon carré,* begins with a confession. Huidobro admits that harsh critical reaction to his 1913 *La gruta del silencio* caused him to question his most satisfying verses and to begin a period in which he granted high value "al subconsciente y hasta a cierta especie de sonambulismo" (737). He is quick to limit its importance: "Pero éste fue un paréntesis de pocos meses"; it was the fall into a distasteful learning experience: "[. . .] ese horrible panteísmo mezcla de hindú y de noruego, en esa poesía de buey rumiante y de abuela satisfecha. Felizmente esta caída duró poco y al cabo de algunas semanas retomé mi antiguo camino con mucho más entusiasmo y conocimiento que antes" (738). Obedience to the unconscious is thus portrayed as an adolescent experiment resulting from self-doubt, not strong enough to permanently deter the poet from his calling. Significantly, self-doubt entails a weakening of the conscious will and a desire for acceptance that leads, naturally in Huidobro's case, to the exploration of the unconscious.

Like these pre-surrealist experiments in Chile, the futurist environment prevailing in Paris at the time of the author's arrival in 1916 is disappointing:

> [. . .] se trataba de un ambiente muy futurista y no hay que olvidar que dos años antes, en mi libro *Pasando y pasando,* yo había atacado al futurismo como algo demasiado viejo, en el preciso instante en que todos voceaban el advenimiento de algo completamente nuevo. (738)

Huidobro's struggle for fluency in French compounds his disillusion and leads to his hyperbolic statement that although he recognized Apollinaire as a poet in the "sentido habitual" of the word, on the contrary, in his own "sentido íntimo," "para mí nunca ha habido un solo poeta en toda la historia de nuestro planeta" (738). This constitutes the first example of a recurring theme in some of his manifestos: the idea that only in the future will there exist poets who fully understand their role and write true poetry. Huidobro develops this idea by quoting himself ten years previously, though perhaps in a less optimistic context than at that time, as reflected in the anti-climactic final statement:

> "Nunca se ha compuesto un solo poema en el mundo, sólo se han hecho algunos vagos ensayos de componer un poema. La poesía está por nacer en nuestro globo. Y su nacimiento será un suceso que revolucionará a los hombres como el más formidable terremoto." A veces me pregunto si no pasará desapercibido. (738)

Here Huidobro displays very strongly the avant-garde's unconditional denial of the past, its urgency of revolution, and its confidence in the future, three traits that yield the paradox of a continuous revolution. Although presented here in a different context, his call for this revolution has not changed in ten years.

From these exaggerated rhetorical claims Huidobro moves on to address the originality and poetic tenets of *Horizon carré*. He concentrates on the title image, a square horizon: "Un hecho nuevo inventado por mí, creado por mí, que no podría existir sin mí" (739). The image, which perhaps not by chance resembles a quaternary mandala with four sides and four corners, is meant to exemplify four aesthetic principles that Huidobro quotes from a letter he wrote to a friend. These principles are: (1) "Humanizar las cosas"—in a fortuitous negation of Ortega y Gasset's term, the poet moves the horizon into the human realm by pairing it with the unique adjective "square";[8] (2) to make precise what would otherwise be vague, or to define fleeting, inner images and ideas; (3) to make abstract what is concrete and vice versa—this creates (again) "el equilibrio perfecto" because otherwise the abstract made more abstract would escape comprehension, and the concrete made more concrete "servirá para beber vino o amoblar su casa, pero jamás para amoblar su alma"; (4) to make essences or phenomena that are already naturally poetic, such as the horizon, *artistically* poetic by modifying them in uncharacteristic, surprising, seemingly impossible ways—"De poesía muerta pasa a ser poesía viva" (739).

Principles (1) and (4) simply relate different ways of saying the same thing, and so do (2) and (3); this conflation yields two similar ideas which, combined, yield the first-page dedicatory phrases of *Horizon carré,* quoted here in the manifesto:

Crear un poema sacando de la vida sus motivos y transformándolos para darles una vida nueva e independiente.

> *Nada de anecdótico ni de descriptivo. La emoción debe*
> *nacer de la sola virtud creadora.*
> *Hacer un poema como la naturaleza hace un árbol.* (739)

These aphorisms express the essence of *creacionismo*. The phrase *"Nada de [. . .] descriptivo,"* seems contradictory after observing that the very novelty of the square horizon relies on the descriptor "square," yet Huidobro would argue that the horizon is square because he created it that way. The basic and ironic paradox is that he must use an adjective to communicate this "hecho nuevo"; he cannot invent an utterly new lexicon (to represent his new images) because it would be incomprehensible. The full force of this paradox, exhaustively manipulated only to cry out in the frenzied anguish of release at the conclusion of *Altazor,* already lies nascent in this kernel of aesthetic policy from *Horizon carré.*[9]

In the intriguing closing sentences of "El creacionismo," Huidobro designates this manifesto as his poetic last will and testament, as if conceding the early death of *creacionismo,* its seeds seemingly smothered in the infertile environment of uncomprehending mimetic artists. His last words leave his poetic inheritance to

> los poetas del mañana, a los que serán los primeros de esta nueva especie animal, el poeta, de esta nueva especie que habrá de nacer pronto, según creo. Hay signos en el cielo.
>   Los casi-poetas de hoy son muy interesantes, pero su interés no me interesa.
>   El viento vuelve mi flauta hacia el porvenir. (739–40)

While embellishing his earlier claims about the inexistence of any true poets, he "out-futures" the futurists by his blind faith in a new generation of artists, at least receptive to his ideas and perhaps embodying them. He bases this faith vaguely on signs in the sky, again privileging the poet-seer's oracular perspective.

The hollow interest of the "casi-poetas" is a blatant snub; Huidobro sees himself as a Pied Piper who must play to the future in order to find a flock of devoted followers. The wind and the flute, both mentioned explicitly, and the implicit figure of the piper (the Pied Piper, Kokopelli), are all symbols of fertility or phallic potency that enhance the fatherly tone Huidobro has adopted to discuss his testament and inheritance.[10] As a poet / "pequeño dios," his legacy is the "poema creado," an incarnation of the created word or the Word of God. As a father, his word is the pending law for his offspring, an idealized, unnamed spiritual progeny of the future, somewhat desperately conceived in the hope of vindication. My reading of Huidobro as a father figure here is supported by Gutiérrez Mouat's intertextual comparison of this flute motif with Darío's at the close of his prologue to *Prosas profanas:* "La gritería de trescientas ocas no te impedirá, Silvano, tocar tu encantadora flauta . . . Y la primera ley, creador: crear" (qtd. in Gutiérrez Mouat 127). Besides an obvious source for his creationist slogan, Huidobro borrows from the Darío passage the authority of Darío as his own father figure. Also, just as Silvano's flute transcends the geese's cacophony, Huidobro's flute turns away from the "casi-poetas."

In contrast to Darío's presentation of the motif, Huidobro includes the wind, a natural presence, which turns the manmade and artistic flute, like the arrow of a weathervane, toward the future. Huidobro seems to admit that the natural and inevitable progression of time will dictate the direction his aesthetics will take in new hands. The final image, then, is one of harmony between the poet's father figure and Mother Nature, between artistic and natural worlds. This manifesto—a sampler, dogma, and history of *creacionismo* in its three parts—thus concludes with a subtle reminder that the only way in which the blustery force of nature should be imitated is in its autonomous creative potential; the poet's wind gives voice to his song for the future.

• Charlatans and Parlor Games

The brief "Yo encuentro . . . ," originally "Je trouve . . ." in *Manifestes,* continues the critique of surrealism begun in "Manifiesto de manifiestos" with several of that text's main statements only slightly reworded here, plus a few new observations. The loose structure comprises a series of aphorisms and observations, many of them beginning with the anaphoric "Encuentro" of the title, thus establishing unequivocally Huidobro's characteristically subjective approach. Typical examples include "Encuentro que el surrealismo actual no es sino el violoncelo del psicoanálisis" (741) and "Encuentro que los verdaderos poetas, contra cierta opinión emitida ya varias veces, jamás aburren. Al menos, a otro poeta" (741).

Huidobro begins with his voice of authority, dismissing young poets (implicitly the surrealists) as "charlatanes de feria":[11]

> Están en la puerta de su tienda gritando a quienes pasan:
> "Entrad, señoras y señores, he aquí la poesía al descubierto.
> Venid a ver. Aquí todos son poetas. Con sólo entrar en esta
> casa escribiréis versos." (740)

As the creator of a poetic mystique, Huidobro reacts against surrealism's (and dadaism's) promotion of random poetry; he finds that surrealism "rebaja la poesía al querer ponerla al alcance de todo el mundo, como un simple pasatiempo familiar para después de la comida" (740). This cheap-circus or parlor-game atmosphere is the result of what Huidobro claims as the surrealists' error in trying to understand the enigma of great poetry: "suponiendo que aquellas cosas misteriosas se debían a un dictado automático" (740); he includes Alphonse de Lamartine (as a Romantic predecessor) and the playwright François de Curel ("'un personaje interior [. . .] hace correr su pluma'" [740]) as examples of this mistaken belief.

In the following section, he glosses his claim, from "Manifiesto de manifiestos," about the inexistence of "lo arbitrario" by pointing out that the designation of what is arbitrary is itself an arbitrary act: "Es cuestión de puntos de vista." He states: "Para los lectores de Lamartine, Baudelaire era arbitrario; para los lectores de Baudelaire, Rimbaud era arbitrario [etc.]" (740). Therefore, he roundly denies the existence of "lo arbitrario" as a factor in artistic production. Yet in his own display of arbitrariness, Huidobro continues by citing verses of Lautréamont, Eluard, Roger Vitrac, and Robert Desnos as examples, both felicitous and poor, of originality. The sole criterion is not allegiance to surrealism—Eluard, for example, "prueba ser un verdadero poeta sin necesidad de declararse surrealista" (740)—but rather, quite simply, whether Huidobro thinks they are original verses. If "lo arbitrario" does not exist in artistic creation, Huidobro affirms that it certainly matters in art criticism.

Aside from subjectively evaluating certain poets (kudos to Eluard but harsh words for Jean Cocteau and Philippe Soupault), Huidobro criticizes the surrealists for being too dependent on the theories of "The Father of Psychoanalysis": "Antes eran los poetas quienes se adelantaban a la ciencia; eran los precursores, mientras que ahora, he aquí, poetas, que habéis salido de una teoría de moda. Los hijos del Fuego se han transformado en los hijos de Freud" (741). Perhaps the "sons of Freud" were overly dependent, but properly contextualized Huidobro's remarks repudiate those who, instead of inventing their own theories as Huidobro has done, adhere to the theories of others; this theme will form the core of the aptly named manifesto "Necesidad de una estética poética compuesta por los poetas." Also, the statement connects to Huidobro's axioms about the poet having the same natural creative powers as the scientist; therefore, he should not be dependent on scientific progress to create. Ironically, Huidobro was himself dependent on scientific vocabulary in "Manifiesto de manifiestos" and other works.

Readdressing the parlor-game context of surrealism, Huidobro sounds the swan song for "poemas compuestos con palabras y títulos recortados de los periódicos" (741). His condemnation does not arise from a lack of participation in similar activities: he recalls an afternoon when he and some famous friends composed poems, "escribiendo cada uno un verso sobre una hoja de papel, la que pasábamos doblada al vecino para que escribiera el suyo sin leer los anteriores" (741). Another day he wrote a poem in collaboration with Max Jacob, "escribiendo cada uno un verso con lo primero que se nos venía a la cabeza" (742). According to Huidobro, all three of these methods—writing down the first thing that comes to mind, writing collectively sequential verses without knowing what has been written before, and composing poems from random newspaper clippings (Huidobro claims that an amused Picasso proposed a coin-operated bar machine that could be filled with clippings to create instant poems)[12]—can produce curious and sometimes beautiful results, but they lack "la voluntad, la voluntad fatal que debe traspasar como un fierro incandescente toda obra que tienda hacia una altura superior" (742). Here "la voluntad" is yet another manifestation of what Huidobro has previously called intelligence, reason, and imagination, the conscious force that he always associates with lifting poetry up, and that must keep poetry from being the pure chance of the surrealists. Huidobro's anecdotes, while reaffirming his insistence on conscious control, reveal that his judgments were based on experience.

The manifesto ends with another valorization of the best poets, alluding to the vacuum left by Apollinaire's death: "Ayer, Apollinaire era el único que daba [. . .] sensación; hoy, entre los que conozco a fondo, no existen más que Tristan Tzara y Paul Eluard" (742). After a sentence about the power of Tzara's poetry, Huidobro concludes with: "Eluard, ¡ah!, si Eluard quisiera . . ." (742). The allusion to Eluard's potential, in the subjunctive "quisiera," complements the ellipsis that ends the manifesto, itself reflecting the ellipsis of the title "Yo encuentro . . ."; these signs of a tentative nature imply that, as much as Huidobro dismisses the younger poets, he recognizes that it is too early for a complete evaluation. As far as the surrealists are concerned, he rewords in this text a statement from "Manifiesto de manifiestos": "Encuentro que los surrealistas harán algo hermosísimo cuando nos den en sus libros una verdadera sensación de altura" (740). Once again, he cannot condemn the surrealists outright, but he continues to criticize their reliance on automatic writing and chance.

• In the Name of Science

Although rebuked, the surrealists have escaped the full force of Huidobro's scorn; not so the futurists. In the two-part "Futurismo y maquinismo," Huidobro aims to debunk Emilio Marinetti's claim of originality and the new mythology of the machine. Originally "Futurisme et machinisme" in *Manifestes,* the text condenses the material presented in "El futurismo," a brief section of the 1914 *Pasando y pasando.* The earlier piece provides more detail about Huidobro's renunciation of Marinetti's primacy for that of Alomar and Vasseur; Alomar's ideas, as Larrea has shown, contributed to the formation of the title and protagonist of "Non serviam."[13]

Huidobro begins by ridiculing the implications of the term *futurismo:* "Futurismo, arte del futuro. Pero si hacemos el arte del mañana, ¿qué harán los artistas del mañana? Tal vez harán el arte de hoy día. ¡Hermosa inversión de papeles!" (742). Regarding the idea that the futurists discovered modern poetry, he comments: "Esto es absolutamente falso; no es más que un sueño imperialista en frío. Ellos nada han aportado; salvo algo de ruido y mucha confusión" (742). Huidobro explains sarcastically that his reproach centers on the fact that cubism was already extant when Marinetti arrived in Paris. Typically, Huidobro cites examples of futurist verses showing, he claims, that their creators have not budged "ni un paso de medio centímetro hacia adelante después del simbolismo" (743). Significantly, he does not disclose the names of the poets who have written the four free-verse fragments that he presents. Their themes, however, are identified and contextualized historically: "Cantar la guerra, los boxeadores, la violencia, los atletas, es algo mucho más antiguo que Píndaro" (744). For this reason he repeats that they contribute nothing new: "No podréis precisarme vuestro aporte a la poesía y decirme, mostrándome vuestros poemas: esto no existía antes de mí" (744).

The second section of the manifesto, just a few paragraphs, addresses *maquinismo,* the cult of the machine. Huidobro reiterates his main point that a poem cannot be modern only because of its theme: "Si canto al avión con la estética de Victor Hugo, seré tan viejo como él; y si canto al amor con una estética nueva, seré nuevo" (744). He elaborates the idea into an accusation:

> Ignoro si otros poetas, al igual que yo, tienen horror a los términos mitológicos, y si también rehuyen los versos con Minervas y Ledas.
> Creo que ciertos poetas actuales están creando una mitología, la mitología de la máquina. Ella es tan antipática como la otra. Estoy seguro de que los poetas del porvenir tendrán horror de los poemas con muchas locomotoras y submarinos, tal como nosotros tenemos horror de los poemas llenos de nombres propios de las demás mitologías. (744)

Contemporary poetry needs new words representing modern realities, but without making the new words an end (a mythology) instead of a means. Instead, Huidobro concludes that modernity, and not machines, is "la base fundamental de nuestra poesía" (744).

In a sense, this condemnation of the machine myth is a catch-22; considering only the manifestos, Huidobro himself, besides frequently employing electrical or energy-related metaphors, likens the writing of poetry to a mechanism of creation in "La creación pura." Yet his mechanism is certainly not the same contraption as Picasso's coin-operated headline shuffler; the controlling elements of reason and imagination, missing from the latter, are integral parts of Huidobro's description of creative production. In contrast, the redundantly mimetic glorification of machines in this new mythology seems to evoke a world in which the human qualities of reason and imagination risk extinction. Such a threat is similar to a process that Oscar Hahn has identified: "Pero eventualmente el culto a la ciencia y a la tecnología termina transformándose en miedo a su poder destructor" ("Del reino mecánico" 727). Hahn's focus is on the societal danger of technology run amok, but no less important in the aesthetic context is the hazardous displacement of original artists by slaves to the machine. The creative self should not submit to either nature or technology, but must rather maintain a perspective in balance.

In the sober "Necesidad de una estética poética compuesta por los poetas" Huidobro agressively appropriates not scientific but rather poetic discourse. As "Futurismo y maquinismo" condemned the machine myth, "Necesidad" vituperates scientists and other nonpoets who dare to write about poetic theory. Huidobro, for his part, stops using pseudoscientific discourse here, since it follows that if scientists should not write about poetry, poets should not write about science. In Gutiérrez Mouat's Marxist reading, here Huidobro "reconoce implícitamente que vive en un mundo regido por la división del trabajo" such that he must claim for poets "un saber especializado" (124). The text, originally appearing in *Manifestes* as "Besoin d'une esthétique poétique faite par les poètes," contains little more than the establishment of an opposition *(personas de fuera* and *personas de dentro),* some vilified examples of aesthetics written by *personas de fuera,* and the declaration that both reason and imagination can be developed simultaneously as skills.

The exclusive dichotomy of the outsiders vs. those who are "in the know" provides the point of departure for Huidobro's main example, an article on inspiration by "los doctores Antheaume y Dromard":

> ¿Y sabéis qué poetas citan y de la manera de escribir de qué poetas hablan en ese artículo? José María de Heredia, Sully Prudhomme, François Fabié, Auguste Dorchaim, Emile Trolliet.
>
> Despúes de esto, el diluvio. (749)

Signaled by another catastrophic biblical reference that transfers the force of divine disaster to the vanguard revolution, Huidobro's objection stems from the lack of discussion of any contemporary poets in the article. Furthermore, he disagrees with the authors' statement that "'la imaginación es la facultad dominante de las sociedades primitivas, y a medida que la razón se perfecciona ella se debilita y descolora'" (749). On the contrary, Huidobro argues that imagination, like reason, becomes more complex, often to such a degree that the highly imaginative poet's work suffers the scorn of his or her contemporaries. (This is an obvious clue to the way in which Huidobro perceived his own artistic reception.) However, Huidobro sees the development of individual imagination as independent from that of a collective idea of imagination, which evolves by generations; whereas future critics may value the misunderstood poet of today, they will nonetheless ignore the young poets who are their contemporaries, "para no dejar así de caer en la misma inconsecuencia de sus abuelos" (749).

The following statement summarizes the manifesto: "En general, los estudios sobre Arte realizados por los que se llaman hombres de ciencia son tan ridículos para los artistas como podrían serlo los estudios sobre la ciencia hechos por artistas sin una cultura científica especial" (749–50). Unfortunately, Huidobro can only conclude weakly: "Es necesario una estética de la poesía hecha por las *personas de dentro,* por los iniciados y no por los que miran de lejos" (750). As a call to action, this statement only implicitly recognizes Huidobro as an insider; as such he could have been much more specific about what direction the formation of this new aesthetic should take, without relying so heavily on the indications of his other manifestos.

• The Lunatic Fringe

An apparent consequence of the dadaist- and surrealist-inspired embrace of nonsense was the appraisal of poetry written by lunatics. The manifesto "La poesía de los locos," first printed as "La poésie des fous" in *Manifestes,* is the result of Huidobro's predictable need to speak out against such a trend. It offers two pages of "banal" French examples in an effort to condemn any valorization of the lunatics' crazed imagination. Then, after differentiating himself from the lunatic fringe, Huidobro restates his binary vision of the conscious and unconscious creative elements.

The initial differentiation sets up the lunatics as a failed source of creativity, poets as improbable as angels, sleepwalkers, or Martians:

> La poesía de los locos no me interesa como poesía, pues no estoy loco; tampoco la música de los ángeles me interesa algo más, ya que no soy ángel.
>
> Soy un hombre, simplemente, un poeta, y lo que me interesa es la poesía de los poetas.
>
> Ahora, y porque en nuestro mundo no hay poetas, vamos a buscar fuera de la poesía, en el mundo de los locos, de los ángeles o de los sonámbulos.
>
> Yo contesto: no. En mi opinión, debemos tratar de que nazca esta poesía que nunca ha existido, de que crezca en nuestro campo y no en el del vecino ni en el planeta Marte, esa planta que nos falta y que buscamos por sobre toda otra cosa con angustia y avidez. (744)

Once more, Huidobro claims that the true poet still does not exist; this negation posits that the mere desire for an ideal poetry is better than lunatic poetry. Furthermore, this poetic desire reassumes its botanical manifestation in the word *planta;* given the related context of the previous manifesto "La poesía" and the poetic contexts examined by Larrea in *Adán, Horizon carré,* and *Altazor* (241–44), the assumption can readily be made that this plant is once again Huidobro's *aleph,* the tree. Simultaneously the center, the source, and the self, the tree symbolizes the poet's avidly desired embodiment of ideal poetry.

Huidobro immediately contrasts this ideal with five deranged samples that show that lunatic poems, except for rare exceptions, "están compuestos de fragmentos de recuerdos de otros poemas, de confusos ecos y mezclas de todas las antologías" (746). In fact, Huidobro argues that these poetic fragments appear to be more orthodox than what he calls "nuestra poesía," which can mean *creacionista* and *ultraísta* poetry at its most specific, or avant-garde poetry in general: "[Los locos] se hallan mucho más próximos a la Academia Francesa que nosotros; y a menudo su poesía, al lado de la nuestra, le parecería a todo el mundo la sabiduría misma" (747). Because of the lunatics' apparent conservative bias, Huidobro can argue that their imagination is "absolutamente restringida" (744), paradoxically designating the lunatics' supposedly unbridled imagination as a poor creative source; imagination in tandem with reason will provide the richer arrangement for poetic creativity.[14]

In the following ten paragraphs, Huidobro denigrates the isolated imagination of the lunatics while stressing the integration of reason into the poetic process. The lunatic imagination is "*decadente,* y cuando no es de una vulgaridad increíble es de una incoherencia banal" (747). The emphasized use of the word *decadente* recalls the similar designation of the final evolutionary phase of art as proposed in the earlier manifesto "La creación pura," in which the unconscious totally dominates the conscious: "Con ello empieza la tercera época; es decir, la decadencia" (718–19). The contextual meaning of decadence as the prevailing of the unconscious helps to explain Huidobro's next paragraph in "La poesía de los locos": "Un médico me afirmaba un día que si la poesía era fruto del inconsciente, cualquiera puede ser poeta. Esta afirmación no merece respuesta" (747). Since Huidobro has clearly stated that the poet has special powers, he views the doctor's observation with complete disdain. As in his critique of the surrealists, Huidobro insists that embracing the unconscious, a decadent act, is not the equivalent of writing poetry.

To further clarify his own views, Huidobro disagrees with two classical authorities. Socrates' statement "'que los poetas componen por instinto, al igual que los oráculos, sin tener conciencia de lo que dicen'" (747) does not allow a place for reason (conscience). Huidobro counters with a totalizing image: "El universo encendido de luces se vacía en nuestra alma como un río irremediable, pero sobre el que flota la razón nadando junto a la imaginación" (747). The emphasis is on the presence of imagination *with* reason, which is the same union presented in the "delirio" or "superconciencia" of "Manifiesto de manifiestos." The context of imagination, in this manifesto, thus implies the frivolity espoused by the lunatics, here offset by reason; both float along the river of the poetic universe.

Huidobro's amendment to the opinion of his second classical source further promotes equilibrium. He quotes Cicero: "'Hay que estar poseído de locura para componer versos hermosos'" (747). Huidobro's reply clarifies: "Para que un hombre normal pueda componer hermosos versos debe hallarse poseído de locura, y para que un loco pueda componerlos debe hallarse en estado normal" (747). The mental states of lunacy and rationality complement each other in balance in order to compose poetry.

Huidobro quotes Goethe, more akin to his views: "'Ninguna obra genial procede de la razón; pero el genio se sirve de la razón para remontarse poco a poco hasta el punto de producir obras perfectas'" (747). The author expands Goethe's idea in order to continue his mystique: "La chispa, el primer impulso del que debe brotar una obra es inconsciente [. . .] El trabajo de la razón viene *a posteriori,* y construye leyes sobre la resultante controlada" (747). The nature of such laws is only vaguely outlined, but Huidobro insists that the laws are not random:

> Sostengo nuevamente que todo lo que se presenta en la superficie como algo libre y gratuito que se nos impone de pronto ha sido controlado de antemano en las profundidades de nuestro alambique intelectual.
> Yo también proclamo el inconsciente, pero el inconsciente de los hombres conscientes. (748)

The reference to the "alambique intelectual" recalls the image of the "alambique espiritual" in "Manifiesto de manifiestos" (728); in both cases, reason seems to exist and assimilate unconscious elements independently. The end result, encapsulated in the last statement of the above citation, is a binary harmony or balance.

Huidobro finishes the manifesto by differentiating poets from lunatics once again: "la diferencia [. . .] no consiste tanto en el grado de la excitación cerebral como en la cualidad y en la forma de la inspiración producida por dicha excitación" (748). The difference appears to be scientifically quantifiable, revealing again the poet's faith in science as an ultimate truth. Yet the closing sentence has a philosophical bent: "No recuerdo qué filósofo escribió que la imaginación es un delirio que expulsa las locuras" (748). Perhaps the poet pretends that he does not remember because the unknown philosopher is really Huidobro himself. In any case, the statement succinctly promotes Huidobro's idea that lunacy and imagination are a mismatched pair. In fact, the "delirio" of the sentence conforms, as in the earlier floating image, to Huidobro's definition of it as the "superconciencia" in "Manifiesto de manifiestos"; it is the incorporation of both imagination and reason (thereby expelling lunacy). In conclusion, Huidobro asserts in this manifesto that lunacy does not encompass the greatest imagination; however, if lunacy is to represent imaginative elements of the poetic process, then it must be complemented by reason or rationality so as to avoid the hackneyed doggerel of the lunatics.

• Creation as Invention

The identical first and third paragraphs of the half-page "Época de creación," perhaps the last openly *creacionista* manifesto, constitute its leitmotif: "Debemos crear" (750). The manifesto reaffirms the poet's role as creator while restating previous axioms about creation, such as: "La poesía no debe imitar los aspectos de las cosas sino seguir las leyes constructivas que forman su esencia y que le dan la independencia propia de todo lo que es" (750). The use of an invention-related lexicon dominates the text and thus seemingly contradicts Huidobro's conclusions about separating art and science in "Necesidad de una estética [. . .]"; however, allowance must be made for the fact that "Epoque de création" first appeared in the November 1921 issue of the Paris magazine *Création* and thus the sequence, in the Montes edition of the *Obras completas,* of "Necesidad de una estética [. . .]" before "Época de creación" is not chronological.

In the text, Huidobro makes a list of inventions, "hechos nuevos," that moves from art to technology: "un poema, un

cuadro, una estatua, un barco a vapor, un auto, un aero-
plano . . ." (750). Without succumbing to the spell of the machine myth, he aims to praise art, as much as technology, as
an individually creative act; however, the assembly-line connotation of mechanical inventions does not flatter his depiction
of poems, paintings, and statues. Rather, his focus is on the
conception of original ideas: "Inventar consiste en hacer que
las cosas que se hallan paralelas en el espacio se encuentren en
el tiempo o viceversa, y que al unirse muestren un hecho
nuevo" (750). The vagueness of this definition is remedied in
part by a footnote: "El salitre, el carbón y el azufre existían
paralelamente desde el comienzo del mundo. Pero era necesario un hombre superior, un inventor que, haciéndolos encon-
trarse, creara la pólvora, la pólvora que puede hacer estallar
vuestro cerebro tal como una hermosa imagen" (750). The
metapoetical image of the image exploding is therefore an example, like the square horizon, of the original, inventive act. In
general this manifesto's imagery marks a move back to a more
creative expository style in Huidobro's final manifestos.

Although Huidobro's call in the penultimate paragraph for a
Law of Scientific and Mechanical Selection—to be based on
the Law of Natural Selection—is not developed in this context,
it is supposed to represent the historical shift in the arts from
imitation to creation, which was explained at length in "La
creación pura." The conclusion is a valorization of the creator
as stronger than, and indeed encompassing, the mere observer.
In summary, this brief piece compares art with science as the
original action of inventive genius, repeating the basics of
creacionismo. Although the remaining manifestos move away
from promoting *creacionista* theory, signaled by the act of
Huidobro's departure from the train in "Aviso a los turistas,"
they maintain, if not intensify, the struggle for balance.

Chapter Two

Orientation and Trajectory in "Aviso a los turistas" and "Manifiesto tal vez"

Huidobro's need for definition, when limited by his desire for mystique, can yield contradictory results. Although "Aviso a los turistas" and "Manifiesto tal vez" metaphorize poetic creation and give examples of how not to create poetry, they do not define poetic creation nearly as precisely as his earlier, more traditional manifestos. Instead, through a focus on location and movement, the texts together define Huidobro's place in the avant-garde, the journey of poetic creation, and the independent ontology of the created poem.

• The Avant-Garde Express

In "Aviso a los turistas," Huidobro tackles the idea of equilibrium between the conscious and the unconscious on two planes: one textual and the other graphic. Visually distinctive (see fig. 2), it was originally printed ("Avis aux turistes" in *Manifestes*) as a sort of poster in which the text is read on three different axes. In addition to this visual singularity, it is also the most introspective of the manifestos; it portrays Huidobro's personal artistic experience as an oneiric train ride. As de Costa has noted, this polysemic text has not been analyzed conclusively; "Aviso a los turistas" presents "a cryptic announcement that can lead to many interpretations, the common denominator of which must be Huidobro's realization that he was alone" (79). In truth, Huidobro loved to set himself apart from everyone else (just what the narrator does at the end of this manifesto); however, according to de Costa here, Bary (*Huidobro* 22), and also Gutiérrez Mouat (128), by 1925 Huidobro intuited that creationism was no longer an extant theory.

AVISO

A LOS

TURISTAS

Tuve tiempo para coger ya en movi-
miento el último vagón y cada vez que
el tren iba a descarrilarse yo le hacía
señas al maquinista mostrándole de
lejos la maniobra. En los vagones de
primera, de segunda e incluso de ter-
cera clase, se habían colado varios
vendedores viajeros de grandes casas
comerciales. Al llegar a la estación me
di cuenta de que el tren había cam-
biado de itinerario y de ruta. Bajé y
tomé solo el camino de los sueños
polares.

Llegué atrasado para coger el tren que yo mismo había puesto en marcha.

El maquinista se parecía vagamente a mí pero no era yo mismo.

Fig. 2. "Aviso a los turistas," by Vicente Huidobro, *Obras completas,* ed. Hugo Montes (Santiago: Andrés Bello, 1976), 1: 751. Reproduced with permission of the Fundación Vicente Huidobro, Santiago, Chile.

A narrative allegory, "Aviso a los turistas" chronicles Huidobro's journey on the avant-garde express, an exhilarating but ultimately disappointing trip. The locomotive, one of the vanguard's most common technological images, was a setting commonly used to present scenes and landscapes in rapid, astounding succession. Huidobro's train, as well, incorporates the idea of movement through space and time; however, it carries the reader along the trajectory of the author's personal poetics process. The manifesto's main text appears horizontally between two solid vertical lines, which approximate railroad tracks, along which the reader/tourist travels upon undertaking the movement of the textual reading. The vertical sentences on both sides of the rails work like stage directions; they follow the narration while revealing background information—a deeper psychological context—in the form of the writer's inner thoughts. The graphic placement of the stage directions corresponds to the landscape seen from the train; to read them, the reader has to physically change her perspective to approximate that of a rail passenger or tourist.[1] The "landscape" that the reader observes offers the hidden impressions of the poet's vision, essential for interpreting the personal nature of the metaphorical journey. The world shared with the reader is the pure realm of poetic creation, as Sucre affirms: "El poeta busca crear un mundo desde su visión, no reproducir otro; no el mundo que existe, sino el que debiera existir, dice Huidobro. Ese mundo no está edificado, por supuesto, sobre la ética: ha de estar regido por la imaginación y el deseo, por el lenguaje" (95). This invented and bipolar world contains the possibility of metapoetic commentary by means of an allegorical exploration of the poet's creative role, narrated by, we assume, the voice of Huidobro himself.

The details given between the tracks—that the narrator arrives barely in time to board the train, already in motion; that the cars are full of vendors; that the narrator, acting as a guide, warns the engineer about possible derailments; that when he realizes that the train has changed route and itinerary, the narrator gets off the train alone—trace, in an elemental way, the locomotive trajectory of the evolution of Huidobro's aesthetics. Yet the most surprising details about the journey are found in the stage directions. Huidobro portrays in them the theme of a dual equilibrium: an early Huidobro and a late Huidobro, the narrator and the engineer. Additionally, the stage directions reflect each other in a graphic sense and thus create a symmetry, as vertical texts, with the horizontal text between the rails. The left vertical text reveals a contradiction: the narrator arrives late to board the train, but it is the same train that he himself has set in motion. This paradox summarizes Huidobro's position in the vanguard, marked by the struggle between, on one hand, his constant claims to have begun his creationist tendencies long before arriving in Europe, and on the other hand, the fact that he arrived late, to witness the final days of cubism and futurism. Although the European vanguard movements made their mark on him, Huidobro refused to belong to any movement but his own. He wanted to seem more European than the Europeans; however, he always availed himself of his Latin American origin, even when it was not advantageous because of European perceptions of his home continent. According to González, "Huidobro was a late but enthusiastic arrival at the European banquet [. . .] His emergence from underdevelopment brought confusion and unresolved contradiction" (42). That contradiction was the root of almost all of Huidobro's personal grudges, as Larrea explains:

> Psicológicamente no es posible ingresar en el cercado de las letras con aires conquistadores y derribando las normas establecidas sin provocar de rechazo los desaires, cuando no las iras de sus congéneres. Que así, movido por un impulso de esa naturaleza, desembarcó Vicente Huidobro en Europa, dispuesto a conquistar la conciencia del Viejo Mundo a favor de la del Nuevo que sentía dentro de sí. (213)

This tension symbolizes Quiroga's description of the vanguard obsession in terms of "belatedness and originality," an obsession that materializes also in the well-known case of the suspicious chronologies of "Non serviam" and *El espejo de agua*. Especially in the stage direction "Llegué *atrasado* para coger el tren que yo *mismo había puesto en marcha*" (my emphasis) one perceives the anxious desire to transcend time, implying an atemporal creation and thus a creation with no prior influence.[2]

The neophyte/veteran dichotomy encompasses the poet's splitting into two *yos*—an early Huidobro and a late Huidobro—and the right vertical text reflects this division in the figure of the engineer, the narrator's vague double. One in the engine and the other in the caboose, they are alpha and omega twins, Genesis and Apocalypse. Are they a Chilean/Latin American Huidobro and a French/European one? Or perhaps one poet, young and naïve, and another, older and disillusioned? The matter of a double Huidobro has intrigued several critics, who nonetheless have not addressed the text "Aviso a los turistas." In the introduction to *Huidobro o la vocación poética*, appropriately titled "Los dos Huidobros," Bary identifies a similar scission in Huidobro and develops it from two viewpoints: that of the public and that of the critic. For the public, and because of his personal scandals, the figure of Huidobro appears to be an innovator or perhaps a charlatan, but from the critical viewpoint the figure becomes a poet and theorist (9–28). Huidobro's double in "Aviso a los turistas" would be an apropos reference in Bary's context, given that Bary addresses in these pages Huidobro's missionary zeal for disseminating his poetic ideas, and given also the poet's cited declaration (in the 1921 manifesto "La creación pura") that he had initiated creationism before reaching Europe (21). Another opposition schematized by Bary is that of a poet who accepts the intellectual rigor of cubism and creationism but who feels attracted to the heroic romanticism inherent in the tendencies of Apollinaire, Cendrars, and Breton (65–66). Similarly, in "A manera de prólogo" from *Vientos contrarios,* Larrea acclaims both Huidobro the theorist and Huidobro the poet, although he prefers the latter (qtd. in Bary, *Nuevos estudios* 22). For González, preoccupied with social distinctions and basing himself on some of Enrique Lihn's observations, Huidobro "is two things at once; the spiritual aristocrat opposed to bourgeois philistinism; and a bourgeois humanist, drawn sentimentally to the notion of a collective future. Huidobro, in this precise sense, is a poet of transition" (43).

All of these points of differentiation are valid; what is most interesting is the implicit acknowledgment, on Huidobro's part in "Aviso a los turistas," of some kind of division.[3] According to several folklore sources, the recognition of the double (in the form of a spirit or shadow), especially in some dangerous circumstance, is an evil omen that foretells the death of the recognizing subject (Campbell 174–75). In effect, there is here a symbolic death in the narrator's and the engineer's definitive separation. Although the narrator denies that the engineer is exactly his double ("pero no era yo mismo"), it seems that the engineer is a possible or potential Huidobro, as if the real Huidobro invented him to be able to show how he could have ended up if he weren't smarter than the rest of the passengers. Could he be the Huidobro poorly understood by his critics, whom the real Huidobro leaves behind as a decoy? Could he not also represent the poet's attempt to distance himself from his creationist tenets, which no one followed anymore? It is interesting to note a possible source for "Aviso a los turistas" in an observation by Freud:

> In a line of associations ambiguous words (or, as we may call them, "switch-words") act like points at a junction. If the points are switched across from the position in which they appear to lie in the dream, then we find ourselves upon another set of rails; and along this second track run the thoughts which we are in search of and which still lie concealed behind the dream. (Qtd. in Kris 246)

In Huidobro's text the second set of tracks is implied by the narrator's final departure; moreover, the thematic doubling, the oneiric ambiance, the quest for a hidden thought or idea, and of course the image of the train tracks that Freud mentions are indispensable elements of "Aviso a los turistas."

Even though varying interpretations of the double can be recognized, there are two undeniable conclusions: first, while the engineer proceeds, unaware of derailments (possible acts of sabotage), the narrator, in constant vigilance, possesses the illuminating voice of hindsight that protects the train. Second, the definite lacuna between the functions of the narrator and the engineer causes their separation; the *doppelgänger* engineer changes route without telling the narrator, so the latter gets off the train. While the engineer seems to follow his whim or intuition, the narrator symbolizes the voice of reason; they personify, respectively, artistic inspiration and elaboration, or imagination and reason, or any of Huidobro's similar binaries. The narrator is the one who follows another destiny, leaving behind the cars full of vendors; one supposes that the vendors, without the guide of consciousness, will not travel very long before suffering an inevitable derailment.

Who are these vendors on the ill-fated locomotive, who have infiltrated the third-class, second-class, and even the first-class cars?[4] They represent the legions of inferior poets who pledge allegiance to whichever style is in vogue, selling themselves out to the ideas, itineraries, and routes of others. They are Bloom's "weak poets," incapable of creating their own readings of prior texts in the form of original poems. Along with the tourists mentioned in the manifesto title (who, like the engineer, are in need of warning), the vendors act as a group. If the tourists, as readers/observers, resemble the "personas de fuera" of the manifesto "Necesidad de una estética poética compuesta por los poetas," or the observer, inferior to the creator, at the end of the manifesto "Época de creación," then the vendors recall the "charlatanes de feria" of the manifesto "Yo encuentro . . ." Although some of them may rate first class, all of them diminish or dilute poetry to a trivial level. Attracted only to movement in and of itself, they will crash obstreperously as soon as the narrator abandons them. In the context of the manifestos as a textual grouping (in which some of the manifestos already mentioned are dedicated to the critique of surrealism), the failed destiny of these vendors delineates the trajectory of the surrealists without the stabilizing force of reason.

When Huidobro's narrator abandons the train, does he also abandon equilibrium? He leaves his Other, vague and intuitive—the engineer—to his fate, as he seeks, alone, an extreme of isolation at the Pole.[5] If he abandons equilibrium, it is only to change routes—from the engineer's unpredictable and varying route to a different, more concrete one: the Pole. His polar orientation, new and magnetic, supports his many references to the compass and the cardinal points, not only in his poetry but also in "Manifiesto tal vez" and "Las siete palabras del poeta." After providing the conscious and decisive voice that guided the train paradoxically from the caboose, the narrator now reincorporates the unconscious element of his equilibrium in the penultimate word "sueños"; in this way he combines a definite and verifiable bearing (the Pole) with the uncertain and unpredictable nature of dreams which, as appreciated in "Non serviam," provide the desired contact with the unconscious, necessary to engender the creative product. Although the exit from the train in "Aviso a los turistas" could be interpreted as a distancing from creationism as dogma, it seems to me more justified to call it a resignation or a recognition by Huidobro that, as de Costa observes, he was alone. His new orientation isolates the poet, but not without yielding a path toward creationism's three goals of the poet: "crear, crear y crear." His other manifestos, even the ones he surely wrote after "Aviso a los turistas" (for example, "Total"), still continue, if not intensify, the struggle for equilibrium, and also an insistence on the autonomy of the poem as an object, an object/destination as fixed and immutable as the Pole.

• Crystal and Pearl

"Manifiesto tal vez," the text that follows "Aviso a los turistas" en *Manifiestos,* seems to have predated the latter manifesto by a year; the February 1924 issue of *Création* contains the original version, "Manifeste peut-être." It enjoyed, moreover, a wider distribution in Spanish America than "Aviso a los turistas," because it was published in 1926 in Spanish as "Prólogo II" in the anthology *Indice de la nueva poesía americana,* and in *Amauta* in December of the same year. The structure of the text exemplifies the aphoristic style of many manifestos, but the content surprisingly constructs a demythification of the poetic theme; this demythification complements and illuminates the narrator's exit at the end of "Aviso a los turistas."[6] The ludic uncertainty of the title speaks to the role of demythification in undermining the poetic methods proclaimed in other manifestos; this manifesto "perhaps" is not what the reader expects. Above all, the text's polysemantic introduction, in contrast to its strongly monosemantic conclusion, frame the manifesto and guide the general direction of discourse from the abstract to the concrete. The textual declarations begin with easily changeable semantics only to become, by the end of the text, clear distinctions between your money and your life, apples and oranges. Such a noticeable change within the brief manifesto has not attracted critical awareness; in my opinion the progression helps concretize a poetic direction, new and original, that yields the crystallization of the poem as an object. The poem metaphorized as a crystal or pearl aspires to orient the poet in danger of losing himself along several dead-end poetic paths.

The manifesto begins: "Nada de caminos verdaderos y una poesía escéptica de sí misma. / ¿Entonces? Hay que buscar siempre" (751). The words "caminos" and "buscar" inaugurate a lexicon of movement and orientation that, in thirteen brief lines, develops a transformation of poets into explorers and vice versa, illustrating the concept of a poetic quest. The explorers "Se habían transformado en poetas y cantaban de pie sobre las olas derramadas"; likewise the poets "Se habían transformado en exploradores y buscaban cristales en las gargantas de los ruiseñores" (751). This confirms Unruh's observation that in spite of a gradual debunking of the poet-as-god myth, "the ideal of the artist as an explorer with unique skills, in particular, a radical vision of reality, persists in Huidobro's work" (197). The interchange between poet and explorer expands: "He aquí por qué Poeta equivale a Vagabundo sin oficio activo, y Vagabundo equivale a Poeta sin oficio pasivo" (751). Although poet and vagabond normally do not frame any semantic opposition, here they seem to because of the epithets "activo" and "pasivo." The ostensible goal of this semantic play is the establishment of the poet as a seeker of poetic truth. This is why Huidobro denounces the alleged "caminos verdaderos" (the traditional methods as much as the charlatans') to recognize the poem as an independent being:[7]

> Ninguna elevación falsa: sólo la verdad, que es orgánica. Dejemos el cielo a los astrónomos, las células a los químicos. El poeta no es siempre un telescopio que se puede cambiar en su contrario, y si la estrella se desliza hasta el ojo por el interior del tubo, ello no se debe a un ascensor sino más bien a una lente imaginativa. (752)

Seen through Huidobro's imaginative and demythifying lens, the competing poetic strategies are deformed:

> Nada de máquinas ni de moderno en sí. Nada de *gulf-stream* ni de *cocktail,* pues el *gulf-stream* y el *cocktail* ya son más máquinas que una locomotora o una escafandra, y más modernos que Nueva York y los catálogos. [. . .]
> No agreguéis poesía a lo que ya la tiene sin necesidad de vosotros. La miel sobre la miel da asco. [. . .]
> Nada de poemas tirados a la suerte; sobre la mesa del poeta no hay un tapete verde. (752)

These denunciations are directed to the futurists, the sentimentalists, and the dadaists, respectively, but there immediately

appears—apart from the rest of the text and in capital letters—
a more global protest, the manifesto's most important, which
summarizes the demythifying *gestalt:* "Y EL GRAN PELIGRO DEL
POEMA ES LO POÉTICO" (752). Seemingly contradictory, the slogan affirms that the poet/explorer must always insist on discovering new poetic entities, since writing about what others
have already poeticized should be avoided as retrograde or in
poor taste. Within the context of the three denunciations cited
above, one concludes that it is not enough to reflect, repeat, or
find what is poetic by chance. That which is poetic must be
invented. The role of the poet is active and, above all, creative;
Huidobro repeats here the central tenet of creationism: "El
poeta no debe ser más instrumento de la naturaleza, sino que
ha de hacer de la naturaleza su instrumento. Es toda la
diferencia que hay con las viejas escuelas" (752).

This context emphasizes not only the creationist poetic process but also the result—independent and organic creation. The
result of the process, "un hecho nuevo," is perhaps a poem:

> ¿Es un poema, o tal vez otra cosa?
> Poco importa.
> Poco importa que la criatura sea niña o niño, abogado,
> ingeniero o biólogo, con tal que sea.
> Es algo que vive y perturba, aunque en el fondo perma-
> nezca muy calmo.
> Tal vez no es el poema habitual; pero es, al menos. (752)

The independent ontology of the poem is thus unconditional
and supreme. As long as the poem has been invented as an
original and autonomous act, the debate about whether it conforms to poetic ideals is moot. The pejorative phrase "el poema
habitual" opposes what Huidobro advocates in the final section
of "Manifiesto de manifiestos"; the poem should always
achieve an essence that is "inhabitual."

The transformative effects of this unconditional poetic ontology on the poet and his world are immediate:

> Así, primer efecto del poema, transfiguración de nuestro
> Cristo cotidiano, trastorno ingenuo, los ojos se agrandan al
> borde de las palabras que se deslizan, el cerebro desciende
> al pecho y el corazón sube a la cabeza, sin dejar de ser cora-

zón y cerebro con sus facultades esenciales; en fin: revolución total. La tierra gira al revés, el sol sale por occidente. (753)

The asyndeton of this fragment hastens the urgency of its revolutionary message, while the metamorphosis of Christ foreshadows the poet's role in "Las siete palabras del poeta." The
poem's revolutionary power dramatizes a new perspective:
the brain thinks in the chest while the heart beats in the head.
The plural other (poets/explorers/vagabonds) as much as the
yo are lost in general confusion:

> ¿Dónde estáis?
> ¿Dónde estoy?
> Los puntos cardinales se han perdido en el tumulto,
> como los cuatro ases de un naipe. (753)

The scientific compass bearings don't work, or they work just
as well as shuffling a deck of cards. Yet the poet's metaphoric
positioning is precise; the images of inversion and disorienta-
tion, although they negate the natural world, nonetheless affirm the poet's place in his alternative world, announced since
"Non serviam" and described with similar images in "La
poesía." Equilibrium still exists: "(El amor y el repudio carecen
de importancia para el verdadero poeta, pues sabe que el
mundo avanza de derecha a izquierda y los hombres de
izquierda a derecha. *Es la ley del equilibrio*)" (753; my emphasis). Huidobro constructs here this "ley del equilibrio" out of
extreme images—love and hate, progressions to the left and to
the right, the terrestrial poles, the cardinal points—to illustrate
again the revolutionary world of poetic creation.

In this bipolar context the pair "corazón" and "cerebro" can
be interpreted as another dichotomy, because these two organs
change place in the poetic revolution. To support this corporeal
opposition, Huidobro proposes the image of the throat as the
point of equilibrium: "Y si el mejor poema puede hacerse en la
garganta, es porque la garganta es el justo medio entre el
corazón y el cerebro" (752). It is in the "gargantas de los
ruiseñores" (751) that the poets/explorers search for crystals in
the manifesto's beginning. The anatomical symbolism privileges the throat (and, by association with the nightingales, the

voice) as the organ of poetic production; the throat reconciles heart and brain, just as the subjective act of poetic creation (and not the poem itself) mediates between the natural world and the poetic object.[8] Sucre, in another context, arrives at the same conclusion: "no es raro que [. . .] la poesía resida sobre todo en el *acto poético* y no en el poema mismo" (228; original emphasis). The corporeal symbolism is, in effect, a representation of the flow chart from "La creación pura" and a continuation of the preeminence of the throat and of the tongue in the oneiric conclusion of "La poesía." The image of the crystals (in the nightingales' throats) is strengthened in a polar metaphor that connects to the imagery in "Aviso a los turistas." When the poet thinks of "robar la nieve al polo," he adds: "Algunos días después me di cuenta: el polo era una perla para mi corbata" (751). The Pole, his goal and adopted guide at the end of "Aviso a los turistas," magnetic and inexorable, crystallizes the poetic act in a new independent occurrence—a poem—a pearl that is "una creación humana, muy pura y trabajada por el cerebro con paciencia de ostra" (752).

With the poetic goal now crystallized in its autonomous and unconditional existence, as precise as the natural magnet of the Pole that orients the poet/explorer, the manifesto's conclusion contrasts diametrically with its exposition. Instead of "Nada de caminos verdaderos" with interchangeable poets and explorers, Huidobro now specifies:

> ¡Nada de paseos indecisos!
> La bolsa o la vida.
> Esto es neto, claro. Nada de interpretaciones personales.
> La bolsa no quiere decir el corazón, ni la vida los ojos.
> La bolsa es la bolsa y la vida es la vida.
> Cada verso es el vértice de un ángulo que se cierra, no la
> punta de un ángulo que se abre a todos los vientos. (753)

Distinguishing "la bolsa" from "la vida" prepares the unequivocal ontology of the poem: "Un poema es un poema, tal como una naranja es una naranja y no una manzana" (753). These aphorisms reaffirm the "realidad cósmica" of the poem, which is not a copy of nature but rather a new and hermetic creation.

The textual change from abstract to concrete synchronizes the change from the subjective act of poetic creation to the objectivity of the poem itself. The quest as creation is uncertain ("Nada de caminos verdaderos") because the poet should deny already mined themes and images, as well as the supposed true methods, while he probes the unconscious source of inspiration. However, after taking this initial, tentative step, the poet creates the poem which, once it is composed, is absolutely certain and exact ("Nada de paseos indecisos").[9] This contrast traces the creative poetic trajectory that unites the image of the poets/explorers at the beginning of "Manifiesto tal vez" with the itinerary of the solitary poet at the end of "Aviso a los turistas": the Pole is the immutable destination of the journey across dangerous and unknown lands; likewise, the fixed character of the finished poem guides the poet through the challenging and unpredictable process of creation. In this way Huidobro demythifies the poem as an unconditional and conscious product—not automatic writing, nor a compendium of contemporary jargon, but the fruit of poetic exploration and invention.

Both "Aviso a los turistas" and "Manifiesto tal vez" commence with some doubled presence (the narrator and the engineer, the poets / explorers / vagabonds) and then resolve themselves in favor of a sole presence: that of the narrator, and that of the poem as a new object. In both texts the poet rejects itineraries, routes, and paths in order to follow his individual orientation and unalterable goal. In every sense this goal is exactly and obsessively originality—a defensive originality very dear to Huidobro's vanguard poetics, and another more theoretical originality in the autonomy of the poem as artifact. If it is true that Huidobro questions which is the true path, he does not hesitate to blindly affirm the true identity of the finished poem; the avant-garde truth resides in the innovative poem and not in the path (recipe or formula) that leads to it. This explains the fragmentary nature of much vanguard poetry—how does one know if the poem is finished, when there is no established form that dictates the syllable to add or the rhyme to complete? The ephemeral attraction to newness and originality ends up consuming, at times, the vanguard in its own trap, leaving as a poem a series of unconnected images. During the creative process, Huidobro himself composed and altered various versions of his poems—*Altazor* is the best-known example. In spite of this, or perhaps precisely because of this, Huidobro metaphorizes the poem as a crystal, a pearl, a frozen polar formation, in order to project a stable and indubitable poetic ontology onto the powerful impact of the image.

Chapter Three

Dimensions of the Poet God

Huidobro's Final Manifestos

The common thread that links Huidobro's diverse manifestos is the binary struggle to maintain a complete equilibrium between the conscious and unconscious processes of poetic composition. This balance is the same one that Ernst Kris identifies in his study of the artistic ego, *Psychoanalytic Explorations in Art*. Artistic inspiration is born in the unconscious, but its elaboration is a conscious act. Writing about regression as access to the unconscious, Kris exposes the dangers of losing the balance during the process of artistic composition:

> When regression goes too far, the symbols become private, perhaps unintelligible even to the reflective self; when, at the other extreme, control is preponderant, the result is described as cold, mechanical, and uninspired. Poetry is, to be sure, related to trance and dream [. . .] But it is also related to rigorous and controlled rationality. No account of the aesthetic process can be adequate without giving due weight to this "intellectual" component. (254)

A predisposition toward this intellectual or rational component of artistic expression, seen first in "Non serviam," continues especially in "El creacionismo" and in the critiques of surrealism in "Manifiesto de manifiestos" and "Yo encuentro . . ."

Huidobro's last manifestos explore the idea of a divine, organic consciousness to which the poet has exclusive access by virtue of godlike qualities. In his comparison to Christ and in his prophecy of the total poet, Huidobro develops his famous conclusion from "Arte poética," "El poeta es un pequeño Dios." Ironically, Huidobro polished the controlled structures of these poetic prose texts, which exemplify Kris's balance of dream and rationality, during the same years he was developing the spectacular impasse that closes *Altazor,* a text that embodies the dangers of Kris's regression: "the symbols become private, perhaps unintelligible even to the reflective self."

• The Poet as Christ

The final phrases of Christ on the cross articulate the structure of "Las siete palabras del poeta," originally in *Manifestes* as "Las sept paroles du poète" and then published in Spanish in *La Nación,* January 31, 1926. After an initial paragraph, each phrase appears in capital letters, unchanged from the Gospel tradition, and followed by a short series of paragraphs that expands the context of the poet's artistic identification with Christ. The specific historical context of this manifesto involves Huidobro's chiding self-defense against his critical enemies, and for that reason the general tone of the piece is hyperbolically egotistical.[1] However, the imagery continues Huidobro's already established use of Adam and the *axis mundi* tree as representations of the poet fulfilling his creative powers. The figures of Adam and the tree transform into Christ and the cross; Jung has shown, by means of alchemical and apocryphal sources, that the ancients had already read such a symbolic transformation into the Bible:

> The [Syrian] "Book of the Cave of Treasures" states that Adam stood on the spot where the cross was later erected, and that this spot was the centre of the earth. Adam, too, was buried at the centre of the earth—on Golgotha. He died on a Friday, at the same hour as the Redeemer. [. . .] God said to Adam: "I shall make thee God, but not now; only after the passing of a great number of years." (*Mysterium Coniunctionis* 388–89)

Jung argues that the collective unconscious incorporates both Adam and Christ, as well as the tree and the cross, as representations of the self. Similarly, the cross symbolizes, according to Hahn's study of Huidobro's 1918 *Ecuatorial,* "la conjunción de los opuestos y [. . .] el centro místico del universo" ("Voluntad inaugural" 25). The self, the dissolution of opposites, the center: these are the evident connections analyzed in Huidobro's "Non serviam" and Mário's "Parábola";

Huidobro's poet incarnates both Adam and the Redeemer, while Mário's Poetry links Adam, her creator, to the Christ-like Rimbaud.

"Las siete palabras del poeta" resembles the "Prefacio" of *Altazor* in its images of birds and heights. The manifesto begins: "Desde lo alto de mi cruz, plantada sobre las nubes y más esbelta que el avión lanzado a la fatiga de los astros, dejaré caer sobre la tierra mis siete palabras, más cálidas que las plumas de un pájaro fulminado" (753). The "pájaro fulminado" recalls Altazor, while the cross suggests an airplane seen from the ground, a popular avant-garde image. The "palabras," in the context of "cálidas" and "fulminado," evoke the traditionally phallic lightning bolts of divine power, as in "Non serviam"; the poet as Christ is both man and god. The first two words (really phrases) deal with Huidobro's ironic and seemingly noble supplication of pardon for his enemies ("PADRE MÍO, PERDÓNALES, PORQUE NO SABEN LO QUE HACEN") and then his consequent invitation for them to join him in his poetic realm, a place that embodies an important concept in Huidobro's poetics, described here in two ways: "HOY ESTARÉIS CONMIGO EN EL PARAÍSO . . ." and "Sube, ven a recoger los caracoles del otro lado de la luna" (754). Like the new era beyond the jasper doors in "Non serviam," the poet's divine paradise here lies just beyond what is visible, on the dark side of the moon. Supplementing the jasper and the shells, a lexicon of jewels and precious stones throughout this manifesto further likens the representation of poetic paradise to the gem-studded New Jerusalem of Revelation: "la noche de las esmeraldas" (754); "Almirante de perlas finas" (754); "el diamante polarizado en el infinito" (754); "La joya estalla y se disuelve en la noche" (755); "los treinta caballos del rubí" (755). The general sense of this gem lexicon, and some specific terms like pearls and polarized, reinforce the image of the finished poem as an independent object in "Manifiesto tal vez."

The third phrase ("MADRE, HE AHÍ A TU HIJO. HIJO, HE AHÍ A TU MADRE") refers to a symbolic mother, perhaps Poetry. The manifesto's change of second-person addressees complicates interpretation of the mother's identity. Previously, the addressee was the "hombre débil" who ignorantly vilified Huidobro but was then invited to follow him; afterwards, the "tú" forms will refer to God. The following passage, therefore, could be the point at which the poet begins to address God, in which case the mother in question is the divine soul:

> Es tu hijo y lo ignorabas. Tu alma era su madre, y ella lo dejaba partir lejos, entre las estrellas que giran hasta perder el aliento.
>
> Al ver tu desinterés, quisieron robártelo. El se había desligado de tu corazón como un aerolito del cielo o como un navío del puerto.
>
> Almirante de perlas finas, mira a aquel que te llama y se proclama hijo tuyo. Abrele los brazos para el regreso, tal como le has abierto la puerta de tu cabeza cuando quería trepar sobre las palomas. (754)

Whether the mother is Poetry or the divine soul, the poet/son addresses an "Almirante" and asks for a renewal of interest and a reunion, which could be the final reunion of the poet as Christ with God the father (or mother) at the end of the manifesto. An interpretation of the mother as Poetry would also suggest the dynamic relationship between innocent Poetry and curious Rimbaud in Mário's "Parábola."

The fourth phrase is the pivotal one: "DIOS MÍO, DIOS MÍO, POR QUÉ ME HAS ABANDONADO . . ." (754). In this middle section, Huidobro uses the phrase "en medio de" three times to strengthen the idea of abandonment of the self. Traditional self-defining mandala images (also key symbols of spatial orientation)—the four cardinal points, the dividing river—are deformed in this moment of divine contact lost:

> Solo en medio de los lobos. Y soy la cascada de sueño que beben los lobos.
>
> Solo en medio de los cuatro puntos cardinales batidos furiosamente por el huracán de los planetas.
>
> Heme aquí abandonado en medio del río que gira en torno a su eje, que sigue su camino en círculo y vuelve sobre sí mismo como una rueda o una serpiente que se muerde la cola hechizada. (754)

The image "cascada de sueño" establishes an oneiric tone; the realm of the unconscious sets the scene for the self's desertion. The set of four cardinal points, an image of the centered self, shatters. The guiding river turns in on itself to become the *ourobouros,* the snake that swallows its own tail, a literally self-destructive symbol of futility. Yet the poetic self abides in the middle ("en medio de"), of wolves, of the four misaligned cardinal points, of the never-ending circle; the middle is the privileged point, the poet's realm, which allows some retention of the self's identity even in the face of God's abandonment in the swirling unconscious.

"TENGO SED...," the fifth phrase, further accentuates the poet's isolation, as if languishing in the middle of a desert. In four anaphoric sentences beginning with this two-word phrase, Huidobro reveals that only the power of poetry can quench his thirst; the poet expresses this power again as an act of lifting up or as a great height: "altura," "vértigo," "sentirme alzado por el motor de mi poesía," "espacio," "infinito," and "a tres mil metros de altura" (754). The inexorable certainty of his thirst leads into the sixth phrase, "TODO ESTÁ CONSUMADO..." The sense of completeness, of his or Christ's mission, extends to the poem as process result, echoing precisely the imagery from "Manifiesto tal vez": "En la paciencia de la ostra el poema está hecho" (755). Continuing several motifs (jewels, nightingales, camels, thirst), Huidobro concludes the section: "Ni los treinta caballos del rubí, ni toda la potencia de los arpegios concentrados del ruiseñor, podrán impedir jamás que el fin se acerque a mí con el mismo paso con que los dromedarios van hacia las nubes llenas" (755). The poet's eschatological obsession, evident from the beginning of *Manifiestos* in the obsolescence of the natural world that yields the new era in "Non serviam," accelerates to the inevitable conclusion of this manifesto in Christ's last words.

"PADRE MÍO EN TUS MANOS ENCOMIENDO MI ALMA..." unites the poet with the divine, the Self with the Other. Before, God had abandoned the poet ("[...] POR QUÉ ME HAS ABANDONADO..."); now, the poet abandons himself to God:

> Me abandono a ti. Abre la caricia de tu calor a la escala de mis sueños que busca, después de la lluvia, tus largos cabellos entretejidos de sueño para secarse.
>
> Te abandono esta procesión de sueños que salen de mis ojos.
>
> Riega mis miradas y déjalas que maduren en un rincón, sobre la tibieza de tus almohadas de humo.

Me abandono a ti, solo entre tus manos, como los anillos
de los satélites arrojados a la noche.
Todo ha terminado. El sistema planetario se quiebra en
un cataclismo de olas verdes.
Mira, Señor. El firmamento es un cenicero sobre los
adioses. El empolla los dolores. Escucha esta mandolina que
toca despúes del fin del mundo. (755)

The rain signals the longed-for end of the crucified poet's suffering, since it has arrived to quench his unrelenting thirst;
therefore, it also symbolizes the poet's union with God, only
possible by means of this cosmic cataclysm. The oneiric tone,
which unites the self with the unconscious, arises again through
three uses of the word *sueño* and the word *almohadas*. Yet the
apocalyptic union of poet and God survives the end of the universe intact. The poet addresses and even commands God twice
("Mira" and "Escucha") regarding what he and God see and
hear; therefore the poet still retains a separate identity. However, he exists with the divine in paradise, the metaphor for the
poet's creative realm.

Through Huidobro's assumption of the role of Christ, the
only figure who is both God and man, he appears to achieve in
this mystic manifesto that which neither Sor Juana Inés de la
Cruz in *Primero sueño* nor Paz in *Piedra de sol* accomplish:
union with God. Huidobro has moved therefore from self-
representation as the paradigm of poets, Adam, to the ultimate creator, God. God's person in Christ assumes the
center-of-the-world position from Adam and the Tree of
Knowledge in the psychological dimension of the collective
unconscious, while satisfying Huidobro's scandalous desire
to be what Bary has called a "mártir a manos del vulgo"
(*Huidobro* 16). Thus the movement through Christ's seven
phrases culminates in the completion of the poet's creative mission—no longer a mere rebellion against Mother Nature but,
rather, a union with the ultimate creative force.

• The Total Poet

The last manifesto of the *Obras completas* collection, "Total"
was written in 1931 and first published in July 1932 (seven
years after *Manifestes*) in the Paris magazine *Vertigral*. The text

deals appropriately with the theme of completeness; the title itself reflects the idea of a sum of parts, as in the total or balance of a mathematical ledger. Specifically, the title and content derive from certain statements in "Manifiesto de manifiestos" (i.e., "nuestra personalidad total y verdadera" [723]) and from the middle section of "El creacionismo," as noted earlier:

> En el creacionismo proclamamos la personalidad total.
> Nada de parcelas de poetas.
> El infinito entero en el poeta, el poeta íntegro en el momento de proyectarse. (737)

Aggressive in tone and encompassing a series of dialectical pairings, "Total" is Huidobro's last plea for poets to show strength, here characterized as a virile and complete, or unified, power. Navarrete Orta, for whom "Total" marks a watershed in Huidobro's oeuvre, observes the text's lack of both anecdotes and references to people or works; this absence strengthens the unified presentation of the theme (176). For Nelson Osorio, the manifesto's potent message marks the end of the experimental phase of the Latin American vanguard and the beginning of a more socially engaged artistic paradigm (383).

The repeated call "Basta" [Enough] characterizes the manifesto's opening while reinitiating the need for poetic revolution in order to change an undesirable situation of fragmentation:

> Basta ya de vuestros pedazos de hombre, de vuestros pequeños trozos de vida. Basta ya de cortar el hombre y la tierra y el mar y el cielo.
> Basta de vuestros fragmentos y de vuestras pequeñas voces sutiles que hablan por una parte de vuestro corazón y por un dedo precioso.
> No se puede fraccionar el hombre, porque hay todo el universo, las estrellas, las montañas, el mar, las selvas, el día y la noche.
> Basta de vuestras guerras adentro de vuestra piel o algunos pasos más allá de vuestra piel. (755)

The enumeration of telluric and cosmic elements establishes each person wholly as a universe, an infinitesimal sum of parts.

Huidobro immediately divides the conflictive disunion, announced in the word "guerras," into opposing pairs, the first of which recalls "Manifiesto tal vez":

> El pecho contra la cabeza, la cabeza contra el pecho.
> El ojo contra la oreja, la oreja contra el ojo.
> El brazo derecho contra el brazo izquierdo, el brazo izquierdo contra el brazo derecho. (755)

Following the same syntax, Huidobro continues on for six more pairs: "sentimiento" / "razón"; "espíritu" / "materia"; "realidad" / "sueño"; "concreto" / "abstracto"; "día" / "noche"; and "Norte" / "Sur." He concludes this list with a question: "¿No podéis dar un hombre, todo un hombre, un hombre entero?" (756).

The annulment of these oppositions provides the last strong example of Huidobro's desire for the union of opposites, for balance or harmony. Collectively they recall the series of "más allá de" pairings at the end of "La poesía," which define the location of the poet's creative realm (some of the pairs are, in fact, repeated): "verdadero" / "falso"; "vida" / "muerte"; "espacio" / "tiempo"; "razón" / "fantasía" and "espíritu" / "materia" (717). Furthermore, as noted, they resemble elements in the second section of "El creacionismo," although the issue of masculine and feminine forces struggling within each personality, a prominent element of "El creacionismo," does not appear in "Total" (this may be due to the emphasis, in "Total," of the poet's strength as manly potency—the subject of further discussion below). The resolution of these binary conflicts in "La poesía" is mutual dissolution, whereas in "El creacionismo" and in "Total" the implied resolution is through encompassment or inclusion. In either case, Huidobro clearly associates this resolution of opposites with the creativity of the complete poet.

Timid, unfulfilled poets receive Huidobro's scorn. Their voices resemble that of a "canario monocorde":

> Es preferible oír los discursos de un picapedrero, porque él al menos siente su cólera y conoce su destino, él está en la pasión y quiere romper las limitaciones.
> En cambio, vosotros no dais la gran palabra que se mueve en su vientre. No sabéis revelarla. (756)

The muscular quarry worker has the strength to break the "limitaciones"—recalling the breaking through to the poetic realm of the "más allá"—but the ineffective poets have no access to their gut strength, the "fire in the belly" of manhood. As a result, these unfulfilled poets are ignored because they have the "lengua de príncipes y es preciso tener lengua de hombre" (756). Similarly: "[. . .] porque vuestra lengua es demasiado diminuta, demasiado pegada a vuestro yo mezquino y más refinada que vuestros confites. Habéis perdido el sentido de la unidad, habéis olvidado el verbo creador" (756). The phallic power that the tongue symbolizes, seen also in "La poesía," is the key to the unity ("unidad") of opposites as the creative Word. The word *lengua* of course also means "language"; in both senses the weak, refined poets have not fulfilled their potency or talent. These are the foppish, impotent, and redundant poets whom Huidobro humiliates in Canto III of *Altazor:*

> Manicura de la lengua es el poeta
> [. . .]
> Matemos al poeta que nos tiene saturados
>
> Poesía aún y poesía poesía
> Poética poesía poesía
> Poesía poética de poético poeta
> Poesía
> Demasiada poesía
> Desde el arco iris hasta el culo pianista de la vecina
> Basta señora poesía bambina (406)

In contrast, Huidobro calls for the voice of the universal poet, the same as the biblical Word: "Porque al principio era el verbo y al fin será también el verbo" (756). The voice/word is "grande y calma, fuerte y sin vanidad," the voice of "una nueva civilización naciente, [. . .] un mundo de hombres y no de clases [. . .] que pertenece a la humanidad y no a cierto clan" (756). The new civilization, again the New Jerusalem of the poet's creative world, is somewhat adapted to accommodate Huidobro's communist sympathies. Huidobro further admonishes the weak poets to be men and not pansies: "[. . .] tu oficio es oficio de hombre y no de flor. Ninguna castración interna del hombre ni tampoco del mundo externo. Ni castración espiritual ni castración social" (756). Castration, as an act of separation, thwarts the manifesto's central idea of totality. In a psychoanalytical sense, castration symbolizes the fear of absorption by the phallic mother, or the semiotic source of language, still unshackled by semantics. A true poet, Huidobro implies, does not dread this temporary abandonment to inspiration (or union with the divine), since the poet does not permanently abandon reason. Neither side disappears, "ninguna castración." Yet the cowardly poets let their fear of losing this balance overly restrict their creative capacities; in contrast to the quarry worker who breaks through barriers, these poets are limited by "la medida": "Sois todos muy medidos" (756). They cannot conceive of the original act of breaking away from poetic norms, of poetic exploration as exhorted in "Manifiesto tal vez": "Habéis nacido en la época en que se inventó el metro. Todos medís un metro sesenta y ocho, y tenéis miedo, miedo de romperos la cabeza contra el techo" (756).

Huidobro can only break away from the targets of his derision by heralding their Nietzschean opposite in his closing lines:

> Pero necesitamos un hombre sin miedo. Queremos un ancho espíritu sintético, un hombre total, un hombre que refleje toda nuestra época, como esos grandes poetas que fueron la garganta de su siglo.
>
> Lo esperamos con los oídos abiertos como los brazos del amor. (756)

Huidobro's final manifesto could not be a more "synthetic" text; herein are reprised all his major symbols and ideas. This idealized figure of the fearless poet, necessarily deferred to the future as is the generation of new poets at the end of "El creacionismo," not only incorporates the completeness of the title "Total" but also of the key word "sintético." Huidobro has introduced the context of synthesis several lines earlier—immediately after the brief paragraph beginning "Ninguna castración [. . .]"—in the form of an even briefer but immensely revealing one-sentence paragraph: "Después de tanta tesis y tanta antítesis, es preciso ahora la gran síntesis" (756). The future poet, of course, will fulfill this synthesis, which represents again the union of opposites ("tesis" and "antítesis") in balance or harmony. The synthetic, total poet can only exist in the future since, like the Hegelian synthesis of the lordship and bondage relationship—in which the barriers of servitude break in an authentically liberated society—the synthesis is only possible in an ideal, nonexistent environment. Huidobro, either brave or foolhardy, retains his optimism regarding the future existence of such a society, no doubt generally influenced, as Navarrete Orta postulates, by the writings of Marx and Lukacs—specifically by their concepts of solidarity and totality (178–80).

Furthermore, Huidobro rationalizes the possibility of the fearless poet's future appearance through comparison to great poets of the past; he will incarnate, like them, the "garganta de su siglo."[2] Once more Huidobro privileges this corporeal symbol that, coupled with his frequent use of *voz* in this manifesto, brings out again the poet's ideal balance point between the heart and the mind. Finally, in anticipation of this stentorian voice, those who wait for it do so with "los oídos abiertos como los brazos del amor." The ears as orifices of the word's penetration further emphasize the phallic potency of the total poet's new language, while the simile of the open, loving arms traces the horizontal beam of the cross. As in "Las siete palabras del poeta," the cross image again evokes the self waiting for divine deliverance; however, this time the voice of Christ is not the narrating voice of the poet, but rather the promised voice of the poetic Christ's second coming, of the apocalypse that will destroy the old order to construct the ideal and creative poetic world.

• The Poetic Mystique

After analyzing each manifesto individually, a collective exegesis of Huidobro's poetics reveals that the central idea of harmony in poetic creation steadfastly dominates, both during and after his openly *creacionista* period and despite intertextual transformations of the elements in balance; for example, *razón* becomes also *voluntad*, and *sensibilidad* is later expressed as *imaginación*. The poetic revolution achieves the ideal conditions of balance, expressed in three ways: (1) graphically in the mechanistic flow chart (the boxed "Mundo subjetivo" balances the natural world and its physical phenomena with the poetic world and *its* physical phenomena—poems) and in the stage directions along the rails of the placard manifesto "Aviso a los turistas," (2) semantically by dozens of examples of opposing terms such as *cerebro/corazón* and *centrífuga/centrípeta*, and (3) symbolically by the orientation toward a creative space that encompasses all of the following: the *más allá*, the center, the *aleph* tree, the new era (paradise or the New Jerusalem), the far side of the moon, and stratospheric space in general. Within the poet's body, the locus of creativity should be the throat and tongue—or, collectively, the voice—as the balance between thought and emotion. The role of the revolutionary poet involves the embrace of the total personality; prolonged focus on one aspect over its opposite is detrimental.

The critical flaws of this mystique surface unavoidably; not the least of them is the poet's unmasked arrogance that, though it sometimes serves as a motive for writing, can eclipse the message of his poetics. The identity of who the poet can be remains unclear, as Gutiérrez Mouat points out, since Huidobro claims special skills for the poet and yet reproaches poets for not achieving the voice of the "total" being, mixing scientific with metapoetic discourses (134). The poet's relationship with Nature, in which he denounces her as a source of imitation but praises her as a model of the act of original creation, seems clear enough in "Non serviam," yet Huidobro still feels compelled to reelaborate this dynamic frequently in subsequent manifestos. Similarly, the revolution that the rebel poet carries out in "Non serviam" diminishes in later manifestos to no more than a call for such a revolution. In general, that battle cry reveals what is both the greatest weakness and also an unavoidable necessity of the avant-garde: postponement of the poetic revolution's victory. In spite of his idealism, the faith placed in the next generation and in the poet of the future belittles Huidobro's own accomplishments. Even considering the inherent theoretical paradox of *creacionismo,* involving the inescapable referentiality of all words and hence their necessary description by more words in the context of the poem, no one would deny Huidobro's original achievements in *Poemas Articos, Horizon carré,* and *Altazor.*

But Huidobro's poetics of equilibrium outlived his concern for *creacionismo.* Mitre claims that Huidobro's sign "no es el del equilibrio, sino el de la desmesura; su poesía y sus mismas ideas lo testifican" (98), but in interviews published from 1937 to the end of his life, Huidobro returns obsessively to the term and to its opposite, *desquilibrio*, to clarify the poetic process. He states succinctly: "Yo creo que el poeta clásico es aquél en el cual todas las facultades están en una relación de perfecto equilibrio."[3] His sense of the word *clásico* in context is laudatory, not derogatory. The same balanced relationship applies to the poet's work: "Pienso que el movimiento verbal obedece al movimiento orgánico y que el equilibrio o desequilibrio de estos dos elementos es lo que produce la mayor o menor realización de una obra."[4] He rearticulates the motif of intelligence or brain vs. sensibility or heart, and the almost impossible but highly desirable ideal of their working in tandem. Poetry is the key to making order of one's life: "Sólo por medio de la poesía el hombre resuelve sus desequilibrios, creando un equilibrio mágico o tal vez un mayor desequilibrio [. . .] la poesía es la conquista del universo."[5] Life can become "gaseoso y caótico" Huidobro says, "un desequilibrio total," but poetry, like a light, "seguirá creciendo y aumentando su calor vivificante dentro del cerebro humano para equilibrar a la tierra que se enfría."[6] Balancing heat and cold, heart and brain, the ideal of poetic equilibrium continued to dominate Huidobro's thought and expression in his final years.

Part Two

Poetry as Contraband from the Unconscious

Mário de Andrade

Although Mário's most important poetics texts—"Prefácio" and *Escrava*—like Huidobro's manifestos, seek to define an avant-garde poetics and address the issue of balance, they differ from the manifestos in structure and style. Whereas "Prefácio" could be said to resemble Huidobro's and other manifestos' typically loose structure characterized by aphorisms, it nonetheless affects an overriding purpose in the defense of the *Paulicéia* poems; furthermore, the tone, while subjective, is more deeply personal. *Escrava* continues this tone yet sets out more pretentiously to be a treatise on poetics rather than a mere manifesto. In contrast to "Prefácio," as Thomas R. Hart notes, *Escrava* does not concern itself directly with Mário's own poetry, which in fact is never cited (267–68). In general, both works are characterized by their penchant for dialogue through the documentation of Mário's sources, many—including Huidobro ("La création pure")—from *L'Esprit Nouveau*.

Grembecki has studied Mário's marginal notes in his issues of *L'Esprit Nouveau* to explore his points of agreement and disagreement with these contributors in both "Prefácio" and *Escrava*—insight that will be explored in more detail in these chapters. Poetics and aesthetics are generally dominant subjects among Mário's extensive writings. The present analysis will be limited to "Prefácio," *Escrava,* and two *crônicas* published in the collection *Taxi e Crônicas no Diario Nacional,* with limited references to Mário's other works and to salient extracts of his prolific correspondence as organized by Charles Kiefer. The principal focus will be on the structural and thematic unity of "Prefácio" and *Escrava* as Mário's two most important texts on poetics. The two texts can be structurally linked as, in toto, a somewhat paradoxical formal treatise on avant-garde poetics.

Critical analyses of "Prefácio" and *Escrava* tend to pursue intertextual approaches, comparing characteristics of Mário's stated poetic goals with his poetry, but including little or no analysis of the narrative fragments' illustrative role within the poetics. Luiz Costa Lima limits his observations regarding "Prefácio" to the qualification of Mário's "eu" [I] as a Romantic remnant; in general, Lima describes Mário's aesthetic as "passadista" [outmoded] (40). While similarly finding Mário's "eu" "enraizado na tradição" [rooted in tradition], Teles develops a "tensão *eu x outro"* [I-vs.-other tension] in which the Other, variously portrayed as Europe, São Paulo, and Brazil, describes a trajectory through Mário's work *(Escrituração* 193). Teles affirms the importance of Mário's poetics texts but does not elucidate any symbolic narrative meanings. João Pacheco paraphrases "Prefácio" and *Escrava* together, criticizing perceived gaps—"patentes e grandes" [patent and large] (123)—in Mário's aesthetics without defining what these gaps may be. José I. Suárez and Jack E. Tomlins focus on *Escrava,* a corrective to the "flippant" "Prefácio," as Mário's reworking of Dermée (46). In his now classic essay "O psicologismo na poética de Mário de Andrade," Roberto Schwarz considers "Prefácio" and *Escrava* as manifestations of a "quadro maniqueísta de oposições" [Mannichean frame of oppositions] that Mário never manages to resolve: "A superação dessas antinomias, a dialética do particular e do universal [. . .] torna-se inconcebível na oposição absoluta em que são mantidos os pares conceituais" [Overcoming these antonymies, the dialectic of the specific and the universal (. . .) becomes inconceivable within the absolute opposition in which these conceptual pairs are maintained] (18). Indeed, such opposition seems to plague Mário's expressive attempts, subverting even the symbolic loci that he creates—the dock and the street—as possible points of contact and reconciliation. Schwarz constructs a scheme of polarities involving later texts by focusing on Mário's clarifications of degree (of conscious or unconscious activity), but does not enter into a detailed analysis of Mário's symbolic narrative fragments.

David T. Haberly's and Adrien Roig's treatments of "Prefácio" are representative of many critical intertextual approaches in that they seek to compare and contrast that text with the poems of *Paulicéia.* As Mário makes clear, "Prefácio" was written after the poems of *Paulicéia* had been completed; it therefore follows that "Prefácio" is equally a preface to his next work, *Escrava.* In fact, although Mário wrote *Escrava* in April and May of 1922, shortly after the Modern Art Week, it was not published until 1925, just prior to which Mário felt compelled to add a "Postfácio."[1] This circumstance gives coherence and closure to the idea that "Prefácio" can serve as a preface to *Escrava,* because in "Postfácio" Mário again laments the lapse of time between two events; both "Prefácio" and "Postfácio" were written to justify Mário's changing theoretical stances between the time he composed a work and the time the work was published. These chronological differences illustrate Mário's sense of avant-garde urgency in distancing himself from futurism while defining Brazilian *modernismo.*

The characteristics of the "Parábola" about Adam and Poetry that are common to "Prefácio" and *Escrava* include the personal, often playful tone; the championing of Rimbaud; the metaphor of breaking free from bondage or prison; and most importantly, the stress on balance and harmony in relating the conscious and unconscious aspects of poetic composition, a balance often expressed in equations or formulae. However, even considering his deeply personal and often quite colorful style, Mário does not promote in these texts the creation of a mythos comparable to Huidobro's poetic realm and *aleph* tree. Rather, he concerns himself with citing apropos poetic examples, redefining the terms of his contemporaries, and addressing aesthetic issues with a growing, profound sense of social responsibility.

Chapter Four

"Prefácio Interessantíssimo"
as Mock Manifesto

Oswald de Andrade's May 1921 piece about Mário de Andrade, "O meu poeta futurista," pushed the latter into the limelight and forced him to distinguish his ideas from those of the futurists, a task that became the "Prefácio" and also, eventually, the 1925 *Escrava*. In "Prefácio," Mário accepts the blame for being labeled a *futurista*: "Oswald de Andrade, chamando-me de futurista, errou. A culpa é minha. Sabia da existência do artigo e deixei que saísse. Tal foi o escândalo, que desejei a morte do mundo" [Oswald, in calling me a futurist, was wrong. It's my fault. I knew about the article and let it go to print. The scandal was such that I desired the death of the world] (PC 61). Mário's strong feelings provoked him to defend himself with "Prefácio," which, consequently, displays a chaotic mixture of disarming sarcasm and pious sincerity.

For the same reasons, "Prefácio" as text challenges classification. Beyond the usual essay style of a preface, it also resembles a manifesto in two important ways: (1) it begins with the founding of a movement and (2) aphorisms constitute a large portion of its content. The text does not strictly conform to either of Castillo's following distinctions, but rather shares aspects of both:

> [. . .] los manifiestos vanguardistas se distancian de los prólogos, porque, en general, éstos aspiran principalmente a la presentación, dilucidación o justificación del texto al cual preceden y no pretenden adquirir un carácter explícitamente dogmático o abiertamente subversivo, mientras que aquéllos aspiran a exponer un programa estético dirigido a una pluralidad de textos virtuales y revelan a un tiempo una naturaleza francamente rebelde y militante frente a los postu-

> lados de la estética tradicional, o incluso de otros manifies-
> tos que, por medios diversos, también la combaten. (156)

In another light, the term "pretext" provides a useful definition for "Prefácio" in three ways. First, "Prefácio" fits the apologetic paradigm of the prologue as "pretext" or excuse; second, in its published form (graphically) it precedes *Paulicéia* in order to exonerate the poet's unfamiliar style. Finally, as suggested earlier, "Prefácio" may also be read as a chronological "pre-text" to *Escrava,* which it anticipates in matters of theory and narrative.

In order to facilitate an analysis of its unique form, I propose an arbitrary but necessary division of "Prefácio" (after the "Dedicatória") into three sections (see fig. 3). The thematic structure of these seamless sections will reveal a reading of "Prefácio" as essentially a mock manifesto in which Mário founds and then revokes the hallucinationism (*desvairismo,* a term derived from the title *Paulicéia Desvairada*) movement while proposing an aesthetic theory and other ideas even as he seemingly derides them.

Of equal thematic importance is Mário's circular movement from a discussion of his multiple creative selves to the exposition of aesthetic ideas, and then back to the personal theme. The document becomes an ontological meditation on what it means to defend one's creative writing from a hostile and uncomprehending public, and to propose, humorously yet earnestly, a new aesthetic interpretation. My interpretation of "Prefácio" as mock manifesto does not neglect its fundamental salience; it allows the text the serious consideration due a statement on aesthetics while examining simultaneously the ephemeral nature that Mário himself assigns to it.

Exposition	Beginning (PC 59)–PC 63 "Um pouco de teoria?"
Theory	PC 63 "Um pouco de teoria?"–PC 75 "Por muitos anos [. . .]"
Conclusion	PC 75 "Por muitos anos"–End (PC 77)

Fig. 3. Proposed division of "Préfacio."

- ## Mário's Dedication to Himself

Opening *Paulicéia* and addressed to "Mestre querido," the "Dedicatória" stands as the first manifestation of Mário's blend of serious and frivolous messages. Undeniably, it is meant as a dedication for the entire work, but it bears the date of December 14, 1921, revealing that it was composed at the same time as "Prefácio," that is, after the poems of *Paulicéia;* for that reason it can be considered here within the framework of "Prefácio," if not in fact as the true beginning of "Prefácio." This parodical dedication to Mário de Andrade from Mário de Andrade (himself) unmistakably sets the tone of "Prefácio" and the theme of its beginning and end sections; the tone is humorously preposterous yet serious at the same time, while the theme is Mário de Andrade as self and as poet.

Roig identifies another duality in the purpose of the dedication; it can be seen either as Mário's expression of egocentric pride or as a humble recognition of his inability to communicate his artistic ideals in verse (79). It can also be interpreted as a rift between the new poet Mário de Andrade and the old poet Mário Sobral, the pen name Mário used for his early Parnassian verse. In any case, Mário undeniably splits his personality, elevating one self to the status of maestro in order to account for, and perhaps to emphasize, the perceived distance between the reality of his poems and the ideal of his poetics. Like Huidobro's split self in "Aviso a los turistas," Mário's doubling also highlights the avant-garde obsession with temporality and immanence.

Arguably a variant of the humility topos, this original take on dedicatory convention yields the irony of the following statement, for example: "Permiti-me que ora vos oferte este livro que de vós me veio. [. . .] Mas não sei, Mestre, si me perdoareis a distância mediada entre estes poemas e vossas altíssimas lições . . ." [Permit me that I may offer thee this book that came to me from thee [. . .] But I do not know, Master, if thou wilt pardon the imposing distance between these poems and thy most high lessons . . .] (PC 58). The statement hints at the tension between Mário's poetic output and the changing aesthetic orientation that motivated him to write "Prefácio." Moreover, the language and syntax of the dedication are decidedly Lusitanian, ironically assuming the style of a colonial writer grateful for Portuguese financial patronage. Mário felt that Brazilian *modernismo* expressed an overdue linguistic independence from Portugal; his parodic style, not unlike Huidobro's poet's discourse with Mother Nature in "Non serviam," also represents the farewell of a long-suffering, apprenticed Brazilian idiom to its colonial master.

Also quite significant is the fact that the brief text anticipates "Parábola" regarding the importance of the individual in poetic truth; the context again becomes ironic due to Mário's split self. He says, as if to differentiate himself from someone else: "Não de mim, mas de vossa experiência recebi a coragem da minha Verdade e o orgulho do meu Ideal" [Not from me, but from thy experience did I receive the valor of my Truth and the pride of my Ideal] (PC 58). The key phrase is "minha Verdade," which is the same that Mário later distinguishes from Christ's truth in "Parábola." In the latter text, it is not Mário's personal truth but rather Christ's "Verdade" that is capitalized; in contrast, Mário's "Verdade" is the truth that is capitalized here, along with the important epithets of the closing sentence: "Recebei no vosso perdão o esforço do escolhido por vós para único discípulo; daquele que neste momento de martírio muito a medo inda vos chama o seu Guia, o seu Mestre, o seu Senhor" [Receive in thy pardon the effort of he who was chosen by thee to be thy disciple; from he who in this moment of martyrdom very fearfully still calls thee his Guide, his Master, his Lord] (PC 58). In a Brazilian setting, the use of the pronoun *vós* [you] and its corresponding verb forms connote the ecclesiastical discourse of prayers or sermons, heightening the effect of Mário as divine master. As with Huidobro, the divinity of the self surfaces in the poet's discussion of his work or his role. Mário's separation of a Christ-like self, while more obvious than Huidobro's *doppelgänger* in "Aviso a los turistas," is less dramatic than "Las siete palabras del poeta."

Finally, the term *mestre* signals yet another dimension of this mixture of solemnity and humor, divinity and mortality, through Hegel's lordship and bondage relationship as discussed in the introduction. The young rebel Mário breaks away from the earlier, Parnassian-influenced master Mário, ironically begging forgiveness for not maintaining the master's standard. Such a standard had been described by Mário in a previous series of essays called "Mestres do Passado," in which he praised the achievements of Brazilian poet paragons such as Olavo Bilac and Raimundo Correia while stressing the need to move beyond their still dominant styles. For Jackson, this ironic and competitive scission in the dedication sets the tone for the entire "Prefácio" in which "Mário dramatically proclaims his martyrdom at the service of the master's ideal" (55). Yet the tone of the dedication is simultaneously sarcastic and sincere; the sincerity is not unlike that of Rimbaud's adulation for the idealized Poetry in "Parábola." The relationship's elements of union (name, personality) and division (apprentice and master) therefore maintain a tension of consciousness of Mário as creator. Throughout "Prefácio," he struggles to conceptualize and categorize this tension, for example in his distinction regarding consciousness and genre (the prose of "Prefácio" and the poetry of *Paulicéia*) and in his minute but essential allegory of Dom Lirismo. In sum, the dedication presents the juxtaposition of roles that Mário seeks to embody simultaneously in an effort to reconcile conscious and unconscious elements of poetic creation.

• Exposition / Exposure

The opening sentences of the text immediately characterize "Prefácio" in two important ways: (1) they establish Mário's intimate tone with the reader and (2) they confirm the tongue-in-cheek slant of the title, the dedication, and the entire text:

> Leitor:
>
> Está fundado o Desvairismo.
>
> *
>
> Este prefácio, apesar de interessante, inútil. (PC 59 [2])

Similarly sardonic messages, about the purpose of "Prefácio" and the nature of founding schools or defining artistic movements, continue in the beginning section and reappear in the end section, while the generally jocular and personal tone prevails throughout the entire text. Starting with "inútil," Mário's statements gradually reveal a spectrum of self-deprecating attitudes that constitute a fundamental incongruity within the context of the typically avant-garde bold and assertive dogma.

Mário asserts, but always with disclaimers. For example, in the sixth section of text:[1]

> E desculpe-me por estar tão atrasado dos movimentos artísticos atuais. Sou passadista, confesso. Ninguém pode se libertar duma só vez das teorias-avós que bebeu; e o autor deste livro seria hipócrita si pretendesse representar orientação moderna que ainda não compreende bem. (PC 60 [3])

As in so many instances of this text, his statement "Sou passadista" seems to go against the avant-garde grain, yet does not prevent him from outlining new ideas. He pretends to be out-of-touch with or to not understand current movements, yet the reader may observe (in a footnote on page 72, referring to Mário's harmonics theory) that Mário was reading *L'Esprit Nouveau* and forming his opinions in relation to those of the magazine's contributors.

Similarly, Mário humbly recognizes the limits of his explanatory "pretext" while aggressively singling out hostile readers:

> Alguns dados. Nem todos. Sem conclusões. Para quem me aceita são inúteis ambos. Os curiosos terão prazer em descobrir minhas conclusões, confrontando obra e dados. Para quem me rejeita trabalho perdido explicar o que, antes de ler, já não aceitou. (PC 59 [4])

This is a warning to the reader not to expect a formal treatise but rather the outline of a work in progress, with any and all inconsistencies that such a work may display. His self-effacing style incorporates his honesty and sentimentality into a more sincere aesthetics.

Mário extends the honesty of his endeavor into the purity of an unfettered creative process. Ideally, his act of writing poetry springs directly from the unconscious, as he states:

> Quando sinto a impulsão lírica escrevo sem pensar tudo o que meu inconsciente me grita. Penso depois: não só para corrigir, como para justificar o que escrevi. Daí a razão deste Prefácio Interessantíssimo. (PC 59 [5])

The first sentence of this explanation inevitably leads one to think of automatic writing, espoused by the surrealists and proclaimed in Breton's 1924 manifesto. But Mário adds the self-corrective stage of critical thinking afterwards, a meta-cognitive step that would establish a balance of feeling and thinking processes, or of input from the unconscious and from the conscious; this restoration of balance is akin to Huidobro's assertion, in "Manifiesto de manifiestos," that automatic writing can only be the product of a "semipersonalidad."

However, the assumption that Mário would mean that only "Prefácio" has undergone this second, corrective step implies presumptuously that *Pauclcéia* is, if perhaps not automatic writing, at least an unencumbered manifestation of his unconscious. Rather, Mário employs two verbs to clarify: "não só para *corrigir,* como para *justificar* o que escrevi" (my emphasis); the fact that Mário somewhat corrected or altered his poems is beyond conjecture, just as the legitimizing purpose of "Prefácio" is undeniable. In his comparative study of Mário's and Breton's aesthetics, Joseph Pestino underscores the difference that Mário's second step makes: "Breton would have paled at the heresy of the words 'corrigir' and 'justificar.' There was no room for them in surrealism and Breton himself claimed he never revised or tampered with any of his works after their initial creation" (19). Though they may have desired the interpenetration of the unconscious and the conscious in their development of a new lifestyle, clearly the surrealists did not espouse the same mutual contact in the artistic creative process.

The theme of the verses and the preface as potential functions of different psychological stimuli and mental processes will be continued in the middle section of the text. Yet, at this point, Mário writes the following afterthought, which could serve as a warning to critics: "Aliás muito difícil nesta prosa saber onde termina a blague, onde principia a seriedade. Nem eu sei" [By the way, it's very difficult to determine where the blague ends and the seriousness begins in this prose. Not even I can tell] (PC 60). Here the balancing of serious and light elements becomes so thorough that not even the author, again seemingly stepping outside himself, can distinguish between them. This passage hints that Mário deconstructs his own categories; after all, his word *prosa* refers to the preface, yet the *prosa* itself mixes the foolery or joking around suggested by *blague* with the seriousness of his aesthetic theory. The ludic nature of *blague* is linked to the unconscious realm of the psyche; Mário seems to admit that the division of the conscious and the unconscious in artistic creation cannot be achieved in reality as exactly as it may be expressed in theory.

The play of conscious and unconscious elements in "Prefácio" is reinforced by Mário's exposure of his multifaceted self as poet. In the remainder of the beginning section, Mário develops the theme of his creatively poetic self by portraying himself in different roles: prophet, lunatic, artisan, and father. First, he facetiously quotes a skeptical view of the Koran and compares himself to Muhammad:

> "Este Alcorão nada mais é que uma embrulhada de sonhos confusos e incoerentes. Não é inspiração provinda de Deus, mas criada pelo autor. Maomé não é profeta, é um homem que faz versos. Que se apresente com algum sinal revelador do seu destino, como os antigos profetas." Talvez digam de mim o que disseram do criador de Alá. Diferença cabal entre nós dois: Maomé apresentava-se como profeta; julguei mais conveniente apresentar-me como louco. (PC 60 [6])

The tongue-in-cheek reading of this passage is that Mário *does* consider himself a prophet. Just as in the "Parábola," when Mário says "Gosto de falar com parábolas como Cristo" while proposing an individual truth, here he compares himself to Muhammad in a moment of personal defense; yet in both cases Mário also humbles himself by this comparison, in this case with the demeaning epithet of "louco."

As if to temper his profession of lunacy by displaying authority, Mário name-drops in the brief ninth text section, after the word "louco": "Você já leu São João Evangelista? Walt Whitman? Mallarmé? Verhaeren? [Have you read St. John the Baptist? . . .] " (PC 61). Maintaining an intimate tone, the author challenges the reader's ability to keep up with him, to understand the source of his inspiration. This important word—inspiration—serves as the title of *Paulicéia*'s well-known opening poem about São Paulo ("comoção de minha vida" [commotion of my life]) and plays a leading role in Mário's search for balance. In the above comparison with Muhammad, Mário places the word "inspiração" in the uneasy dichotomy of being either divine or human; the division of these sources of inspiration echoes Mário's own division in the dedication as

111

much as his desire for balance. By questioning the distinction between poetry and prophecy, and by listing the sacred John the Baptist alongside the profane Whitman, Mário—a divided self—implies that inspiration has a more heterogeneous nature.

Mário demonstrates for the reader how he has already tried and rejected certain elements of inspiration in the creative process. For example, as he continues to expand the role of his self, he claims: "Perto de dez anos metrifiquei, rimei. Exemplo?" [For about ten years I metered and rhymed. Example?] (PC 61) and provides a sonnet, "ARTISTA," which crystallizes his longing for artistic perfection in the desire to be a classical painter. Mário's presentation of himself as an artisan calls attention to the craftsmanship with which he has constructed this perfect, Parnassian-influenced sonnet. Those ten years of apprenticeship to the poetic styles of Bilac, Correia, and others from his series "Mestres do Passado" have been the developing years of his creative self, similar in effect to the bondsman's time spent with the master in Hegel's paradigm.[2] In its immediate context, the sonnet is the identifying proof of Mário's having passed through this period of apprenticeship. However, the poet now clearly rejects this style; as seen in the dedication, Mário's new master is Mário himself. He later boasts: "Podia, como eles, publicar meus versos metrificados" [Like them, I could have published my metered verses] (PC 61).

After such a rejection, the reader may expect an affirmation of some other style or worldview instead. But the text that follows is an even more outright rejection—the oft-cited negation of Oswald de Andrade's labeling of Mário as *futurista,* in which the latter accepts some of the blame for the misleading situation. He also expresses his disappointment and frustration:

> Era vaidoso. Quis sair da obscuridade. Hoje tenho orgulho. Não me pesaria reentrar na obscuridade. Pensei que se discutiriam minhas idéias (que nem são minhas): discutiram minhas intenções. Já agora não me calo. Tanto ridicularizariam meu silêncio como esta grita. (PC 61–62 [7])

In his bitterness, Mário delays some sort of affirmation of his style, of what *desvairismo* is, until the next page—marking the beginning of the middle, theoretical section of "Prefácio." Meanwhile, the words "vaidoso" and "ridicularizariam" foreshadow sensitive references to vanity and ridicule, which appear shortly afterward in the further extension of Mário's self that incorporates the role of father:

> Perdoe-me dar algum valor a meu livro. Não há pai que, sendo pai, abandone o filho corcunda que se afoga, para salvar o lindo herdeiro do vizinho. A ama-de-leite do conto foi uma grandíssima cabotina desnaturada. (PC 62 [8])

Mário as father of his verses anticipates the Adam of his "Parábola" as the father of Poetry. The apologetic tone manifest in the command "Perdoe-me," coupled with the pathetic images of the deformed, drowning son and the wet nurse (an abhorrent cabaret-style actress), continues the self-deprecating anxiety of Mário's "pretext" while reprising the humility topos of the dedication.

In sum, the first section's closure is characterized by its defensive tone. The poet, under attack by the conservative elite of São Paulo, must defend himself by writing this preface, in which he makes himself even more vulnerable through the exposure of the different aspects of his self as poet: prophet, lunatic, artisan, and father. As both apprentice and master, Mário invites the reader to consider the complexities of artistic creation in the simultaneity of a split self.

• Theory: Polyphonics

The teaser phrase "Um pouco de teoria?" opens this section while defining its content. In the first few pages Mário develops his ideas about the conscious, the unconscious, and inspiration, while adding a discussion on beauty and order vs. chaos. His theory of a harmonic poetry constitutes the bulk of this section, which closes with the Dom Lirismo allegory and reflections on modernity in general.

Mário begins with the nature of lyricism. Since lyricism originates in the unconscious, it produces free-form verses "sem prejuízo de medir tantas sílabas, com acentuação determinada" [without the impairment of measuring so many syllables, with a determined accentuation] (PC 63). Reelaborating this idea, Mário identifies the delicate instability of inspiration as a reason for not impeding its lyric development. He makes his first reference to a formula of Dermée's that he read in *L'Esprit Nouveau,* an equation that he returns to obsessively in *Escrava.*[3] The equation, Lyricism + Art = Poetry, receives a frenetic animation in Mário's gloss:

> A inspiração é fugaz, violenta. Qualquer impecilho a perturba e mesmo emudece. Arte, que, somada a Lirismo, dá Poesia, não consiste em prejudicar a doida carreira do estado lírico para avisá-lo das pedras e cercas de arame do caminho. Deixe que tropece, caia e se fira. Arte é mondar mais tarde o poema de repetições fastientas, de sentimentalidades românticas, de pormenores inúteis ou inexpressivos. (PC 63 [9])

Both times that he expresses this idea, Mário uses related terms in similarly constructed phrases to emphasize an original lyric purity: "sem prejuízo" and "não consiste em prejudicar." Prejudice—pre-judgment as impairment—has no place in this process. On the contrary, Mário insists on the role of judgment in the later, metacognitive stage of creating poetry that he mentioned in the beginning section, which prevents poetry from being merely automatic writing; here he likens this final judgment to the weeding of a garden. The only exception that the author mentions, and exemplifies with the "mestres" Shakespeare and Homer, is exaggeration, which he defines as "símbolo sempre novo da vida como do sonho. Por ele vida e sonho se irmanam. E, consciente, não é defeito, mas meio legítimo de expressão" [the always new symbol of life as a dream. Because of it life and dreams are siblings. And, when conscious, it's not a defect but rather a legitimate means of expression] (PC 63). Exaggeration relates life and dream, makes reality more like fantasy; its function approximates that of the equals sign (=) in an equation and therefore exemplifies again the desire for balance.

Mário's discussion of beauty aims to debunk the idea of "o belo horrível" [the horrible beautiful] and to differentiate natural from artistic beauty. Responding to the belief that ugliness attracts artistic expression, the author declares: "Chamar de belo o que é feio, horrível, só porque está expressado com grandeza, comoção, arte, é desvirtuar ou desconhecer o conceito da beleza. Mas feio = pecado . . . Atrai" [To call beautiful what is ugly, horrible, only because it is expressed with magnificence, commotion, art, is to disparage or ignore the concept of beauty. But ugly = sin . . . It attracts] (PC 64). Beauty in the arts, he concedes, is completely subjective and for that reason not related to natural beauty.

> Belo da arte: arbitrário, convencional, transitório—questão de moda. Belo da natureza: imutável, objetivo, natural—tem a eternidade que a natureza tiver. Arte não consegue reproduzir natureza, nem este é seu fim. Todos os grandes artistas, ora consciente (Rafael das Madonas, Rodin do Balzac, Beethoven da Pastoral, Machado de Assis do Brás Cubas), ora inconscientemente (a grande maioria) foram deformadores da natureza. Donde infiro que o belo artístico será tanto mais artístico, tanto mais subjetivo quanto mais se afastar do belo natural. Outros infiram o que quiserem. Pouco me importa. (PC 64–65 [10])

The adjectives used here to distinguish artistic from natural beauty evoke the same qualities as the distinction between Mário's "verdade" and Christ's "Verdade" in "Parábola"; divine truth exists in nature while personal truth can be expressed through art. Mário affirms (like Huidobro) that art is creatively independent from nature, that artists even deform nature, and the more so the better; the list of artists and works in this passage, which serves to recognize that this act of deforming nature can exist in both the conscious and unconscious aspects of creation, underlines Mário's awareness of these coexisting forces.

Moreover, Mário points out that to the extent that our senses are involved, the deformation of what we perceive in the natural world is involuntary:

> Nossos sentidos são frágeis. A percepção das coisas exteriores é fraca, prejudicada por mil véus, provenientes das nossas taras físicas e morais: doenças, preconceitos, indisposições, antipatias, ignorâncias, hereditariedade, circunstâncias de tempo, de lugar, etc. . . . (PC 65 [11])

The words "prejudicada" and "preconceitos" here reinforce the impure nature of perception; collectively the use of these words and their derivatives (as above) attacks the closed minds of

115

Mário's critics. In contrast to our flawed sensual capacities, art offers the idealization of concepts "na sua plenitude heróica, que ultrapassa a defeituosa percepção dos sentidos" [in their heroic fullness, which surpasses the defective perception of our senses] (PC 65). For this reason the author concludes the paragraph with a separation from nature and a warning image of mimetic art: "Fujamos da natureza! Só assim a arte não se ressentirá da ridícula fraqueza da fotografia . . . colorida" [Let's run away from nature! Only then will art not resent the ridiculously poor insult . . . of the colored photograph] (PC 65).

The above ideas about art and nature correspond to Huidobro's propositions in "Non serviam" about freedom from mimesis in poetic *content*. In contrast, the next series of paragraphs emphasizes the need to escape poetic *formal* limitations. Mário compares the restrictive rules of versification and syllabification to the bed of Procrustes, although he admits a fondness for some forms and concludes that he is simply opportunistic: "Nesta questão de metros não sou aliado; sou como a Argentina: enriqueço-me" [In this matter of meters I am not an ally; I am like Argentina: I get rich] (PC 66). This leads into a discussion of the types of order and the imposition of order onto the frenzy of lyricism. He identifies different levels of orders:

> Existe a ordem dos colegiais infantes que saem das escolas de mãos dadas, dois a dois. Existe uma ordem nos estudantes das escolas superiores que descem uma escada de quatro em quatro degraus, chocando-se lindamente. Existe uma ordem, inda mais alta, na fúria desencadeada dos elementos. (PC 66 [12])

Similarly, he stresses the importance of chronological order for students of Brazilian history, yet contrasts with "Quem canta seu subconsciente seguirá a ordem imprevista das comoções, das associações de imagens, dos contactos exteriores. Acontece que o tema às vezes descaminha" [Whoever sings his unconscious will follow the unforeseen order of the commotions, of the associations of images, of the exterior contacts. Sometimes the theme goes astray] (PC 66–67). The "ordem imprevista das comoções" is the source of inspiration or "impulso lírico," similar to Kristeva's concept of the chaotic drives composing the semiotic chora: "O impulso lírico clama dentro de nós como turba enfurecida. Seria engraçadíssimo que a esta se dissesse: 'Alto lá! Cada qual berre por sua vez; e quem tiver o argumento mais forte, guarde-o para o fim!'" [The lyric impulse cries out within us like an infuriated mob. It would be incredibly comic to say to it: 'Hold on! Only one person shouting at a time; and whoever has the strongest point, save it for last!] (PC 67). The modifier "enfurecida," and the "fúria desencadeada" of the whirling elements above, evoke the same images of cosmic chaos found in Huidobro's "Las siete palabras del poeta" and *Altazor*. The chaos of the semiotic chora enthralls the poet and yet impedes clarity of expression, because the lyric impulse cannot be frozen or contained without disappearing.

Ideally, this autonomy of the lyric impulse should be carried over into the poem; hence Mário's distaste for rhyme schemes. In fact, he suggests that the freedom of the word (from semantic or phonetic association) is inextricably part of its original essence, and not a new idea of the futurists. In this way he further disassociates himself from the "futurista" label with which he had been branded, even though there are strong similarities between some of Mário's assertions and those of Marinetti, especially in the latter's widely available 1912 "technical" manifesto. Essentially Mário confirms many of Marinetti's ideas while claiming that they are not really innovations:

> Marinetti foi grande quando redescobriu o poder sugestivo, associativo, simbólico, universal, musical da palavra em liberdade. Aliás: velha como Adão. Marinetti errou: fez dela sistema. É apenas auxiliar poderosíssimo. Uso palavras em liberdade. Sinto que o meu copo é grande demais para mim, e inda bebo no copo dos outros. (PC 67–68 [13])

Again, the author prefigures his "Parábola" through the mention of Adam as the original poet, a poet who had no automatic associative context for words or even sounds—"a palavra em liberdade."

Challenging the associative context of words is the poetic ideal that motivates Mário's theory of poetic harmonics, which constitutes the only ostensibly theoretical part of "Prefácio." He begins immediately with another teaser: "Sei construir

teorias engenhosas. Quer ver?" [I know how to construct ingenious theories. Do you want to see?] (PC 68). As an accom-
plished musician and musicologist, Mário constructs his theory
facetiously and yet earnestly by pointing out that music has
long since freed itself from the dictatorship of melody to accommodate the plurality of harmony; why not poetry? Instead
of the literal *denotation* implied by melodic dominance
("arabesco horizontal de vozes (sons) consecutivas, contendo
pensamento inteligível" [horizontal arabesque of consecutive
voices (sounds), containing intelligible thought]), Mário strives
for the unexpected jump between words or phrases, more akin
to *connotation:* "estas palavras, pelo fato mesmo de se não
seguirem intelectual, gramaticalmente, se sobrepõem umas às
outras, para a nossa sensação, formando, não mais melodias,
mas harmonias" [these words, by the very fact that they don't
follow intellectually or grammatically, overlap among themselves according to our sensation, forming, no longer melodies,
but rather harmonies] (PC 68). Mário defines harmony somewhat generously: "combinação de sons simultâneos" [combi-
nation of simultaneous sounds]. In music, the definition could
just as easily apply to cacophony, but—without having to worry
about pitch, interval, tone quality, etc.—the definition suits his
poetic purposes. His example, from the poem "Tietê" in
Paulicéia, clarifies: "Arroubos . . . Lutas . . . Setas . . . Cantigas . . . Povoar! . . . Estas palavras não se ligam. Não formam
enumeração. Cada uma é frase, período elíptico, reduzido ao
mínimo telegráfico" [Delirium . . . Battles . . . Arrows . . .
Songs . . . Settle! . . . These words don't connect. They don't
form an enumeration. Each one is a phrase, an elliptic sentence,
reduced to a telegraphic minimum] (PC 68). The words build a
kind of harmonic suspension without release, each one providing a new semantic shading without concluding or erasing the
previous ones in the succession. Beyond harmony, Mário
identifies polyphony, which is the same idea but with phrases
(= melodies) instead of words (= notes); he then gives examples
of melodic, harmonic, and polyphonic verses from *Paulicéia.*
As logically and carefully as Mário has constructed this theory,
he nevertheless concludes with a typically playful and self-conscious disclaimer: "Que tal? Não se esqueça porém que outro
virá destruir tudo isto que construi" [How about that? Don't

forget, however, that someone else will come along to destroy all this I've built] (PC 69).[4]

Even so, the author continues to elaborate by appending five numbered paragraphs labeled "Para ajuntar à teoria" [To add to the theory] (PC 69). The third and fourth paragraphs best defend his ideas. In the third, Mário illuminates an important difference between the harmony of musical intervals and that of unconnected words on a page:

> Harmonia oral não se realiza, como a musical, nos sentidos, porque palavras não se fundem como sons, antes baralham-se, tornam-se incompreensíveis. A realização da harmonia poética efetua-se na inteligência. A compreensão das artes do tempo nunca é imediata, mas mediata. Na arte do tempo coordenamos atos de memória consecutivos, que assimila-mos num todo final. Este todo, resultante de estados de consciência sucessivos, dá a compreensão final, completa da música, poesia, dança terminada. (PC 70 [14])

The blending of notes in a chord, or primary colors in a secondary color, results in a distinct simultaneous entity that words—of a single voice or presentation—can only approximate. What is perhaps the best description of Mário's desired simultaneity forms the fourth paragraph:

> Entretanto: si você já teve por acaso na vida um aconteci-mento forte, imprevisto (já teve, naturalmente) recorde-se do tumulto desordenado das muitas idéias que nesse momento lhe tumultuaram no cérebro. Essas idéias, reduzidas ao mínimo telegráfico da palavra, não se continuavam, porque não faziam parte de frase alguma, não tinham resposta, solução, continuidade. Vibravam, ressoavam, amontoavam-se, sobrepunham-se. Sem ligação, sem concordância aparente—embora nascidas do mesmo acontecimento—for-mavam, pela sucessão rapidíssima, verdadeiras simultanei-dades, verdadeiras harmonias acompanhando a melodia enérgica e larga do acontecimento. (PC 70–71 [15])

A series of contradictory thoughts and ideas harmonically and tangentially accompanies an unsettling event, just as Mário's strings of words suggest variations on his poetic theme.

The musical analogy suggests another fruitful comparison—the word association technique in psychological analysis.

Mário's word sequences purposefully flaunt semantic association, not unlike the utterances of a patient instructed to say the
first word that comes to mind. Obvious word relations do little
to help the analyst, but striking, apparently unfounded associations may open a window to the unconscious. However, this
psychological analogy, like the musical one, proves to be inexact. The words in the "Arroubos" example do not necessarily
reflect unconscious word associations on Mário's part and, on
the contrary, could be likened to the conscious selection of elements in a scene. In any case, the words are not completely
random and thus some associative context must exist; the extent to which conscious choice or unconscious relation dominates the selection of the words remains a matter of debate.

The other three paragraphs of this "Para ajuntar à teoria"
section further promote the harmonics theory by pointing to
precedents in Pythagoras, Victor Hugo, and Bilac, the leader of
Brazil's Parnassian generation. Mário credits Bilac for discovering poetic harmonics in Brazil, but criticizes him for not exploring its possibilities further: "aceitou harmonias de quartas
e de quintas desprezando terceiras, sextas, todos os demais
intervalos. O número das suas harmonias é muito restrito" [he
accepted harmonic fourths and fifths, scorning thirds, sixths,
all the other intervals. The number of his harmonies is very re-
stricted] (PC 71). Unrestricted harmonies, freer word associations, no rhyme schemes: these are the limitless goals of
Mário's poetics, necessary in a personally creative sense in order to encompass the author's expansive self as presented in a
variety of roles in the beginning section of "Prefácio."

Concerning this issue of multiple selves and Mário's racial
identity, Haberly has definitively illuminated the fundamental role of the harlequin in the poems of *Paulicéia* as the multi-
colored image of racial juxtaposition: "If no single identity
could exist for Mário, it was vital for the separate and parallel
racial selves to survive intact, balanced in an uneasy truce"
(138). Haberly concludes that "Prefácio," written after the
poems, distracts from, or even obscures, the theme of race and
self-definition:

> There are no specific references to the book's central image
> of harlequinate diversity and conflict, an image drawn from
> the poet's own racial multiplicity. Moreover, because the

> most obvious stylistic technique in the poems—the juxta-
> position of contradictory and discordant elements—might
> lead readers to perceive the personal implications of the text,
> Mário cleverly uses allusion and misdirection to create the
> complicated theory (which he openly admits is nonsensi-
> cal) of melodic, harmonic, and polyphonic verse. (143)

While it is true that "Prefácio" does not address race or mention the harlequin image, it nonetheless espouses this same idea
of juxtaposition, albeit in a way more akin to the text's aesthetic and theoretical framework. For the same reason that, as
Haberly shows, Mário endorsed the simultaneous possibilities
of the concept of racial juxtaposition rather than the negatively
eschatological connotations of racial fusion, the simultaneous
presentation of Mário's words in what he calls "harmonic
verse" creates a distinctly articulated mosaic—retaining the semantic and phonetic qualities of each word—more than the fusion of notes in a chord. In sum, the harmonics theory must be
seen within the ludic yet didactic tone of "Prefácio" as an aesthetic explanation of simultaneity, on the level of words,
phrases, or selves, that embellishes the main theme of equilibrium or harmony.

The balance of conscious and unconscious activity in artistic creation is the theme of the remainder of the middle section
of "Prefácio." Beginning again with "sublime" lyricism, Mário
returns to the use of "prejudica" to warn against altering the
pure source of inspiration: "Preocupação de métrica e de rima
prejudica a naturalidade livre do lirismo objetivado. Por isso
poetas sinceros confessam nunca ter escrito seus milhores
versos" [Worrying about rhyme and meter impedes the free nature of objectified lyricism. This is why sincere poets confess
they never wrote their best verses] (PC 72). Paraphrasing
Théodule Ribot, a prominent French psychologist, he shows
that the conscious phase of lyrical creation, though necessary,
can be reduced:

> Ribot disse algures que inspiração é telegrama cifrado trans-
> mitido pela atividade inconsciente à atividade consciente
> que o traduz. Essa atividade consciente pode ser repartida
> entre poeta e leitor. Assim aquele que não escorcha e es-
> miuça friamente o momento lírico; e bondadosamente con-
> cede ao leitor a glória de colaborar nos poemas. (PC 72 [16])

The poet does not merely relay the telegram's message; some interpretation must occur, but more is left for the active reader. Continuing this idea, Mário uses Wagner's comparison of the poet to the plastic artist and to the musician; the poet "'se avizinha do artista plástico com a sua produção consciente, enquanto atinge as possibilidades do músico no fundo obscuro do inconsciente'" ['is like the plastic artist with his conscious production, while he attains the possibilities of the musician in the dark depths of the unconscious'] (PC 73). The poet occupies a space somewhere around the middle on a scale of conscious and unconscious activity; this is the first reference to the poet's specific need for balance on such a scale as opposed to the needs of other creative artists. Mário's point, through both Ribot and Wagner, underlies what he has already said elsewhere: the poet should strive to represent his inspiration as purely as possible, though some degree of conscious control, in expressing that inspiration in words, is inevitable.

Mário creates the allegory of Dom Lirismo to explore this question of conscious and unconscious activities. Because of its unique importance, the Dom Lirismo allegory is treated separately in the following chapter, "At the Dock and on the Street." I will state here that the brief narrative generally resembles "Parábola" in three ways: (1) both texts center on a personified element—the slave Poetry and the traveler Lyricism; (2) both texts aim to characterize aspects of poetic creation; and (3) Mário's first-person voice appears in both texts to relate the narratives directly and unequivocally to his aesthetic ideas. Not as global as "Parábola," the allegory of Dom Lirismo focuses only on the "smuggling" of the lyric impulse from the unconscious realm to consciousness.

The theme of modernity unites the last paragraphs of the "Prefácio" middle section. While Mário defends the appearance in his poetry of words that describe modern objects ("automóveis, cinema, asfalto"), he specifies that these objects do not constitute the theme of modernity as such; rather, he recognizes the universality of certain eternal themes—"universo, pátria, amor [. . .]" (PC 74). In contrast to modernity, he regards the avant-garde movement *primitivismo* with contempt, but he acknowledges the aesthetic influence of the "primitivos das eras passadas, expressão mais humana e livre de arte" [primitives of past eras, more human and free expression of art] (PC 74). (The terms *humana* and *livre* recall once again the lexicon used to describe "primitive" Poetry in "Parábola.") Finally, the conclusion of this section, too, is a more open-minded and honest statement than the typically destructive vanguard dogma: "O passado é lição para se meditar, não para reproduzir" [The past is a lesson to contemplate, not to reproduce] (PC 75). This aphorism, while bringing to mind Mário's studies of the "Mestres do Passado" series, also recalls the thematic leitmotif of the years of servitude as prelude to the revolution.

The middle, theoretical, section of "Prefácio" has attempted to justify not just the poetic practices evident in *Paulicéia* but also the poet's entire aesthetics at that time. The playful and self-conscious tone typifies Mário's creative freedom and yet masks to some extent the earnestness of that same freedom. The simultaneity developed in his harmonics theory resembles Marinetti's "palavras em liberdade" but achieves a greater musical and ontological resonance, while successfully pushing the limits of grammar and other restricting linguistic elements to let Mário be, like Dom Lirismo in the allegory, a smuggler from the "Eldorado do Inconsciente."

• The Conclusion of a Very Short-Lived Movement

The theme of Mário's multiple selves, prevalent in the beginning section, returns to dominate the end of "Prefácio." Without a doubt, the theme has also appeared in the middle section (i.e., Mário as theorist, musicologist, smuggler), but always subordinate to the larger issue of aesthetics. Now, Mário signals the shift back to the theme of his self with discussion of his originality, the reception of his work, and even an emotional guide to his poems, before closing "Prefácio" in the same role in which he began it—the tongue-in-cheek founder of a new movement. The focus this time, as far as the self-centered theme, is the need for the reader to expand his or her own self—to become like Mário's self—in order to understand *Paulicéia*.

Mário portrays himself as confident and mature: "Por muitos anos procurei-me a mim mesmo. Achei. Agora não me digam que ando à procura da originalidade, porque já descobri onde ela estava, pertence-me, é minha" [For many years I searched for myself. I found myself. Now don't tell me I'm searching for originality, because I already discovered where it was, it pertains to me, it's mine] (PC 75). Consequently, he reacts with good humor and feigned indifference to the critical reviews of his poetry, losing no faith but revealing the imagined response of his ideal reader:

> Quando uma das poesias deste livro foi publicada, muita gente me disse: "Não entendi." Pessoas houve porém que confessaram: "Entendi, mas não senti." Os meus amigos . . . percebi mais duma vez que sentiam, mas não entendiam. Evidentemente meu livro é bom. (PC 75 [17])

The missing response is to have understood *and* felt—the ideal balance, for which Mário strives, of intelligence and feeling, sense and sensibility.

Although Mário speaks at times for himself, in a deeply personal manner, at other times he speaks for many, or at least aims to move from solitude to solidarity. In an attempt to identify himself with his fellow writers of the *modernista* movement, Mário proclaims that, like the reactions to his work, there seems to be no middle road:

> Escritor de nome disse dos meus amigos e de mim que ou éramos gênios ou bestas. Acho que tem razão. Sentimos, tanto eu como meus amigos, o anseio do farol. Si fôssemos tão carneiros a ponto de termos escola coletiva, esta seria por certo o "Farolismo." Nosso desejo: alumiar. A extrema-esquerda em que nos colocamos não permite meio-termo. Si gênios: indicaremos o caminho a seguir; bestas: naufrágios por evitar. (PC 75 [18])

The strongly polar dichotomy of "geniuses" or "idiots" leaves no room for moderates. Yet this vision of congenial unity ostensibly disintegrates in the first sentence of the next paragraph: "Canto da minha maneira" [I sing my own way] (PC 75); at least the poet's song of his self leads the effort to build a chorus of voices: "Como o homem primitivo cantarei a princípio só. Mas canto é agente simpático: faz renascer na alma dum outro predisposto ou apenas sinceramente curioso e livre, o mesmo estado lírico provocado em nós por alegrias, sofrimentos, ideais" [Like the primitive man I will sing alone at first. But song is a sympathetic agent: in the soul of someone predisposed or even just sincerely curious and free, it brings about the rebirth of the same lyric state provoked in us by joys, sorrows, ideals] (PC 75–76).

Teles has identified the general influence of Romains and the *unanimismo* movement in *Paulicéia;* the ideas related to this movement have special relevance at this point of "Prefácio." The essentially cosmopolitan *unanimismo* movement embraces "a teoria de que a vida humana não devia ser vista na sua individualidade, mas nas suas relações através das quais se poderiam perceber afinidades psíquicas que pareciam formar um ser novo e superior—a alma coletiva" [the theory that human life should not be seen in its individuality, but in its relations through which can be perceived psychic affinities that seem to form a new and superior being—the collective soul] (*Vanguarda* 50). Teles's link connects with Mário's collective vision of São Paulo in the poems of *Paulicéia*. In "Prefácio," too, Mário seeks a unified spirit; his confidence that such a spirit exists allows him to write as if he were writing only for himself, but in the knowledge that those who can identify with this spirit will also understand him.[5] He writes:

> Sempre hei-de achar também algum, alguma que se embalarão à cadência libertária dos meus versos. Nesse momento: novo Anfião moreno e caixa-d'óculos, farei que as próprias pedras se reunam em muralhas à magia do meu cantar. E dentro dessas muralhas esconderemos nossa tribo. (PC 76 [19])

Mário in the person of Amphion, a mythological figure who combines attributes of Orpheus and the Pied Piper, protects his people as the father figure of a collectively mythified freedom-loving tribe. Although the walls enclose the tribe, the tribal image remains inclusive because of the possessive adjective "nossa"; the walls shut out the past poetic tradition in order to nurture the fledgling artistic expression of Mário and his group of sympathetic souls. The future tense of "farei" and "esconderemos" reveals that Mário's imaginary tribe, like Huidobro's ideal generation of poets (for whom Huidobro is also a father figure and musician in "El creacionismo"), must be deferred to posterity.

The author next addresses his change of opinion regarding the publication of *Paulicéia,* which he did not originally intend to publish, by referring to other authors' reflections on their own contradictions. However, as if he still resented so much public exposure, he adds the next paragraph: "Mas todo este prefácio, com todo o disparate das teorias que contém, não vale coisíssima nenhuma. Quando escrevi *Paulicéia Desvairada* não pensei em nada disto. Garanto porém que chorei, que cantei, que ri, que berrei . . . Eu vivo!" [But this whole preface, with all the nonsense of the theories it contains, is not worth the slightest little thing. When I wrote *Paulicéia* I didn't plan any of this. I guarantee, however, that I cried, I sang, I laughed, I roared . . . I live!] (PC 76). Many critics have taken the first sentence of this paragraph at face value, disregarding "Prefácio" as merely a hastily written defense of *Paulicéia*. But such a reading denies Mário's original exposition of the ideas he was struggling to express and understand. Primarily, the poet's ludic tone throughout the text should caution against a straightforward interpretation of such a statement. Furthermore, that first sentence, read with the added context of the second sentence, more correctly alludes to chronology, i.e., the fact that this preface was written *post facto* (as most are) and therefore cannot re-create the poet's original inspiration. Nevertheless, the preface can and does still serve as a "pretext" for both *Paulicéia* and *Escrava*.

The last of Mário's sentences in the above citation leads into the miniature emotional guide to the *Paulicéia* poems. It consists of a series of parallel negative commands: "Quem não souber cantar não leia Paisagem n.° 1. Quem não souber urrar não leia Ode ao Burguês [etc.]" [He who doesn't know how to sing shouldn't read "Paisagem No. 1." He who doesn't know how to yell shouldn't read "Ode ao Burguês"] (PC 76). However, such a guide ignores the unanimity of spirit on the part of the understanding reader, so Mário ends: "Não continuo. Repugna-me dar a chave de meu livro. Quem for como eu tem essa chave" [I won't continue. It disgusts me to give a key to the book. Whoever is like me has that key] (PC 77). Mário's self, having been presented in multiple manifestations, now unites in a definite *eu* to symbolize the equalizing spirit of unanimity.

For the conclusion of his text, Mário returns to the subject of *desvairismo,* which has not been mentioned as such since the preface's opening sentence. The end completes the circle:

E está acabada a escola poética "Desvairismo."

*

Próximo livro fundarei outra.

*

E não quero discípulos. Em arte: escola =
imbecilidade de muitos para vaidade dum só.

*

Poderia ter citado Gorch Fock. Evitava o
Prefácio Interessantíssimo. "Toda canção de
liberdade vem do cárcere." (PC 77 [20])

Mário pokes fun at the avant-garde mania of founding "ismo" movements and schools; *desvairismo* has not lasted more than the duration of the preface, nor does it have any followers. Mário's avoidance of disciples throughout his career, while opposing the practices of his contemporaries Oswald de Andrade *(antropofagia)* or Menotti del Picchia and Plínio Salgado *(verdeamarelismo),* strongly reinforces the precepts of unanimity; the poet's ideas can be anyone's, and can already be more universal, without the need for what Mário perceives as sycophantic imitators. But again the reader should bear in mind Mário's sarcasm, especially in the final paragraph about replacing the entire preface with one remark. That paragraph helps to close the textual circle by echoing the preface's second line: "Este prefácio, apesar de interessante, inútil" (PC 59); but more importantly, the quote from Gorch Fock (an early-twentieth-century German novelist) supports the essential avant-garde slogan of revolution. In broad terms, "liberdade" connotes freedom from rhyme, syllabification, and other traditional norms of prosody; this is the slave's emancipation and the break with the past, so dear to the vanguard artists, that Mário's and Huidobro's parables and other texts represent. The quote thus anticipates Mário's rendition of the slave Poetry's oppression and eventual freedom in "Parábola."

In conclusion, "Prefácio" as text challenges the limitations of both form and content in three genres: dedication, preface, and manifesto. In his enumeration of selves and his appeal to the collective soul or self, Mário emphasizes the simultaneity of lyric impulse and poetic expression, while at the same time approaching the tenets of *unanimismo;* the dialectic of one and many creates a tension between the possibility of myriad interpretations and the monolithic mandate of "Quem for como eu tem essa chave." The idea seems to follow the relation of many within one, or the simultaneity of messages and persons all moving in the same direction or experiencing the same emotion. The resolution of self and collectivity constantly haunts Mário and, according to Schwarz, only resolves itself in some of Mário's musings in "Elegia de Abril" without further development: "É pela expressão mais rigorosa de sua verdade pessoal, diz Mário, que o indivíduo se universaliza; ao mergulhar em sua própria subjetividade o artista encontrará, ao fundo, o social" [It is through the more rigorous expression of one's personal truth, says Mário, that the individual becomes universal; when he dives into his own subjectivity the artist will find, at bottom, the social] (9). Yet this reconciliation is clearly already nascent in the struggle for unanimity/simultaneity in "Prefácio."

In reference to the dialectic of conscious and unconscious creative processes, the validity of the following general affirmations is irrefutable: Lima proclaims "o elogio do inconsciente" [praise of the unconscious] (37) as the first directive of "Prefácio"; Pacheco notes "E, em confissão de ordem pessoal, [Mário] mostra a predominância que dava ao subconsciente" [And, in a personal confession, Mário shows the predominance he gave to the unconscious] (117–18). However, the distinction that Mário maintains between lyricism and art clarifies that whereas lyricism should be the uninhibited fruit of the unconscious, the work of art itself is necessarily a product of both the lyric impulse and conscious processes. It is not too much to insist on Mário's view of balance. If, in "Prefácio," the unconscious receives more attention, it is because of the "pretext" of Mário's defense of the *Paulicéia* poems, which necessitates the exaltation of free poetic forms and disconnected imagery in the face of the conservative poetic norms of the day.

At the Dock and on the Street

The Loss of Purity and Solidarity in Mário's Poetics

Although "Prefácio" displays a loose, aphoristic structure whereas *Escrava* more closely approximates a formal treatise, the two texts share a defense of avant-garde poetry, a personal, tragicomic tone, and an expository style that includes brief narrative fragments and anecdotes, of which the most well known is "Parábola d'*A escrava que não é Isaura*." These narrative fragments yield a wealth of densely symbolic images that articulate Mário's avant-garde poetics, specifically pertaining to the functions of the conscious and the unconscious in the act of writing poetry. One of these crucial images is the dock. It appears first in the allegory of Dom Lirismo in "Prefácio," characterizing a procedural loss of lyric purity, and then a second time, in relation to an emotional loss of understanding, in the hallucination sequence in endnote Q of *Escrava*. The dock is a liminal zone; within these contexts, it may be seen as the contact point, yet also the barrier, between a semiotic source and symbolic expression, or between the collective unconscious—source of poetic inspiration and ultimately of the artist's solidarity with the public—and the individual nature of conscious expression. Similarly, the street, as a commonplace, serves as a point of reunion for Mário and his public. Although the writer's sense of solidarity on the street most often eludes him, his desire to achieve it leads to some of his most creative meditations on the artist's role in society.[1]

• El Dorado

Mário's clearest insights, regarding this question of the degree of conscious and unconscious activity in the process of poetic creation, appear in the allegory of Dom Lirismo in "Prefácio":

> Dom Lirismo, ao desembarcar do Eldorado do Inconsciente
> no cais da terra do Consciente, é inspecionado pela visita
> médica, a Inteligência, que o alimpa dos macaquinhos e de
> toda e qualquer doença que possa espalhar confusão, obs-
> curidade na terrinha progressista. Dom Lirismo sofre mais
> uma visita alfandegária, descoberta por Freud, que a deno-
> minou Censura. Sou contrabandista! E contrário à lei da va-
> cina obrigatória. (PC 73 [21])

The word "desembarcar" and the pivotal image of the dock ("cais") establish Dom Lirismo's journey as having been over water. Although no boat is directly mentioned, it would seem that either the name of the boat—in which Dom Lirismo traveled from the land of unconsciousness—is "Eldorado," or that the name of the boat is "Eldorado do Inconsciente," in which case the boat itself represents unconsciousness. In either case, Mário establishes an important frame of reference by unequivocally uniting both the signifier "Eldorado," and a body of water, with unconsciousness.

This associative framework, which expands the scope of the narrative considerably, refers to the New World legend of El Dorado. According to the chronicler Juan de Castellanos—his version of the legend was one of the most popular of several slightly differing accounts—El Dorado was the leader of a tribe in the vicinity of Bogotá. During certain ceremonies, the leader's assistants would disrobe him and coat him from head to toe with gold dust; afterwards they would all ride out in a raft onto a lake in his domain, and would throw emerald-studded jewelry and golden ornaments into the lake as an offering. At least one other version of the legend implies that the golden chieftain would dive into the lake himself in an act of ritual purification. Iberians in the Americas came to associate the name El Dorado with an Edenic land of great riches, especially gold (Hemming 97–109). The core elements of this legend—the lake, the raft, the gold and jewels, and the submersion of the gold, jewels, and chieftain in the lake—provide the background for the allegory of Dom Lirismo. Mário's often-used term for the unconscious—"subconsciência"—displays the prefix, meaning "under," which has influenced the manner of thinking about the unconscious as below the surface of consciousness. Indeed, below the surface of the lake lie the ceremonial (and therefore symbolic) riches of the tribe; probing the waters, one gains insight by glimpsing the glittering flashes of the tribal community's (therefore collective) unconscious. Significantly, the tribal leader emerges from the waters naked and pure, just like the slave Poetry, unveiled in her moment of liberation in "Parábola." An expert in Brazilian and South American folklore, Mário very probably was familiar with the preceding details of the El Dorado legend.[2] Yet even if the phrase "Eldorado do Inconsciente" is interpreted in the least specialized sense, in which it would mean simply a paradisiacal land of unconsciousness, the water implied by "desembarcar" and "cais" retains its fundamental function in the allegory as the barrier between consciousness and unconsciousness. Dom Lirismo arrives, then, from the water, implicitly purified like the tribal leader El Dorado.

His arrival in a land of contrast sets up the rest of the narrative. The distance he has traveled is highlighted not spatially but temporally; from the legendary past of El Dorado and sixteenth-century conquest, he has landed, in a reverse discovery, "na terrinha progressista" of independent, industrialized Brazil (whose national motto declares "Ordem e Progresso" [Order and Progress]). A personification of the lyric impulse, pure and fresh from the unconscious, Dom Lirismo has set foot on the dock; paradoxically, he must undergo two inspections of his person. Intelligence, a doctor, purges Dom Lirismo's body of "qualquer doença que possa espalhar confusão, obscuridade" [any and all disease that could spread confusion, obscurity] (PC 73); in like fashion, the customs official Censorship revises Dom Lirismo's personal effects. A parallel develops between medical clearance/Intelligence (deeply affecting the inside of the body) and customs clearance/Censorship (superficially affecting articles outside the body). Thus the lyric impulse, source of inspiration, is characterized both as a product of sensibility or passion reduced by intelligence (or reason), and as a product of the unconscious diminished by Freud's censorship mechanism, the superego.

The allegory's message clarifies that, to a certain inevitable extent, conscious processes contaminate the already pure lyric impulse. Put within parameters of the semiotic and the symbolic, such distortion by conscious influence defines the thetic moment as described by Kristeva. In *Revolution in Poetic Language,* Kristeva develops the concept of the self as a simultaneous pulsion and stasis of drives called the chora. These internal drives are semiotic, but their moment of articulation is necessarily symbolic (25–30). In a Kristevan model, therefore, the self has a limited ability to express its needs or desires; this represents Mário's loss at the dock. Some meaning is "lost in translation" from the semiotic chora to the speech act, or, in a parallel sense, from the collective unconscious to an individual consciousness.[3] Kristeva posits that poetry (especially that of the Symbolists) and other art forms can allow some of the semiotic to slip out, but this happens rarely and even then the expression is seldom complete (82–89). By the same token, if the presentation of the semiotic were complete, it would be incomprehensible; as Kelly Oliver shows, the semiotic must rely on the symbolic to shape meaning (96–97). In Mário's allegory, Dom Lirismo does manage to pass through the medical and customs inspections, but his essence has been inexorably, and yet necessarily, altered.

Moreover, the *necessity* of this alteration signals a key difference between Mário's aesthetic ideas and those of his contemporary Breton, perhaps the most influential European avant-garde leader. Pestino emphasizes that, unlike the resistance that Breton leveled against any editing of "the spontaneous flow of the unconscious," Mário developed the idea that "revision was a [. . .] process not to be feared, but actually to be called art" (19). In *El arco y la lira,* Paz points out that even Breton's surrender to the unconscious constitutes a planned event: "el problema que desvela a Breton es un falso problema, según ya lo había visto Novalis: abandonarse al murmullo del inconsciente exige un acto voluntario" (174). The act of writing a poem moves beyond a moment of inspiration to include an awareness of will: "el poema es una obra [y] la obra, toda obra, es el fruto de una voluntad que transforma y somete la materia bruta a sus designios" (158). Mário recognizes the artistic merit of the conscious will, but perceives an inevitable loss of purity in this refinement of the "materia bruta."

The Dom Lirismo allegory focuses exclusively on this transfer of the inspirational lyric impulse from the unconscious realm to consciousness; the range of the allegory's themes does not reach the same global level as that of Mário's later "Parábola." Nonetheless, the brief allegory generally resembles "Parábola"; both texts characterize aspects of poetic creation, centering on a personified element—the traveler Lyricism and the slave Poetry. Poetry and Dom Lirismo are pure and yet disquieting presences in a conservative society, the former associated with the words "escandalosamente" and "estranheza" (OI 202), the latter with "confusão" and "obscuridade." The "terrinha progressista" represents the same "sociedade educadíssima, vestida e policiada da época actual" (OI 202) that closes "Parábola"; the adjectives "educadíssima" and "policiada" suggest the same repression and censorship that Dom Lirismo meets at the dock. Moreover, Poetry, like Dom Lirismo above, is a visitor not through space so much as time, from Genesis to the "época actual" [contemporary era] (OI 202); in both cases Mário's avant-garde preoccupation with originality transplants Edenic or primitive essences into the modern moment, or into São Paulo, city of simultaneity in *Paulicéia*.

Demonstrating another similarity to "Parábola," Mário's first-person voice relates the allegory directly and unequivocally to his aesthetic ideas. He leaves no doubt about his message of embracing, as much as possible, the pure unconscious: "Sou contrabandista! E contrário à lei da vacina obrigatória" (PC 73). The declaration subverts both legal confiscation and medical intervention (censorship and intelligence); these motifs continue into the next two paragraphs of "Prefácio," in which Mário shifts his focus from an emphasis on the unconscious back to a balance of unconscious and conscious elements:

> Parece que sou todo instinto . . . Não é verdade. Há no meu livro, e não me desagrada, tendência pronunciadamente intelectualista. Que quer você? Consigo passar minhas sedas sem pagar direitos. Mas é psicologicamente impossível livrar-me das injeções e dos tônicos. (PC 73 [22])

Nelly Novaes Coelho uses the first three sentences of this citation as the epigraph of *Mário de Andrade para a Jovem Geração,* her 1970 defense of Mário's ideas. Signaling the words "instinto" and "intelectualista," she identifies these qualities as the members of a stabilizing, central duality in

133

Mário's work: "Dualidade que ao acarretar o contínuo confronto dos dois pólos extremos de sua personalidade, equilibrava-os, impedindo o poeta das atitudes radicalizantes" [Duality which, in causing the continuous confrontation of the two extreme poles of his personality, balanced them, keeping the poet from radicalizing tendencies] (1). In her study of *Paulicéia,* Coelho develops this binary tension, which she claims kept Mário from the more typically avant-garde excesses of "anarquia revolucionária" [revolutionary anarchy] (1); again, the comparison to Breton's unflinching embrace of the unconscious provides a useful contrast. In fact, more than just the epigraph, the entire paragraph cited above supports Coelho's view, for in the continuation of his subversion motif, Mário implies that while he can escape conscious censorship (the silk he conceals from the superficial customs inspection) he cannot avoid the "intelectualista" effects of intelligence (the more profound medicinal treatment of injections and tonics). Some kind of balance must therefore be achieved between the unconscious force of the lyric impulse and the consciously intellectual attempt to express it in poetry.

The injections and tonics that Mário mentions figuratively are immediately redefined, in the second of these two paragraphs, in a more literal fashion: "A gramática apareceu depois de organizadas as línguas. Acontece que meu inconsciente não sabe da existência de gramáticas, nem de línguas organizadas. E como Dom Lirismo é contrabandista . . ." [Grammar appeared after languages were already organized. It happens that my unconscious knows nothing of the existence of grammars, nor of organized languages. And like Dom Lirismo it is a smuggler . . .] (PC 73). The intellectual element (represented by the medicine) that Mário cannot avoid arises in the very act of linguistic (or symbolic) representation: it is grammar, syntax, semantics, pronunciation, orthography, and other restrictions entailed by "línguas organizadas." Paradoxically, without these restrictions no understandable expression would be possible; Kristeva observes, through Mallarmé's text "Le Mystère dans les lettres," that "the 'mysterious' functioning of literature [works] as a rhythm made intelligible by syntax" (30). Like Mallarmé and the other Symbolists (Mário held a special esteem for Rimbaud), Mário struggles in his poetry against the restrictions of this syntax. However, the expository language of the prose "Prefácio" must necessarily maintain some syntactical structure or else deny its explanatory function in a poetics. The poet thus uses "Prefácio" as "pre-text" to forewarn and excuse his grammatical, lexical, and orthographic innovations—typically vanguard though also part of Mário's nationalist agenda within Brazilian Modernism—in the poems of *Paulicéia:*

> Você perceberá com facilidade que si na minha poesia a gramática às vezes é desprezada, graves insultos não sofre neste prefácio interessantíssimo. Prefácio: rojão do meu eu superior. Versos: paisagem do meu eu profundo. (PC 74 [23])

While reaffirming the spatial designations of the conscious and unconscious in "eu superior" and "eu profundo," Mário implies that the conscious control of language in "Prefácio" sets up a necessary counterweight to the lyrically dominated use of language in *Paulicéia.*

At the limit of consciousness, the dock stands as a juncture of giving and taking; the poet can receive the lyric impulse in its original brilliance, but cannot attempt an expression of that inspiration without diminishing it in some way, in order to accommodate its form in words and/or its psychological acceptability. The second of these two accommodations is the weaker; Mário declares himself to be, like Dom Lirismo, a smuggler from "Eldorado do Inconsciente," and thus he perceives little inclination on his part to censor the unconscious images of his inspiration. But like all great artists, he battles the limitations of the very medium of his expression: language.

• Waves of Oceanic Humanity

In Mário's next encounter at the dock, this linguistic quandary absorbs the emotional implications of his profound search for solidarity through art. Less allegorical and more radically oneiric, this second encounter appears as a hallucination sequence in endnote Q of *Escrava.* Endnote Q is the final endnote and exclusively a continuation of endnote J (no reference to Q appears in the main body of the text); the two endnotes describe Mário's conception of "cansaço intelectual" [intellectual fatigue], which constitutes both the detrimental effect of new information and transportation technology, and the fruitful cause of artistic innovation. In a lengthy discussion in endnote J, Mário credits this intellectually blasé attitude as the stimulus for the destructive poetics of the earlier vanguard writers who, although they abandoned reason, consequently developed poetic techniques that are nonetheless "os únicos capazes de concordar com a verdade psicológica e com a natureza virgem do lirismo" [the only ones capable of agreeing with psychological truth and with the virginal nature of lyricism] (OI 288). The intense vanguard desire for originality also derives from such high-brow boredom: "A inovação em arte deriva parcialmente, queiram ou não [. . .], do cansaço intelectual produzido pelo já visto, pelo tédio da monotonia" [Innovation in art derives partially, like it or not, from the intellectual fatigue produced by the already seen, by the tedium of monotony] (OI 289).

Referred to endnote Q, the reader finds continued exposition of this theme with a tone of personal anguish. In confirming art's debt to moments of intellectual fatigue, Mário posits a series of questions seeking to define the artist's duty:

> Será possivel forçar a perfeição a surgir para as artes? Saltar a evolução para que as obras actuais ganhem em serenidade, clareza, humanidade? Escrevemos para os outros ou para nós mesmos? Para *todos* os outros ou para *uns poucos* outros? Deve-se escrever para o futuro ou para o presente? Qual a obrigação do artista? (OI 295 [24])

The actions—a surge of perfection and a leap to clarity—suggest the force necessary to break through some kind of boundary limiting the artist's true expression. Such a boundary both reflects and predicts the limitations experienced at the dock, frontier between conscious and unconscious zones; it reflects the linguistic barrier met at Dom Lirismo's dock, while it foreshadows—with questions about the general identity and nature of the artist's public—the humanistic barrier that the author himself will confront in this second dockside encounter. His conflict of responsibility to the public, within an ostensible dichotomy of elitist art and popular art, further reveals the need to express, without limiting or masking ("mascarar"), the moment of actuality, of actualized participation:

Ha nestas duas estradas, numa a obrigação moral que nos (me) atormenta, noutra a coragem de realizar esteticamente a actualidade que seria ingrato quasi infame desvirtuar, mascarar, em nome dum futuro terreno que não nos pertence. (OI 295 [25])

Such a challenge to Mário's firmness of purpose evokes the marvelous extended hallucination sequence that dramatizes his divided loyalties:

Dores e sofrimentos! Dúvidas e lutas. Sinto-me exausto. Meu coração parou? Um automovel só, lá fóra . . . É a tarde, mais serena. E si vedono comparire delle immagini. Ha uns mocinhos a assobiar nos meus ouvidos uma vaia de latidos, cocoricós . . . Os cães rasgam-me as vestes na rua terrível, mordem-me os pés, unham-me as carnes . . . Eis-me despido. Nú. Diante dos que apupam. Despido também da ilusão com que pretendi amar a humanidade oceánica. Mas as vagas humanas batem contra o meu peito que é como um cáis de amor. Roem-me. Roem-me. Uma longinqua, penetrante dor . . . Mas o sal marinho me enrija. Ergo-me mais uma vez. E ante a risada má, inconsciente, universal tenho a orgulhosa alegria de ser um homem triste. E continuo para frente. Ninguem se aproxima de mim. Gritam de longe: — "Louco! Louco!" Volto-me. Respondo: — "Loucos! Loucos!" É engraçadíssimo. E termino finalmente achando em tudo um cómico profundo: na humanidade, em mim, na fadiga, na inquietação e na famigerada liberdade. (OI 295–96 [26])

While emphasizing the modern moment of the automobile, the initial act—mistaking the loud and sudden braking of a car out on the street for a heart attack—symbolizes the confusion of the author's interior, personal longings and his altruistic sense of debt to the humanity that awaits him on the street. The sentence in Italian reprises part of a longer citation, presented earlier in endnote Q, from Angelo Mosso about the way in which intellectual fatigue leads to imaginative daydreams; the reappearance of the phrase here triggers the dreamlike sequence, sustaining Mário's argument that this same fatigue leads to curious artistic innovations. Mário's naked stroll down the horrible street contrasts with nude Poetry's exposure to modern society at the end of "Parábola"; instead of the adoration that Poetry commands, the author meets with jeering urchins, rude strangers, and the vicious mutts that bite his feet and shred his clothes. His cherished dream of achieving solidarity through representation of the man-in-the-street, expressed in the conclusion of the first part of *Escrava,* here becomes a nightmare of isolation in the "rua terrível"; he has been stripped of the "ilusão com que pretendi amar a humanidade oceánica."

These limitless ocean waves ("vagas") of humanity signal the transformation of the author's terrestrial motion into the rhythm of the tides, inducing an association between the waves and the collective unconscious—"humanidade," "humana," and later "inconsciente" and "universal"—that recalls the water-unconsciousness symbolism of the Dom Lirismo allegory.[4] As in the earlier text, a dock articulates the point of contact, and of loss, between the unconscious and the conscious; yet it is no longer the site of customs inspections and vaccinations, but rather the "cáis de amor"—the simile of Mário's chest, the breakwater of his wounded love for humanity. Mário's loss of hope and conviction, vis-à-vis the scorn of the humanity he wishes to embrace, reflects the loss of the lyric impulse's original purity. Like the tribal leader El Dorado, Mário bathes in a body of water that symbolizes the collective unconscious, but instead of the sparkling waters of the treasure-laden lake, the salt water of oceanic humanity immerses Mário in waves that cleanse and yet also aggravate his wounds. While the first dockside encounter illustrated that lyric inspiration must be modified before it can be expressed, the second encounter shows that the artistic product that Mário creates from his already diminished inspiration once again diminishes before it can be interpreted, or even rejected outright, by humanity—his irreverent, gnawing public. Always, it seems, something is irrevocably forfeited at the dock; here Mário *becomes* the dock and assumes a sacrificial loss of communication, painfully aware of the frustration of artistically translating the collective unconscious in a way that can be universally understood by the very humanity who creates it.

Mário recommences his headlong path, spurred on by humanity's "sal marinho" in his wounds; his path straddles the line of the scission he wishes to reconcile between elitist and popular art, portrayed respectively by the images of the author writing calmly in his study and of the bustling, inhospitable, noisy street. The only dialogue possible consists of a volley of repeated epithets accusing mutual insanity. The poet's antithetical emotions ("alegria" with "triste") lead him somewhat desperately to invoke his own comic sense against the wicked guffaws that mock him; his contradictory feelings can only resolve into more laughter, perhaps representing, laugh against laugh, the unity and balance with humanity that he desires.

Encapsulated within two auxiliary texts (endnotes J and Q), the entire hallucination sequence projects a sort of secret status; the writer, stripped naked and stripped of pretension, exposes his deepest, darkest concerns to the reader. Yet the text also doubles as an alternate ending to *Escrava,* and thus receives more symbolic weight, since the hallucination sequence quoted above presents—in terms of physical presentation on the pages—Mário's last words in *Escrava* before a summary quotation of some verses by Apollinaire and then "Postfácio," written two and a half years later. As an alternate ending (and one must wonder why Mário split endnote Q off from endnote J in the first place), the hallucination sequence contrasts with the ending of "Prefácio" regarding the important theme of artistic liberty. Whereas in the earlier text Mário concludes more soberly, quoting Gorch Fock, "'Toda canção de liberdade vem do cárcere'" (PC 77), here he laughs desperately at, among other ideas, the "famigerada liberdade." The artistic freedom that had been opposed to the rigors of fossilized poetry in *Paulicéia*—and dramatized in its concluding oratory—has here resulted in too great a separation from the artist's public. In general, the Brazilian Modernists (and other avant-garde writers and artists) gleefully forfeited a widespread public following. Yet here the presumably sympathetic reader, led behind the scenes in this cloistered text and brought into the writer's confidence, ironically observes the writer's conflict in reconciling his ideals and his commitments regarding a potentially much larger reading public.

The encounter at the dock causes loss, pain, and humiliation: Dom Lirismo suffers the inspections of his person and the consequent pollution of the pure lyric impulse, Mário endures the relentlessly beating pain of a public who scorns him, unable or unwilling to comprehend him. The loss always occurs in the act of contact between the universal (humanity, the collective unconscious) and the individual (the poet and his expression); this contact dramatizes the unavoidable concentration of semiotic urges into symbolic form, an act Kristeva calls "the positing of signification" (43). Positing, deposit, position—after the infinite (and only ostensible) apositionality of the ocean, a dock embodies an exact locus of contact, each dock concretizing an individual position facing the universal. Such a juncture of perspectives in simultaneity becomes one of Mário's constant and generally positive themes, treated exuberantly in some of his most important works (*Paulicéia*, "Carnaval Carioca," *Macunaíma*). However, within the explanatory purpose of his poetics and, moreover, within the intimate, even privileged, company of reader and writer in a preface and in an endnote, Mário ultimately concedes inherent, inescapable casualties of artistic expression.

- ## Men-in-the-Street and the Poet Alone

> O bonde abre a viagem,
> No banco ninguém,
> Estou só, stou sem.
>
> Depois sobe um homem,
> No banco sentou,
> Companheiro vou.
>
> O bonde está cheio,
> De novo porém,
> Não sou mais ninguém.
>> From *Lira Paulistana* (PC [27])

In this brief poem Mário's beloved streetcar sets the scene for a telling mathematics exercise in which one plus one is a fruitful sum but one plus many is fruitless. In his search for solidarity, the poet is encompassed by the growing crowd but his voice is overwhelmed and the poem ends. Like many artists Mário invariably portrays his aesthetic sensibilities as being out-of-sync with the crowd. In the oratory that closes *Paulicéia Desvairada,* "As Enfibraturas do Ipiranga," Mário's solo voice "Minha Loucura" contrasts with many urban societal groups, among them the indifferent proletariat. Yet the operatic nature of the "Enfibraturas" invites comparison with Mário's call for action at the end of the first part of his *A escrava que não é*

Isaura: "Acontece porém que no palco de nosso século se representa essa ópera barulhentíssima a que Leigh Henry lembrou o nome: Men-in-the-street. . . Representemo-la" [It happens, however, that on the stage of our century is now playing that very noisy opera of which Leigh Henry remembered the name: Men-in-the-street . . . Let's put it on] (OI 224). The men in the street, and women too, are average folks who stand in deliberate contrast to the bourgeoisie, whom Mário and all the other ex-bourgeois vanguardists vilified with uncommon glee. The men in the street are the authentic Brazilians who live authentically in authentic Brazil and of course speak authentic Brazilian Portuguese. These average folks are the lynchpin in Brazilian *modernismo*'s plan to interpret and promote the national character and language, yet these typical folks, who would never go to the opera, are almost always at odds with Mário.

Mário is driven to literally expose himself in some passages from his poetics and from his *crônicas:* naked before the crowd. For Matildes Demetrio dos Santos, nudity is the perfect metaphor for Mário's exposure to the individual readers of his prolific letters: "[. . .] é possível [. . .] surpreender momentos em que o remetente se desnuda para o outro, projetando o que estava escondido ou o que o preocupava no momento [e ele] levanta o véu que encobre sua figura múltipla" [it's possible to capture moments in which the writer bares himself for the other, projecting what was hidden or what was preoccupying him at the moment [and he] lifts the veil that covers his multiple figure] (95–96). Yet dos Santos and other analysts who draw attention to Mário's frank and engaging style employ this imagery obliquely, since there does not appear to exist any exploration of Mário's own use of nudity as metaphor.

His conflict with the men-in-the-street, as characterized in endnote Q by nudity or exposure and also by a lack of dialogue, thus parallels the struggle to introduce lyric inspiration into formal language, or the semiotic into the symbolic, illustrated in the Dom Lirismo allegory. In one of his *crônicas,* "A Pesca do Dourado" [Catching the Dourado Fish, 6 July 1930], Mário again reproduces elements of the El Dorado ritual. Without denying the anecdotal value of this text, wedded to the particular structural exigencies of the Brazilian *crônica* as genre, I intend to foreground an artistic allegorical reading. In this fish tale, Mário, the only city slicker on a boat with experienced fisherman in the middle of a lake in northern São Paulo state, endeavors to catch a *dourado*. With "raiva individualista" [egotistical anger] he swings his rod wrong and smacks himself in the nose with the bait. The canoe paddler looks at him and stonewalls: no reaction. Mário protests to the reader:

> Essa inexistência de manifestação exterior destes que me rodeiam, a deferência desprezível, a nenhuma esperança pelo moço da cidade, palavra de honra, é detestável. Castiga a gente. Oh vós, homens que viveis no sertão porque me tratais assim! Eu quero ser como vós, vos amo e vos respeito! (*Táxi* 219 [28])

Mário's pretentious pronoun use only exacerbates his distance from the common folk who would never speak that way. His frustrations are compounded when a man whom he believes to have a *dourado* on his line, and whom he therefore suddenly sees as a god with the golden dawn breaking behind him, loses the fish after much struggle. But then Mário himself has a turn with the *dourado* on his own line:

> A segunda vez que o bicho pulou fora da água, eu já não podia mais de comoção. Palavra de honra: estava com medo. Tinha vontade de chorar, os companheiros não falavam mais nada, tinham me abandonado! ôh que ser mais desgraçado! . . . (*Táxi* 220 [29])

Not in vain does Mário repeat the phrase "palavra de honra": he seeks desperately to invoke a fraternal code of conduct among the fishermen, an honor code that, just when he needs it most, does not function: "os companheiros não falavam mais nada, tinham me abandonado!"

Finally someone does help the author land the catch, and Mário's mood changes. He sits, "muito simples, dum lado, jogado fora pela significação do dourado que era um peixe importante" [very unaffected, to one side, blown away by the significance of the *dourado,* which was an important fish] (*Táxi* 220). The author's use of "significação" conveys the sense of a deeper, unconscious meaning heroically and forcefully brought to light, as much as the earlier use of "comoção" in relation to the *dourado* displays the high emotion of this boon from beneath the surface of the waters. Yet the *crônica* ends and we cannot know at what price the *dourado* has been caught. Perhaps the fishermen resent his catch, or chalk it up to beginner's luck, or perhaps they respect him for it, or all of the above. But these backwoods men-in-the-boat are also Mário's beloved men-in-the-street, his desired collective entity, to whom he directs his ornately written but unspoken cry, "Eu quero ser como vós, vos amo e vos respeito!" These men parallel the hostile, crashing waves of oceanic humanity in the *Escrava* hallucination sequence and, as in Dom Lirismo's encounter at the dock, there remains very little to be voiced of Mário's unadulterated inspiration. If he has won the gleaming golden lyricism from the depths of the unconscious, his silence indicates that it has not come accompanied by the conscious tools with which to communicate it, to render it understandable for his desired audience.

• The Invisible Man

In another of his *crônicas* Mário portrays himself among others, this time back in the city streets of São Paulo. The street, too, is a liminal zone, a transforming point of contact between Mário the writer and his public. As such it constitutes an important locus in endnote Q's hallucination sequence and also in this *crônica,* "O Terno Itinerário ou Trecho de Antologia" [The Endearing Itinerary or Anthology Extract, 15 February 1931]. In this oneiric text, Mário traces a seemingly aimless wandering around the city that becomes the itinerary or *roteiro* leading from an initial sensation of loss of self-identity to an eventual sense of regained self. His journey commences: "Saí desta morada que se chama O Coração Perdido e de repente não existi mais. Perdi meu ser. Não é a humildade que me faz falar assim, mas o que serei eu por entre os automóveis?" [I left this dwelling called The Forsaken Heart and suddenly I no longer existed. I lost my being. It's not humility that makes me speak this way, but what can I be among the automobiles?] (*Táxi* 337). He describes the errands he needs to run as if he were only gradually becoming aware of his own will:

> Estava com dois embrulhos na mão. Um era pro Conserva-
> tório, outro era pro Correio, e eles criaram em mim alguma
> decisão. Minha roupa cor-de-cinza riscava mal na tarde nu-
> blada e uma quase sensação da nudez me caceteou. Feliz-
> mente as auras vieram, batidas da várzea largada, me
> afagaram, me levaram pra outros mundos animais em que é
> bom viver. (*Táxi* 337 [30])

Here Mário externalizes the color of his clothing to mix it with
São Paulo climatic conditions, as he does throughout *Paulicéia
Desvairada* with the colored lozenges of his harlequin suit.
Paradoxically this identification of his gray clothing with the
mist is what makes him feel naked, a clothed nudity, but in the
fog his nudity is really an erasure—"Perdi meu ser"—or an in-
visibility, that parallels his frustration in the fishing *crônica*
with the "inexistência de manifestação exterior destes que me
rodeiam." Here he is rescued by the breezes that caress him—
"me afagaram"—the feeling of air on his skin, that awakens
instinct and carries him away ("outros mundos animais") by
engaging his senses.

His clothed nudity in the *crônica,* a realistic genre, contrasts
strongly with the more imaginative hallucination sequence
from *Escrava,* in which he is stripped violently by the street
mutts, and in which the people actually pay attention to
Mário (by making fun of him), unlike the men-in-the-street
in "Itinerário" who do not penetrate Mário's shrouded in-
visibility. Mário is wrapped up in himself in "Itinerário," a
conceptualization that is supported by the image of the
embrulhos or bundles he is carrying. In his efforts to unwind,
so to speak, Mário is thwarted by the formality of the packages:

> Era eu, tomando café, a vítima. Era a muito mais lógica fe-
> licidade de primeiro me libertar dos embrulhos pra depois
> gozar melhormente a bebida, o vilão. E, do outro lado da
> cena, ainda e sempre a primavera, Ariel, Chico Antônio,
> Nosso Senhor, enfim, todo o desequilíbrio contra a vida.
> (*Táxi* 338 [31])

Given how dear the concept of equilibrium is to the expression of Mário's aesthetics, it follows that *desequilíbrio* unfavorably depicts amateur style or uncontrolled imagery. The
imbalance or chaos of the street scene here is life, however, not

art, and it is into this imbalance—"o desequilíbrio da nossa cultura" [the imbalance of our culture]—that Mário desires to thrust himself.[5] But he must fulfill the duties of his errands, so he heads to the post office: "Felizmente havia doze embrulhos pra registrar antes do meu e fumei, divertidamente fumei, enquanto a consciência me afagava devagar, sussurrando-me no ouvido: 'Homem de bem!'" [Fortunately there were a dozen bundles to process before mine, and I smoked, amusedly I smoked, while my conscience comforted me slowly, whispering in my ear: "Man of good deeds!"] (*Táxi* 339). Mário's realization that there are "doze embrulhos pra registrar"—that his is just one of many bundles—leads to his smoking and feeling relieved. Previously the breeze had caressed him, saving him from his feeling of "quase sensação da nudez"; now it's his conscience that can whisper like the wind in his ear, caressing him (again the verb *afagar*) and reinforcing a feeling of camaraderie among the other postal patrons: "Homem de bem."

Does Mário-as-narrator's smoke cloak him like the fog had done previously? Does waiting in line, participating in civic order, reassure him? Certainly these final words "homem de bem" close the *crônica* in a more participatory vein than the fishing *crônica,* where Mário ends up "jogado fora." *Fora e dentro,* out of touch but in the line, waiting to free himself of his *embrulhos* and partake in the "desquilíbrio contra a vida," Mário writes his aesthetic and poetic sensibilities into his chronicling of life. His musings here reflect what Vivian Schelling, agreeing with Schwarz, calls a noticeable change in his artistic leanings after 1930, an attempt at synthesis "entre o inconsciente individual 'lírico' e a construção técnica consciente necessária para que o produto artístico tenha um significado público" [between the "lyric" individual unconscious and the conscious technical construction necessary so that the artistic product has a public meaning] (184). While I agree that such a change seems evident in Mário's work, in this *crônica* he explores group dynamics and the chaos of the crowd but prefers, as in the streetcar poem, the sum of one plus one, embodied in the persons of Mário and his implied reader.

Chapter Six

Balancing the Equations

Mário's Struggle to Define
Aesthetic Simultaneity

In comparison to the structure of "Prefácio Interessantíssimo," the two-part structure of *A escrava que não é Isaura* more closely replicates an exact balance of attention to the themes of conscious and unconscious processes. Published in 1925 as a treatise on *modernista* poetics, *Escrava* elaborates the main points of "Prefácio" while introducing new ideas, and attempts to finally cut off any unfounded ties to futurism originated by the claims of Oswald de Andrade, to whom the text is significantly dedicated. As previously noted, the text was written in April and May of 1922, while its "Postfácio" was written in November of 1924, just before publication, to defend once again Mário's right to change his mind on aesthetic issues.[1] The text begins with "Parábola," studied in depth in the introduction. Although Mário did not section "Prefácio," he did divide *Escrava* into two parts (after "Parábola") and then concluded with "Postfácio." *Escrava*'s endnotes, all of which (except for endnote A) arise from the second part, constitute another important feature; as in the analysis of "Parábola," they will be considered as they occur in the text.

After abolishing the *desvairismo* or hallucinationism movement at the end of "Prefácio," Mário had stated, only somewhat seriously: "Próximo livro fundarei outra [escola poética]" (PC 77). Undeniably, this act is not fulfilled in *Escrava* as far as the founding or naming of a movement; however, the treatise, after the notoriety of the Modern Art Week, replaces *desvairismo* by naming *modernista* poetry in its subtitle and targeting the *modernista* movement as part of the general, international vanguard tendency. Though the term *desvairismo* never appears in *Escrava,* the text nonetheless resuscitates, and significantly elaborates, all the major ideas of "Prefácio" (and thus validates the function of "Prefácio" as pretext): the origin and nature of the lyric impulse, its relationship to conscious will, the subordinate role of beauty in art, the restrictions of traditional prosody, simultaneity/polyphony, the characteristics of modernity, and contemporary critical reaction. The important "Prefácio" theme of Mário's self-portrayal does not wholly disappear in *Escrava* (it resurfaces most notably in endnote Q and in "Postfácio") but, given the change in perspective from a defense of Mário's own poetry in "Prefácio" to a defense of vanguard poetry in general in *Escrava,* the theme diminishes understandably.

Grembecki has suggested that the main themes of the two parts of *Escrava* are "máximo de lirismo" and "máximo de crítica" (27). The definition of the former will be retained from "Prefácio," while the latter becomes a corrective addition to Dermée's formula. The two elements thus correspond respectively to the initial, unconscious birth of inspiration in the lyric impulse, and the subsequent, conscious attempt to express it as art. The division of themes therefore embodies a structural balance which reflects that of the creative process itself. Grembecki also observes that *Escrava* sets out to analyze two sides of the same coin: "criador" [creator] and "criação" [creation] (36). Although this opposition is not demarcated by the two parts of the treatise, it does indicate another essential aesthetic duality that Mário explores. The present analysis aims to reveal the full extent of these thematic divisions, but especially Mário's insistence on their complementary and fundamental nature.

Within *Escrava*'s focus on *modernismo* and the international avant-garde, one could argue—returning to Mário's statement in "Prefácio" that he would found another movement in the next book—that among the six *modernista* concepts that Mário elaborates here, the principle of simultaneity approximates a predominant, movement-like idea. Structurally, the space and argument dedicated to the discussion of simultaneity outweigh that of any other single principle in the text, and the term itself frequently appears in capital letters, isolated like a slogan: "SIMULTANEIDADE." Thematically, simultaneity redefines or reincorporates *polifonismo,* which was the dominant theoretical aspect of "Prefácio" and therefore of the *desvairismo* movement.

Yet simultaneity successfully expands beyond the polyphonics theory because, more than a musical metaphor for certain poetic techniques—such as the elimination of connecting words (adjectives, prepositions) between nouns and the use of verbs in the infinitive—used to lend an idea of imagistic immediacy, it also encompasses, in its incorporation of societal and technological change, the vanguard mainstay of *cosmopolitismo*. This latter trait, moreover, nourishes the conception and growth of a universal artistic spirit akin to *unanimismo*. The euphoric "SIMULTANEIDADE" is thus the broader essence or synthesis of Mário's most important personal and creative theme: harmony, balance, and equilibrium.

The focus on simultaneity/polyphonics in this analysis of Mário's complete poetics corpus from "Prefácio" to "Postfácio" supports Coelho's conclusion on Mário's use of harmony, although her observations are based on a study of his poems rather than his poetics:

> Quando analisamos detidamente a *matéria* de seus poemas e a *técnica* estilística criada para expressá-la, torna-se claro o esfôrço da adequação realizado pelo poeta: harmonizar a *visão fragmentada e multiforme da realidade* (exigida pelo momento histórico e pela renovação estética) com a sua *inteligência ordenadora* (exigida por sua natureza). (97 [32])

Applied to his poetics, this harmonic union illustrates Mário's consolidation of what he observes as the societal "rapidez" [speed] of the time with his own intellectual "síntese" [synthesis]. A clear thinker, well-read, organized, and sincerely creative, Mário de Andrade presents a somewhat conservative but no less enthusiastic alternative to avant-garde excess in the very act of writing a formalized poetics, and especially in focusing on equilibrium, a daringly constructive concept arising from the ashes of the avant-garde's initial denial of the past.

The figure of the slave in the treatise title links "Prefácio" and *Escrava* in that she is especially symbolic, through her juxtaposition with Isaura, of the avant-garde desire for originality. In Bernardo Guimarães's novel *A Escrava Isaura,* the slave, of African origin, is the victim of her master's physical and emotional abuse. In comparison, the slave Poetry is metaphorically submitted to the restrictions of prosody symbolized by the mountain of garments, or, more violently, to the "leito de Procusto" (PC 66) of "Prefácio." She is not explicitly associated with Africa although she is a "primitive" source in that she has contact with ancient civilizations; she represents the vanguard fascination for the art of non-European aboriginal cultures. In the Brazilian context, Poetry's primitive—and therefore unspoiled—nature relates to the recovery of Native American and African traditions in the construction of a new and independent national identity, a process led by Mário, who declared himself, in "Prefácio," to be an "Anfião moreno" (PC 76). The slave's poetic rebellion thus breaks the bonds of Parnassian and other restrictive prosody to allow a new expression that is simultaneously primitive (original) and cosmopolitan (universal). The slave Poetry also symbolizes the semiotic source of language; like Dom Lirismo, she brings the unfettered unconscious into modern society.

• Equations for the Arts

After *Escrava*'s opening "Parábola," Mário literally begins the text anew at this point, marking the significance of "Parábola" as preamble; his first word "Começo" repeats the first word of "Parábola." But instead of a narrative, this time he starts off with an equation for the fine arts:

Necessidade de expressão + necessidade de comunicação + necessidade de acção + necessidade de prazer = Belas Artes. (OI 203 [33])

Mário's struggle to amplify *simultaneismo* from *polifonismo* begins with his attempts at aesthetic definitions of the fine arts and poetry. The equation, a rhetorical as much as a mathematical construct, dominates the exposition and certain other key points of *Escrava*. His subsequent explanation of this formula appears to follow the same general trajectory as Huidobro's box flow chart in "La creación pura," although differing in the specifics of process.[2] Of the four elements in Mário's equation—expression, communication, action, and pleasure—the first corresponds roughly to Huidobro's "Sistema," or the link between the objective and subjective worlds:

> O homem pelos sentidos recebe a sensação. Conforme o grau de receptividade e de sensibilidade produtiva sente sem que nisso entre a mínima parcela de inteligéncia a NECESSI- DADE DE EXPRESSAR a sensação recebida por meio do ges- to. (OI 203 [34])

Mário accentuates, moreover, that this need for expression is "inconsciente, verdadeiro acto reflexo" [unconscious, a truly reflexive act] (OI 203); again, the sensitivity/unconscious side of the balance receives the stress at this point. The remaining elements in the equation embellish what would be Huidobro's "Técnica." Communicating, acting (the "action" is critical thinking), and pleasing (both oneself and others) make up the conscious process of relaying the original expression back to the objective world. Significantly, Mário's ludic sensitivity in- corporates the final element—pleasure—as an essential part of the process.

Since the above equation applies to all the fine arts, Mário defines poetry more specifically, although the succinct quality of his definition elicits a characteristically self-conscious reflection:

> Das artes assim nascidas a que se utiliza de vozes articula- das chama-se poesia.
> (É a minha conjectura. Verão os que sabem que embora sistematizando com audácia não me afasto das conjecturas mais correntes, feitas por psicólogos e estetas, a respeito da origem das belas-artes.) (OI 204 [35])

The seemingly flippant remark barely conceals the well-read Mário's need to evoke authority. In any case, the definition ap- plies to the original and purest essence of poetry; this is to dif- ferentiate it from what could be called prosody, a more recent and restrictive development. Mário refers to "Parábola" in or- der to contrast the slave's articles of clothing—here clearly as- sociated with prosody—with the primitive nakedness of Poetry's original essence: "Os ritmos preconcebidos, as rimas, folhas de parra e velocinos alvíssimos vieram posteriormente e pouco a pouco, prejudicando a objectivação expressiva das representações, sensualizando a nudez virgem da escrava do Ararat" [The preconceived rhythms, the rhymes, fig leaves, and purest fleeces came later and little by little, impeding the ex- pressive objectification of representations, sensualizing the virgin nudity of the slave of Ararat] (OI 204). As noted in "Prefácio," Mário's frequent use of the verb *prejudicar* and related forms draws attention to the distinction between the initial, unconscious lyric impulse and the posterior effort to express it in some meaningful way; in the above citation "preconcebidos" strengthens the negative context anchored by "prejudicando."

Regarding the poetics of his contemporaries—"Adão . . . Aristóteles . . . Agora nós" [Adam . . . Aristotle . . . Now us] (OI 205)—a restructuring of Dermée's equation occupies Mário's attention. The original formula ("Lirismo + Arte = Poesia") becomes, after some explanation:

Lirismo puro + Crítica + Palavra = Poesia. (OI 205 [36])

Mário's reasons for promoting this revised formula for poetry *in addition to* the equation for fine arts that opens this first part of *Escrava* are unclear. Although he does not compare them, the two equations seem redundant because "Lirismo puro" corresponds roughly to "expressão," "Crítica" to "acção," and "Palavra" to "comunicação"; the only element missing from the second formula is "prazer" [pleasure]. Dermée's formula had also made a brief appearance in "Prefácio"; perhaps Mário mentions the formula here, as in "Prefácio," to show his familiarity with contemporary European ideas, only to revise it in order to construct and restate his own critical space. For example, he clarifies his use of "lirismo puro" in order to distinguish poetry from prose:

([. . .] Enfim: na prosa a inteligência cria sobre o lirismo puro enquanto na poesia modernista o lirismo puro é grafado com o mínimo de desenvolvimento que sobre êle possa praticar a inteligência. Esta pelo menos a tendéncia embora nem sempre seguida.) (OI 205 [37])

Even in the act of contrasting prose with *modernista* poetry as conscious- and unconscious-dominated artistic products, Mário must still concede a minimum of conscious control in poetry. Without that minimum, the poetry would not exist as such but rather as automatic writing, or as even more incomprehensible scribbles and utterances.

Mário revises Dermée's formula one last time in order to develop more precisely the relationship between its different elements:

> Dei-vos uma receita . . . Não falei na proporção dos ingredientes. Será: máximo de lirismo e máximo de crítica para adquirir o máximo de expressão. D'ai ter escrito Dermée: "O poeta é uma alma ardente, conduzida por uma cabeça fría." (OI 206 [38])

The element "Palavra" has disappeared and the equation, though not expressed this time with mathematical symbols, seems to be a simple restatement of Dermée's original:

> Máximo de lirismo + Máximo de crítica = Máximo de expressão [39]

Grembecki has established an analogical relationship between the elements of this particular equation and Huidobro's box flow chart in "La creación pura"; "máximo de lirismo," which is the element of "sensibilidade," represents Huidobro's "Sistema," while "máximo de crítica," or "inteligencia," represents Huidobro's "Técnica" (69-70).[3] In this final revision of the formula, Mário's immediate linkage of his series of maxima to Dermée's dichotomy of warmth and cold, passion and reason, proves the strength of Mário's vision of balance. In the quantitative context of maxima, the amount of lyricism must equal the amount of critical thinking in order to achieve the same amount of creative expression; therefore, ideally, lyricism (sensual, unconscious) balances critical thinking (intellectual, conscious) just like the union of opposite temperatures represented by Dermée's figure of the poet.

The main idea of the rest of the first part of *Escrava* is the concept of poetic theme. Mário refers again to "Parábola" to analogize the artificial limits set on theme:

> Ora: observando a evolução da poesia através das idades que se vê? O aumento contínuo do Guarisancar de tules, nanzuques, rendas, meias de seda, etc. da parábola inicial. Foi a inteligência romantizada pela preocupação de beleza, que nos levou às duas métricas existentes e a outros crochets,

filets e frivolités. Pior ainda: a inteligéncia, pesando coisas
e factos da natureza e da vida, escolheu uns tantos que
ficaram sendo os *assuntos poéticos*. (OI 208 [40])

The designation of a preconceived group of themes clearly continues in the vein of Mário's enemy, prejudice ("O assunto
poético é a conclusão mais anti-psicológica que existe" [The
poetic subject is the most anti-psychological conclusion there
is] [OI 208]). In contrast, Mário insists that the lyric impulse
can be born from whatever circumstance: "a inspiração surge
provocada por um crepúsculo como por uma chaminé mata-
razziana, pelo corpo divino de uma Nize, como pelo divino
corpo de uma Cadillac. Todos os assuntos são *vitais*. Não ha
temas poéticos" [inspiration surges provoked by a sunset as
well as a smokestack, by the divine body of a Nize as well as
the divine body of a Cadillac. All subjects are *vital*. There are
no poetic themes.] (OI 208).
    The revolutionary claim that there are no themes means, ef-
fectively, that everything is an appropriate theme. Mário continues to debunk poetic myth about theme by illustrating the
often spontaneous and furtive nature of inspiration. After referring briefly to Ribot's analogy of telegrams from the unconscious (already mentioned in "Prefácio"), Mário explains:

A inteligéncia do poeta—o qual não mora mais numa tôrre
de marfim—recebe o telegrama no bonde, quando o pobre
vai para a repartição, para a Faculdade de Filosofia, para o
cinema. Assim virgem, sintetico, energico, o telegrama dá-
lhe fortes comoções, exaltações divinatorias, sublimações,
poesia. (OI 209 [41])

The city and the streetcar, in contrast to the ivory tower, are
Mário's real inspiration. The tumult of urban life suggests the
rapidity of successive images; Mário hails the "palavra sôlta"
[free word] and the free association of images. Although he
does not reprise the idea of harmonic verse here, he nonetheless gives examples of this "associação de imagens" that recall
his discussion of that theory in "Prefácio." He compares the
sword of Horace to a radio antenna, and telephone wires con-
stricting the city to Othello's fingers on Desdemona's neck.
Unable to resist another equation, Mário concludes:

> Os Horácios + Otelo + Antena radiográfica + Fíos eléctricos
> = 4 assuntos. Resultado: riqueza, fartura, pletora. (OI 209
> [42])

The abundance of themes and images affects not just the poet, but also the reader, whom Mário emphasizes must interpret the telegram that the poet has merely relayed.

The new abundance of poetic themes does not eliminate the pre-existing, select thematic group. The analogy Mário uses to express this coexistence conveys a typically avant-garde idea of constructing anew: "Destruir um edifício não significa abandonar o terreno" [Destroying a building doesn't mean abandoning the terrain] (OI 210). The fertile grounds of religion, love, patriotism, war, and peace provide dozens of examples for Mário to enumerate over the next several pages; in fact, the rest of the first part of *Escrava* is mostly given over to these examples, although Mário continues to provide intervening commentary.

The image of a brand-new building on the same old lot allows Mário to develop a dialectic of thematic continuity and change. In the case of love, for example, the author says: "O amor existe. Mas anda de automóvel. [. . .] Novas sensações. Novas imagens. A culpa é da vida sempre nova em sua monotonia" [Love exists. But it gets around by car. New sensations. New images. The fault is life's—always new in its monotony] (OI 211). The corresponding examples, including Luis Aranha's metaphor of amorous desire as the circuit flow between positive and negative poles in "POEMA ELÉCTRICO," effectively display the venerated theme in a modern context. Continuing with examples showing the themes of women and patriotism, the author stresses the prominence of metaphors in *modernista* poetry as a characteristic that unites the cosmopolitan vanguard writers of the Americas and Europe. Moreover, the vanguard writer connects with transatlantic colleagues by living vicariously and universally:

> Luis Aranha bebeu o universo. Matou tzares na Rússia, amou no Japão, gosou em Paris, robou nos Estados Unidos, por simultaneidade, sem sair de S. Paulo, só porquê no tempo em que ginasiava às voltas com a geografia, adoeceu gravemente e delirou. Surgiu o admiravel "Poema Giratorio." (OI 216 [43])

Videla de Rivero defines the essential avant-garde trait of *cosmopolitismo* as "el deseo de ser 'ciudadano del mundo'" complemented by "la voluntad planetarista por medio de técnicas literarias simultaneístas" (41-42); Mário's comments fulfill this definition in the fraternal union of the above-mentioned "simultaneidade" and in the ideals of *unanimismo*.[4]

Such a universal scope of experience goes hand in hand with the main point about absolute freedom of poetic subject, which Mário recapitulates: "E tudo, tudo o que pertence à natureza e à vida nos interessa. D'ai uma abundância, uma fartura contra as quais não há leis fánias. D'ai também uma Califórnia de imagens novas, tiradas das coisas modernas ou pelo menos quotidianas" [And everything, everything that pertains to nature and life interests us. Thence an abundance, a fullness against which there are no laws. Thence also a California of new images, derived from modern or at least everyday things] (OI 217–18). Thematic freedom yields imagistic freedom, described with another reference to New World myth in the abundance of "Califórnia."[5] Examples of such images follow, punctuated by Mário's hyperbole: "É impossivel resistir a êste repuxo de imagens" [It's impossible to resist this fountain of images] (OI 218) and "O tesoiro é alibabesco" [The treasure is Alibabesque] (OI 220).

Though Mário embraces this overwhelming cornucopia of theme and image, he does not condone any corresponding lack of emphasis on style. Rather, predecessors like Mallarmé and Verlaine ("deliciosos poetas do não-vai-nem-vem não preocupam mais a sinceridade do poeta modernista" [delicious poets of the neither-coming-nor-going no longer concern the *modernista* poet's sincerity] [OI 220]) and contemporaries such as Vladimir Mayakovsky ("exagerou" [he exaggerated] [OI 223]) receive the author's reprimand for errors of eloquence:

—Abaixo a retórica!
—Com muito prazer. Mas que se conserve a eloquéncia
filha legítima da vida. (OI 220 [44])

As usual, the author's frequently conservative tone stands out in his promotion of a new aesthetics. Eloquence, such as "a eloquéncia vária das falas da alma que mais psicologicamente se chamariam movimentos do sub-eu" [the varying eloquence of the voices of the soul, which more psychologically would be called movements of the subego] (OI 221), must remain extant. In the end, though, he reconciles; even Mayakovsky can be accommodated: "É preciso justificar todos os poetas contemporaneos, poetas sinceros que, sem mentiras nem métricas, refletem a eloquéncia vertiginosa da nossa vida" [It is necessary to justify all the contemporary poets, sincere poets who, without lies nor meters, reflect the vertiginous eloquence of our life] (OI 223).

The combination of new themes alongside old ones, and the ability of any of them to cause inspiration, constitute the main points of Mário's conclusion to this section. Poetry, even in its *modernista* conception, remains "a mesma de Adão e de Aristóteles e existiu em todos os tempos" [the same as for Adam, for Aristotle, and that existed during all times] (OI 224). The *modernista* conception only modifies Poetry by reestablishing a duality of old and new:

> [. . .] dois resultados—um novo, originado dos progressos
> da psicologia experimental; outro antigo, originado da
> inevitavel realidade:
>   1.°: respeito à liberdade do subconsciente.
> Como consequéncia: destruição do assunto poético.
>   2.°: o poeta reintegrado na vida do seu tempo.
> Por isso: renovação da sacra fúria. (OI 224 [45])

Mário's revolutionary rhetoric remains as it was defined in the introduction: the restoration of balance. His first conclusion above does not negate the importance of the conscious, but rather exalts the role of the unconscious in expanding thematic horizons. Such an expansion, appearing in the same discussion as Adam and Dante, implies a return to thematic freedom as it was known before the unnatural restrictions placed on it by Mário's immediate predecessors; hence the words "reintegrado" and "renovação" in the second conclusion.

In sum, the first part of *Escrava* reinforces Mário's sense of continuity, which challenges, once again, the typically vanguard break with the past. His opening equations, although avant-garde in style and character, define the fine arts and poetry as atemporal absolutes not necessarily related to the *modernista* period. Similarly—just as in "Parábola" Rimbaud recovers the original, pure essence of poetry—Mário, like Rimbaud, seeks to restore an ostensibly old and forgotten idea: the poet's subjective and unrestricted (or minimally restricted) interaction with the immediacy of life. The vanguard revolution, simply, promotes true poetry as it has always been. Prosody is not even completely revoked, since there still exist certain creative guidelines (rapid verse, abolished adjectives, etc.). Yet the revolution does not pretend to return to some mythical golden age of poetry; rather the poet must be "reintegrado" into his or her time, with the full force of shock embodied by nude Poetry exposed to the modern world. The "radical" nature of the vanguard exposes its root—the initial lawlessness of language confronts the increasingly restricted society (and prosody) of the industrialized age.

• Weighing Words

The second part of *Escrava,* longer than the first and with abundant endnotes, tackles issues related to the poet's conscious self. Most importantly for the context of the present analysis, the second part begins with Mário's direct commentary on Huidobro's ideas. The opening paragraph, which refers back to the first part's dual conclusion, reveals, as Grembecki has shown, Mário's textual source for Huidobro's ideas: "É por ela [a liberdade do subconsciente] que o homem atingirá na futura perfeição, de que somos apenas e modestamente os primitivos, o ideal inegavelmente grandioso da 'criação pura' de que fala Uidobro [*sic*]" [It is through the freedom of the unconscious that man will arrive at a future perfection, of which we are only and modestly the primitives, the undeniably great ideal of the 'pure creation' that Huidobro talks about] (OI 225). By the time he wrote this, Mário had read (at least) Huidobro's "La création pure: essai d'esthétique" in the April 1921 edition of *L'Esprit Nouveau.* Grembecki emphasizes Huidobro's (and Dermée's) general influence in *Escrava:* "Da análise das idéias acessórias na Escr. ressaltamos ainda uma vez o quanto seu desenvolvimento se deveu ao esquema do mecanismo da criação proposto por Huidobro e às fontes subconscientes apontadas por Dermée" [In the analysis of supporting ideas in *Escrava* we stress once again how much their development derived from the scheme of the creation mechanism proposed by Huidobro and from the unconscious sources highlighted by Dermée] (68). Mário directly refers to Huidobro only one other time in *Escrava;* however, the indirect importance of Huidobro's ideas commands critical attention and will be explored in greater detail in this chapter.

Modern poetry's dedication to the unconscious is here rephrased as the "objectivação mais aproximada possivel da consciéncia subliminal" [closest possible approximation to the subliminal consciousness] (OI 225). Yet Mário dramatically announces the concern of the text's second part by contrasting it with the above statement:

> Mas isso ainda não é arte.
> Falta o máximo de crítica de que falei e que [o compositor Georges] Migot chama de "vontade de análise." (OI 225 [46])

The "máximo de crítica," from his earlier equation, involves two proposed sets of "princípios estéticos e técnicos," which form the subjects of address in this second part. The three technical principles are: "Verso livre, Rima livre, Vitoria do dicionario" [Free verse, Free rhyme, Victory of the dictionary]; the three aesthetic principles are: "Sustituição da Ordem Intelectual pela Ordem Subconsciente, Rapidez e Síntese, Polifonismo [Simultaneidade]" [Substitution of the Intellectual Order for the Unconscious Order, Speed and Synthesis, Polyphonics (Simultaneity)] (OI 226). These six principles, beginning with the technical ones, delineate the rest of the treatise.[6] Mário concedes the first two principles as known factors (givens); nonetheless, he offers six slightly different definitions of *verse* before claiming that he is wasting time on "conquistas já definitivas" [already definitive conquests] (OI 234). As in the earlier reworkings of the equations, these variations articulate the text as a work in progress. Defining something means, after all, equating it to some described essence; definitions are another rhetorical device akin to equations. It is precisely in his description of the "Vitoria do dicionario" that Mário develops the cognitive and linguistic aspects of the act of definition in a way that again foregrounds the act of balancing.

Mário uses Dermée's pairing of the verbs *to think* and *to weigh* (*pensar* and *pesar* in Portuguese) as a starting point for his explanation of simple and complex sensations. The *modernista* poets favor elliptical phrases, verbs used as nouns, nouns used as adjectives, etc., to allow a newfound linguistic freedom for the poet's expression of the complex phenomena of everyday life. The poet's conscious interpretation and verbal expression of these phenomena give rise to the author's analogy of balance:

> A inteligência forma ideas sobre a sensação. E ao exterioriza-las em palavras age como quem compara e pesa. A inteligência pesa a sensação não por quilos mas por palavras. Mesmo para o acto de pensar posso empregar metaforicamente o verbo pesar (Dermée) pois que a inteligência ligando predicado e sujeito para reconhecer a equipolência dêstes pesa-lhes os respectivos valores. (OI 235 [47])[7]

The discussion of these sensations crystallizes around a lexicon of equilibrium, with terms such as *pêso* [weight], *equipolência, conchas da balança* [scales of a balance], and *fiel* [pointer of a balance] that recall the *concha da balança* from the metanarrative commentary on the "Parábola" in endnote A. The mundane example Mário gives, in which a store clerk measures a loaf of bread on one side of a scale against a one-kilo weight on the other side, will lead to a more abstract example by analogy and constitute the author's strongest use of the balance or scale as a symbol of aesthetic equilibrium:

> Nossos olhos veem um cachorro.
> Sensação.
> A inteligência pesa a sensação e conclúi que ela corresponde exactamente ao universal cachorro, pertencente a essa vultuosa colecção de pesos que é o dicionário.
> O fiel que temos na razão verticalizou-se.
> O pêso está certo. (OI 235 [48])

The dictionary, more than a book, stands for the compendium of one's experience or one's a priori knowledge; the necessary condition of words as elements of poetic expression justifies the symbol.

The simple sensation described above contrasts with the complex sensation, which dominates Mário's attention. Just as the sales clerk sometimes needs to collect pieces from several small loaves in order to round out to one kilo, the poet also needs to add verbs, adjectives, etc., to the "universal" in order to represent a complex sensation; i.e., not just "dog" but "the black dog was running." The author immediately provides a better example of a complex sensation in the first line of Sergio Milliet's poem "JAZZ-BAND": "'Rires Parfums Decolletés'" [Laughter Perfume Decolletage] (OI 237). Mário points out that these three words involve as many senses (auditory, olfactory, and visual) and successfully suggest, together, the non-Parnassian ambiance of a jazz hall. Three words cannot represent all of the complex sensation, but the poet "não fotografa: cria. Ainda mais: não reproduz: exagera, deforma, porém sintetizando" [does not photograph: he creates. Moreover, he does not reproduce: he exaggerates, deforms, although synthesizing] (OI 237). Mário then reproduces the complete poem "JAZZ-BAND," noting a deliberate dearth of verbs as much as of grammatically complete phrases, and praising the poem's extraordinary style created exclusively by the equilibrium of "pesando sensações com palavras do dicionario" [weighing sensations with words from the dictionary] (OI 239). Thus the "vitória do dicionário," affiliated with Cocteau's "adoração ao léxico" [adoration of the lexicon] and Marinetti's "palavra em liberdade" [word in freedom] (although the latter compares unfavorably, according to Mário, because Marinetti confuses a means with an end), effectively frees words from grammar and syntax and consequently amplifies their evocative power.

Mário's summation of this process discloses the implicit presence of Huidobro, through the latter's box flow chart in "La creación pura":

> O poeta parte de um todo de que teve a sensação, dissocia-o pela análise e escolhe os elementos com que erigirá um outro todo, não direi mais homogéneo, não direi mais perfeito que o da natureza mas
>
> DUMA OUTRA PERFEIÇÃO,
> DUMA OUTRA HOMOGENEIDADE.
> A natureza existe fatalmente, *sem vontade própria*. O poeta cria por inteligência, *por vontade própria*. (OI 237; original emphasis [49])

The activity described in the first paragraph above mimics Huidobro's creative process in which the work of art is returned, as a distinct entity, to the objective world; it is interesting to note that Mário does not dwell as much on what would be the poet's "Mundo subjetivo" as described by Huidobro. The ending sentences in capital letters and in italics coincide with the message of Huidobro's "Non serviam"; it is uncertain whether Mário ever read that text, but in any case the same ideas also figure prominently in "La creación pura."[8]

In a pair of endnotes, the author explores this semantic freedom by affirming an affinity with *primitivismo*. Several influential and relevant cultural factors informed Mário's opinions at the time: (1) the appraisal and absorption of African, Polynesian, and Native American indigenous arts by contemporary vanguard plastic artists and musicians; (2) the rise of modern anthropology as a unified discipline; and most importantly, (3) the general interest of the *modernista* generation in a revalorization of native Brazilian cultural traditions, which later led to the creation of movements (*antropofagia, verdeamarelismo,* and others) advocating the scrupulous selection of European and other foreign ideas to be incorporated into a renewed national identity.[9] Mário's stance subscribes to the general, literal sense of primitivism in that it echoes the Adam paradigm of absolute creative power without associative context. Thus, in endnote E, Mário supports Ribot's observation that in primitive language "os termos não são geralmente ligados mas juxtapostos" [the terms are not generally linked but rather juxtaposed] (OI 282). Endnote E generates further discussion in its own extension, endnote P:

> Somos na realidade uns primitivos. E como todos os primitivos realistas e estilizadores. A realização sincera da matéria afectiva e do subconsciente é nosso realismo. Pela imaginação deformadora e sintética somos estilizadores. O problema é juntar num todo equilibrado essas tendências contraditórias. (OI 294 [50])

The primitivist reference intensifies Mário's endorsement of an inescapable creative equilibrium. The comparison to primitive language further brings to mind the telegraphic nature of avant-garde poetry in general and the consequent ambiguities in the reader's interpretation.

161

• Warnings against Excess

The reader's imaginative role, as the translator of Ribot's telegraph, necessarily becomes more important, hence Mário's rejection of an ignorant and lazy public. At the same time, however, Mário develops, in the main text, a series of three warnings regarding the opposite extreme's danger of intellectual hermeticism, inherent in the "vitoria do dicionario." Each warning cautions against excess; each maintains the theme of balance by steering a course of moderation. The first warning, although condoning the use of analogy (or analogic metaphor, which remains a tool of the trade in order to avoid clichéd similes), condemns periphrasis (circumlocution) as analogy's extreme form ("a irmã bastarda"). According to the author:

> A diferença está em que a analogia é subconsciente e a perífrase uma intelectualização exagerada, forçada, pretenciosa.
> É preciso não voltar a Rambouillet!
> É preciso não repetir Góngora [!]
> É PRECISO EVITAR MALLARMÉ! (OI 240 [51])

The capitalized urgency against the famous Symbolist is surprising, given the recognized importance of his generation as precursors of the *modernista* worldview; however, Mário's message reinforces his own main ideas by pointing out the path to moderation once again. The poet should challenge the active reader, but Mallarmé's extreme type of periphrasis is overly "pedante" [pedantic];[10] to illustrate, Mário points out a defective periphrastic instance from "JAZZ-BAND" and contrasts it with the subtler "Analogias finíssimas" of Guilherme de Almeida's "BAILADO RUSSO" (OI 241). Precisely this latter kind of analogy, in which "o poeta substitui a *causa* da sensação pelo efeito subconsciente" [the poet substitutes the cause of the sensation for the unconscious effect] (OI 241), represents the change from the intellectual to the unconscious "order," the first of Mário's three aesthetic principles of *modernista* poetry.

Such a polar shift from one order to another does not seem to follow the pattern of equilibrium as stated, but Mário makes it fit, in the act of proffering his second warning, by condemning the extreme use of the unconscious order, which again encompasses hermeticism: automatic writing. To counteract this, the conscious, or will, must act as editor to move from initial lyricism to true poetry:

> *O poeta não fotografa o subconsciente.*
> A inspiração é que é subconsciente, não a criação. Não pode haver esfôrço de vontade sem atenção. (OI 242-43 [52])

Furthermore, with "vontade" and "atenção," the lyric unconscious can be reined in enough to maintain a unity of theme. The substitution of orders therefore shifts the weight of composition from the overly intellectual exercises of, for example, Góngora's *culteranismo,* to the moderation of the lyric impulse by conscious will, a judgment process that "é na realidade em psicologia 'associação de imagens'" [is really in psychology "image association"] (OI 243).[11] Even so, Mário reminds the reader, reprising the terminology of his opening equations: "O poeta usa mesmo o máximo de trabalho intelectual pois que atinge a abstração para notar os universais" [The poet uses the very maximum of intellectual work since he attains abstraction in order to observe universals] (OI 243); "máximo de trabalho" rephrases the "máximo de crítica" of the equation, with the word "mesmo" above emphasizing the quantity "máximo," which is the same quantity as that of lyricism. The formula yields the two hypothetical quantities—of unconscious lyric impulse and of conscious critical interpretation—in equilibrium.

Even though the role of reason or rational thought therefore remains an essential element in poetic creation, Mário must still negate, like Huidobro in "La poesía de los locos," the idea that the *modernista* poets embrace lunacy. "NÃO SOMOS LOUCOS" (OI 245), he retorts, insisting simply that an intellectual framework has been reduced or replaced by unconscious patterns. The wrong kind of reader clings to the past:

> Mas o éforo parnasiano nos lê e zanga-se por não encontrar em nossos poemas a lógica intelectual, o desenvolvimento, a seriação dos planos e mais outros Idola Theatri.
> Mas se procura no poema o que nêste não existe! (OI 246 [53])

Likewise, the author denies accusations that his generation's goals relate only to destruction; he focuses instead on innovation, couched in legitimizing pseudoscientific language: "A ultramicroscopia da liberdade aparentemente desordenada do subconsciente permitiu-nos apresentar ao universo espaventado o plasma vivo das nossas sensações e das nossas imagens" [The ultramicroscope of the apparently disordered freedom of the unconscious permitted us to present to the astonished universe the living plasma of our sensations and our images] (OI 246). Finally, the author implies that any ostensible lack of reason would better describe his accusers:

> Mas pedem-nos em grita farisaica uma estética total de 400 páginas in quarto . . .
> Isso é que é asnidade.
> Onde nunca jamais se viu uma estética preceder as obras de arte que ela justificará? (OI 246 [54])

This metatextual moment defends Mário's approximately 100-page *Escrava* by implying that it is inevitably inconclusive, since it analyzes contemporary ideas. Furthermore, the final question above condenses, indirectly, the important issue of Mário's justification of his changing ideas over the three-year period between the writing of "Prefácio" and "Postfácio."

The author presents one last warning against excess, regarding the "associação de imagens," before proceeding to the next aesthetic principle. Marinetti's confusion, "o meio pelo fim" [the means for the end], describes the temptation of allowing free association, which should be serendipitous by nature, to digress into mere word games.

> Inegavel: a associação de imagens é de efeito efusiante, magnífico e principalmente natural, psicológica mas . . .
> olhai a cobra entre as flores:
> O poeta torna-se tão habil no manejo dela que substitúi a sensibilidade, o lirismo produzido pelas sensações por um simples, divertidíssimo jôgo de imagens nascido duma inspiração única inicial. É a lei do menor esfôrço, é scismar constante que podem conduzir à ruína. (OI 247 [55])

Curiously, Mário advises that this wordplay, upon becoming deliberately conscious, is a "virtuosidade" (OI 247); yet the virtuosity in this case is detrimental. In fact, in an extended discussion of this point in endnote I, the author affirms that one of the traditional norms of prosody, rhyme itself, exemplifies this kind of overly cerebral word association, "da pior especie pois provocada e consciente, estimulante de inspiração falsa como o café, a morfina, o opio" [of the worst kind since it's provoked and conscious, stimulant of false inspiration like coffee, morphine, opium] (OI 287). The author's three warnings have thus censured pedantic hermeticism, automatic writing, and exclusive word games as the consequences of excess, leading to the undesirable "desequilíbrio."[12]

• Simultaneity Defined

Mário's treatment of his second principle, rapidity and synthesis, leads to his hallucination sequence in endnote Q, discussed in the previous chapter. The author continues in the main text with his last and most important aesthetic principle: simultaneity. Referring back to "Prefácio," Mário again records the effect of the passage of time on his aesthetic views; he elucidates that what he called *polifonismo* in the earlier text is the same as what he has since learned about—the "simultaneism" of theorists like Epstein and Fernand Divoire. His choice of a musical term derived from his expertise as a musicologist, which he brings out over the next few pages in a brief history of music as an art form. Mário's pan-artistic approach allows him to argue, for example, that in music as in all art, the best creative approach involves his well-known prescription of balanced thought processes. The description of his two musical heroes, Bach and Mozart, illustrates: "São êstes homens os 2 tipos mais perfeitos de criação subconsciente e da vontade de análise que cria euritmias artísticas de que a natureza é incapaz" [These men are the 2 most perfect examples of unconscious creation and of the will to analysis that creates artistic eurythmics of which nature is incapable] (OI 257). (Beethoven, in contrast, begins a decadent period of mimetic and anecdotal composition.) Bach's and Mozart's masterpieces prophesy a definition of art that Mário gleans from *L'Esprit Nouveau:* "A OBRA DE ARTE É UMA MAQUINA DE PRODUZIR COMOÇÕES" [THE WORK OF ART IS A COMMOTION-PRODUCING MACHINE] (OI 258). In a footnote, the author states that this definition represents the general ideas of the Parisian magazine's contributors; Huidobro's box flow chart as mechanism of artistic creation and the accompanying discussion of the mechanics of art in "La creación pura" present a probable specific influence in this case. In the footnote Mário also clarifies the use of "comoções" to imply artistic emotions, and mentions, to support the idea of mechanics, Poe's confession that he composed "The Raven" "com a precisão e a rigidez dum problema de matemáticas" [with the precision and rigor of a math problem] (OI 258).[13]

Mário reveals an earlier source for this idea of mechanical aesthetics in François de Malherbe, a sixteenth-century French theorist who focused on the themes of harmony and craftsmanship in poetic composition. The allusion to Malherbe sets up another pan-artistic comparison: "O Malherbe da história moderna das artes é a *cinematografia*" [The Malherbe of modern art history is *cinematography*] (OI 258). In a series of anaphoric paragraphs, Mário details the changes in perception wrought on the other arts by their newest, youngest sister—the cinema, "o *Eureka!* das artes puras" (OI 258); for example: "Só então é que se percebeu que a pintura podia e devia ser unicamente pintura, equilíbrio de cores, linhas, volumes numa superfície" [It was only then that it was perceived that painting could and should be only that: equilibrium of colors, lines, and volumes on a surface] (OI 258). The cinematic effect on music, in contrast, does not shed new light but rather restores the precedence of Bach and Mozart: "E finalmente só então é que se observou que a música já realizara, 2 séculos atrás, êsse ideal de arte pura—máquina de comover por meio da beleza artística" [And finally it was only then that it was observed that music had already achieved, 2 centuries before, that ideal of pure art—a machine that moves us to emotion by means of artistic beauty] (OI 259). The effect of this, Mário explains, is that *modernista* poetry displays an often detrimental, but sometimes enriching, relationship with music. While the author candidly admits that the musicality of his own *Paulicéia* detracted from its message, he contrasts his work with two exemplary instrumental solos of several pages—the flute-like poem "LA FONTANA MALATA" by Aldo Palazzeschi and the viola-like "BERCEUSE" by Cocteau—and his own translation, "DELFIM NA AGUA AZUL," of a poem by Amy Lowell as an example of sonority and rhythm.

Nevertheless, the desired rhetorical effect of all this comparison of poetry, music, and cinema seems only to be the justification of Mário's term *polifonismo*. To further explicate this aesthetic principle in its guise as "simultaneidade," Mário divides its connotations into two branches: "a vida actual" [contemporary life] and "a observação do nosso ser interior" [observation of our inner being] (OI 265). The former encompasses the influences of modern social and technological circumstances:

> A vida de hoje torna-nos vivedores simultâneos de todas as terras do universo.
> A facilidade de locomoção faz com que possamos palmilhar asfaltos de Tóquio, Nova York, Paris e Roma no mesmo Abril.
> Pelo jornal somos omnipresentes.
> As linguas baralham-se.
> Confundem-se os povos. (OI 265-66 [56])

This kind of simultaneity, recalling the author's earlier example of a poem by Luis Aranha, leads to a reference to Mário's family's genealogy, in a natural, not forced, way:

> O homem contemporâneo é um ser multiplicado.
> . . . tres raças se caldeiam na minha carne . . .
> Tres? (OI 266 [57])

These are of course the "three sad races" from Bilac's well-known sonnet—Native American, European, and African—that Haberly studies as factors of authorial identity in his book of the same name; Mário's multi-ethnic background anchors Haberly's analysis of the harlequin figure in *Paulicéia*. In the text immediately following, Mário corroborates that he, like Aranha, lives vicariously (simultaneously):

> Fui educado num colégio francês. Palpito de entusiasmo, de amor ante a renovação da arte musical italiana. Admito e estudo Uidobro [*sic*] e Unamuno. Os Estados-Unidos me entusiasmam como se fossem pátria minha. Com a aventura de Gago Coutinho fui português. Fui russo durante o Congresso de Genova. Alemão no Congresso de Versalhes. Mas não votei em ninguem nas ultimas eleições brasileiras. (OI 266 [58])

This affirmation of the sociological vector of "simultaneidade" transparently defines the avant-garde characteristic of *cosmopolitismo;* the two traits are one and the same. Mário's second mention of Huidobro, besides aggravating a persistent misspelling, perhaps also confuses his nationality; by pairing Huidobro with Miguel de Unamuno in the paragraph's context of one nation per sentence, Mário seems to render the europhilic Chilean a Spaniard—an error more probable than believing Unamuno to be Chilean. Nevertheless, the reference reconfirms Huidobro as an important source and, not least, as a fellow "simultaneous" or cosmopolitan personality (in which case his supposed nationality is irrelevant). Mário ends the section by affirming that in spite of his international interests it is possible for him to remain an authentic Brazilian, and by pointing to precedents for simultaneity in Walt Whitman's *Song of Myself* and in the book of Job.

As opposed to this sociological aspect of "simultaneidade," the psychological vector dominates the rest of the text proper as much as endnote N, which explores and develops from "Prefácio" the idea of immediate equilibrium (in the spatial arts) vs. the mediated equilibrium of the temporal arts: "Nela [a obra de arte do tempo] pode dar-se simultaneidade pois a propria compreensão duma obra de arte do tempo é uma simultaneidade de actos de memória" [In it the work of temporal art can have simultaneity since the very comprehension of a work of temporal art is a simultaneity of memory acts] (OI 290). Mário uses examples from the nineteenth-century Portuguese poet Antero de Quental and from the medieval Iberian parallelistic *cantigas de amigo* (expanding the temporal scope of his poetics beyond *modernismo*) to show that a mediated equilibrium should exist between the poets' *eu* (like Huidobro's "Mundo subjetivo") and the "mundo exterior" (the "Mundo objetivo"). This division of realms, or "scisma," represents a very common psychological state of being in which various emotions and sensations coexist:

Não ha passeio, não ha atrevessar ruas em que ela [a scisma] não seja mais ou menos nosso estado psicológico. Realiza-la na polifonia politonal aparentemente disparatada das sensações recebidas é construir o poema simultâneo. Haverá nisso impressionismo? Não, porquê não abandonaremos

posteriormente a crítica e a procura de equilíbrio, inevitaveis
dignificadoras da obra de arte. (OI 292 [59])

Once again Mário privileges the street as site of immersion in
collective sensation, here the musical birthplace of the simultaneous poem. The equilibrium of simultaneity must be
guarded, however, since it does not necessarily arise naturally
or spontaneously from simultaneous perceptions.

Such perceptions are the same as Mário's "sensações
complexas" from the bread-on-the-balance analogy, which he
exemplifies again in the main text:

Olhar aberto de repente ante uma paisagem, não percebe

primeiro uma árvore,
depois outra árvore,
depois outra árvore,
depois um cavalo
depois um homem,
depois uma nuvem,
depois um regato, etc.,

mas percebe simultaneamente tudo isso. (OI 267 [60])

As demonstrated by the graphic limitations of lines of typed
phrases on a page, poetry as a temporal art cannot overcome
space through immediate equilibrium, but rather must intend
to create an "EFEITO [EFFECT] TOTAL FINAL" (OI 268) of simultaneity. The author clarifies: "À audição ou à leitura de um poema
simultâneo o efeito de simultaneidade não se realiza em cada
sensação insulada mas na SENSAÇÃO COMPLEXA TOTAL FINAL"
[While hearing or reading a simultaneous poem the effect of
simultaneity is not achieved in each isolated sensation but
rather in the FINAL TOTAL COMPLEX SENSATION] (OI 269). Though
Mário does not make it explicit, he has moved from the simultaneity of the creative process in endnote N to the simultaneity
of the receptive process in these pages of the main text.

The poet participates in both of these processes; after all, he
or she is first a receptor and then a creator. The incorporation
of both processes or viewpoints allows Mário to offer more examples for examination, including some brief verses by Ronald
de Carvalho; the verses describe a haiku-like natural moment
of raindrops and a passing swallow, and provoke Mário's

reader-response type question: "Mas donde vem êsse estado de alma em que ficamos ao terminar o poema?" [But from where does that state of the soul come, in which we remain upon completing the poem?] (OI 270). The key to the reception lies in the poet's own creative process:

> É que o poeta, escolhendo discrecionariamente (crítica, vontade de análise para conseguir euritmia e Arte) discrecionariamente alguns valores pobres não se preocupou com a relativa pobreza dêles mas sim com a riqueza da sensação complexa total final. (OI 270 [61])

The author likewise discusses this process of equilibrium in a three-column poetic fragment by Nicolau Beauduin (very similar to Paz's attempt at spatial distribution in "Blanco" and not that different from the effect of Huidobro's "Aviso a los turistas"), a few verses by Soupault, and more examples from Aranha, "já um filho da simultaneidade contemporânea" [already a son of contemporary simultaneity] (OI 273).

The propagandistic closing paragraphs of *Escrava* reaffirm Mário's revolutionary rhetoric. The dominant aesthetic principle, simultaneity, "será uma das maiores sinão a maior conquista da poesia modernizante" [will be one of the biggest if not the greatest conquest of modernizing poetry] (OI 273). Mário and his fellow poets, in international union, will march on "em busca duma forma que objective esta multiplicidade interior e exterior cada vez mais acentuada pelo progresso material e na sua representação máxima em nossos dias" [in search of a form that objectifies this interior and exterior multiplicity, more and more marked by material progress and in its maximum representation in our times] (OI 273). They are the "escoteiros da nova Poesia" [scouts of the new Poetry]: "Não mais irritados! Não mais destruidores! Não mais derribadores de ídolos!" [No longer irritated! No longer destroyers! No longer demolishers of idols!] (OI 274). The poets will thus enact what is stated in the last paragraph of "Parábola": "Essa mulher escandalosamente nua é que os poetas modernistas se puseram a adorar" [It is that scandalously nude woman that the *modernista* poets dedicated themselves to adoring] (OI 202).

Further linking the conclusion of his treatise with its parable beginning, Mário proclaims grandiosely:

E é revestidos com o aço da indiferença,

> os linhos da serenidade,
> as pelúcias do amor,
> os setins barulhentos do entusiasmo, que

partimos para o oriente, rumo do Ararat. (OI 274 [62])

The incorporation of the thematic elements of "Parábola" at this moment provides a satisfactory closure; however, the list of garments differs significantly from that of "Parábola" because of its enumerated symbolism. The *modernista* poets are not just more pilgrims to Ararat. The specifically symbolic qualities of their garments (of indifference, serenity, love, and enthusiasm) set them apart enough to imply the poets' special ceremonial consecration to their pilgrimage. Rimbaud's act reversed and negated the conscious accumulation of poetic restrictions; in contrast, Mário and his generation, recognizing the need for an active but reduced conscious presence, must pack at least a few garments for Poetry in their endeavor to find a happy medium between a mountainous excess of clothing and inflexible, total nudity. Significantly, the poet-pilgrims first wear these garments themselves and will then transfer them, along with their symbolic qualities, to Poetry in the act of renewing the interplay of conscious and unconscious thought processes that restores poetic harmony.

In this symbolic new beginning, there can be no doubt about the poetic quest's clean break with the past. Even though Mário has said that the poets are no longer "destruidores," someone or something has caused the fire that the other, traditional poets are left trying to extinguish: "Insistem ainda em apagar o incêndio cujas garras nervosas, movediças pulverizam fragorosamente as derradeiras torres de marfim" [They still insist on putting out the fire whose nervous and unstable claws clamorously pulverize the remaining ivory towers] (OI 275). The ivory tower as poetic realm (and as symbol of the traditional structures and norms of restrictive prosody) is abandoned to its fate in favor of the city street, the streetcar, the adventure of life that the quest to Ararat symbolizes. The text ends with this one-sentence paragraph: "Ao rebate dos sinos que imploram a conservação das arquitecturas ruidas respondemos com o 'Larga!' aventureiro da vida que não para" [To the ringing of the bells that implore the conservation of the ruined architecture, we respond with the adventurous 'Let's go!' of the life that doesn't stop] (OI 275). The bells, although sounding the alarm, also toll the death knell for traditional prosody.

The second part of *Escrava* has summarized Mário's main ideas. His attempt to separate his principles into technical and aesthetic categories facilitates his argument but cannot pretend to be a complete division; each category deals inevitably with elements from the other. The plethora of endnotes typifies Mário's self-conscious meta-commentary, effectively linking "Parábola" (with its continuation in endnote A) to the detailed discussions of this second part that carry over into endnotes B through Q. Most importantly, "Parábola" provides the narrative link; no new allegorical narratives replace it, Mário refers to it often, and he returns to it to end the text. The analogy of the store clerk's balance, and the hallucination sequence of endnote Q, constitute examples of important metaphorical narrative fragments.

• Changing Perspectives in "Postfácio"

As noted earlier, the overriding purpose of "Postfácio" is to clarify changes in Mário's ideas during the two and a half years since the composition of *Escrava;* this was the amount of time that passed before Mário could arrange its publication. He immediately and corporeally takes stock of the ideas presented in *Escrava:* some have been transformed, some have died, others have withered up, still others have put on weight, and some new ones have appeared. He explains simply that *Escrava* is "uma fotografia tirada [taken] em Abril de 1922" (OI 297).

In "Postfácio" Mário, as expected, refers to *Escrava,* but also to "Prefácio," not least because of the chronological proximity of the composition dates for these two works, but also because, as mentioned earlier, "Prefácio" serves as much as a preface to *Escrava* as to *Paulicéia,* and thus "Postfácio" presents a unified closure. Specifically, "Postfácio" refers to "Minha Verdade," a representation of the author's convictions in comparison to Christ's eternal truth, which appears not only in "Parábola" but also in the "Dedicatória" of *Paulicéia.* The April 1922 photo that *Escrava* represents is now replaced with a more mature portrait; it is the personified "Verdade" that has changed:

> Este livro, rapazes, já não representa a Minha Verdade in-
> teira da cabeça aos pés. [. . .] A mudança tambem não é tão
> grande assim. As linhas matrizes se conservam. [. . .] Mas
> afinal os cabelos vão rareando, a boca firma-se em linhas
> menos infantis e suponhamos que a Minha Verdade tenha
> perdido um dente no boxe? Natural. Lutado tem ela bastan-
> te. Pois são essas as mudanças: menos cabelos e dentes, mais
> musculos e certamente muito maior serenidade. (OI 297 [63])

The physical changes that Mário/"Minha Verdade" have experienced collectively represent the most important changes in the
author's convictions.

In another reference to an earlier text, Mário implicitly associates the now personified "Minha Verdade" with another
personification: "Minha Loucura," the solo soprano in his oratorio "As Enfibraturas do Ipiranga" from *Paulicéia*. "Minha
Loucura," clearly Mário's authorial voice in the oratorio, becomes a related manifestation of "Minha Verdade": "É que
tambem muita gente começa a reconhecer que a louca não era
tão louca assim e que certos exageros são naturais nas revoltas"
[It happens also that many people are starting to recognize that
the crazy woman wasn't really that crazy and that certain exag-
gerations are part and parcel of revolutions] (OI 298). The epithet "a louca" refers to "Minha Verdade" from the sentences
quoted above; the double identity of Mário's truth and insanity
unifies two of Mário's personified authorial voices: "Minha
Verdade" and "Minha Loucura." Just as Mário had compared
his truth to Christ's truth, he now likens the direction his convictions have taken to Christ's painful path to Calvary: "As
revoltas passaram, estouros de pneu, cortes de cobertão,
naturais em todos os caminhos que têm a coragem de ser
calvarios. Calvarios pelo que ha de mais nobre no espirito
humano, a fé" [The revolutions have passed, blown-out tires,
interruptions of coverage, natural for all paths that have the guts
to be Calvaries. Calvaries because of what is most noble in the
human spirit: faith] (OI 298). The poetic revolution ("revolta"),
in its eminently modern progress via automobile, has had its
setbacks, but the ultimate goal of the revolutionary spirit has
been achieved.

Christ's forgiveness parallels Mário's relaxed attitude toward
his former enemies: "Não me incomoda mais a existência dos
tolos e cá muito em segrêdo, rapazes, acho que um poeta

modernista e um parnasiano todos nos equivalemos e equiparamos" [I am no longer bothered by the existence of fools
and just between us, guys, I think that between a *modernista*
and a Parnassian we balance ourselves out and merit the same
scrutiny] (OI 298). The reconciliatory power of equilibrium
("equivalemos e equiparamos"), heightened by a few years'
perspective, unites poets of opposing camps albeit under a
frivolous rubric:

> É que nós tambem os poetas nos distinguimos pela mesma
> caracteristica dominante da especie humana, a imbecilida-
> de. Pois não é que temos a convicção de que existem Verda-
> des sobre a Terra quando cada qual vê as coisas de seu geito
> e as recria numa realidade subjectiva individual! (OI 298 [64])

However, Mário justifies himself by pointing out that some
guardian angel had guided him to use the restrictive term
"*minha* verdade": "Em nome dela é que sempre escrevo e
escreverei" [It's in her (its) name that I always write and will
write] (OI 298). The author recognizes that he cannot pretend
to represent the convictions of anyone other than himself, even
in the act of summoning a collective soul to characterize the
poetry of an entire generation.

The remaining four paragraphs of "Postfácio" discuss the
most important (and the only named) change in Mário's convictions: the increased role of intelligence, or reason, in the
creative process. The author blames "a desilusão pela sciencia
no fim do sec. XIX europeu" [the disillusion of science in late
nineteenth-century Europe] for the predominance of the senses
and intuition in the arts. Attempts to justify intuitive prominence have failed:

> As justificativas sentimentais eram insuficientes porquê na
> inteligencia é que moram razão e consciencia. [. . .] Todos
> êstes raciocinios provocaram uma revisão total de valores
> de onde proveio o novo renascimento da inteligencia. (OI
> 299 [65])

Always self-conscious, Mário questions his own previous sub-
scription to these ideas by singling out a flaw in his logic: "Eu
mesmo poderia objectar o que dentro dêste livro já disse mais
ou menos: que afinal todo êste lirismo subconsciente é ainda
filho da inteligencia ao menos como teoria" [I myself could

object to what I already said in this very book: that in the end all this unconscious lyricism is still the product of intelligence at least as theory] (OI 299). The very source of the idea of lyric prominence resides in conscious decision.

Mário concludes with a reprise of some key themes: the medical role of personified Intelligence from the allegory of Dom Lirismo, and the slave and master relationship of "Parábola." Regarding intelligence, he emotionally states:

> Foi serva disposta apenas a ministrar os pequenos e paliativos remedios da farmacopea didactico-tecnico-poetica ohoh! quando a ela cabe sinão superioridade e prioridade, cabe o dominio a orientação e a palavra final. Nos discursos actuais, rapazes, já é de novo a inteligencia que pronuncia o tenho-dito. (OI 299-300 [66])

Intelligence, merely a medical assistant, should have played a much larger part, larger even than the role of doctor in the Dom Lirismo allegory. The word *serva* above can be interpreted as a synonym of the word *escrava*, given the ubiquitous political use of the former term in nineteenth-century Brazilian discourse about slavery and abolition; the turn of the slave's rebellion has now come to intelligence, paradoxically more conscious now of its own ontological consciousness. The reappraisal of reason as Mário's hindsight seems only appropriate, because his changed attitude moves more obviously now toward the restoration of equilibrium, for example, to his aesthetic principle "Substituição da Ordem Intelectual pela Ordem Subconsciente."

But did this lead to too much self-censorship? Maria de Lourdes Patrini L'Abatte suggests an inherent risk in Mário's emphasis on the role of reason: "Será justamente esta razão consciente que levou Mário de Andrade a estar sempre explicando a sua própria criação artística [. . .] talvez o poeta chegou, enquanto criador, em alguns momentos de sua vida, a um certo imobilismo" [It could be exactly this conscious reason that led Mário to always be explaining his own artistic creation [. . .] perhaps the poet arrived, as a creator, in some moments of his life, at a certain immobility] (56). The periodic occurrence of this kind of impasse may well have been one of Mário's chief inspirations, as L'Abatte paradoxically states. Mário would later use his growing obsession with social engagement to reinforce his claim that reason (or the intellect/ consciousness) must shape lyric inspiration so that it can be comprehended by the public. His defense of this link continued throughout his career and culminated in his much analyzed 1942 lecture "O Movimento Modernista," an exaggerated rejection of aesthetic tendencies accompanied by an espousal of sociocultural responsibilty. In this retrospective essay, Mário regrets a lack of organization and of social presence in the movement. Yet the essay's conclusion, questioning the role of freedom in both art and society, reveals the author wrestling with the same problems some twenty years later. "Será que a liberdade é uma bobagem?" [Could it be that freedom is hogwash?] (*Aspectos* 255), he asks, directly reflecting the conclusion of his hallucination sequence in endnote Q, in which he laughs in exasperation at the "famigerada liberdade" [celebrated freedom] (OI 296).

Mário had always used the term *equilíbrio* and its related forms, synonyms, and antonyms to qualify artistic conditions, be they cognitive, stylistic, or social. In "O artista e o artesão" from the collection *O baile das quatro artes,* he characterized restrictions placed on artists working under dictatorships: "Não derivam de um justo equilíbrio entre o arte e o social, entre o artista e a sociedade" [They do not derive from a just equilibrium between art and the social, between the artist and society] (30). The artist loses his craft and his technique, assuming instead a social stance, which upsets the balance. On the other hand, the surrealists' obsequiousness to the unconscious deflects attention from the work of art to the artist himself, an action for which Mário tellingly uses the verb "desnortear" [to disorient], resembling Huidobro's compass imagery (31). These imbalances contrast with Mário's characteristically laudatory use of equilibrium to describe well-conceived works or styles. For example, he describes Sérgio Milliet as an "equilibradíssima figura de intelectual" [very balanced intellectual figure] in comparison to the "grande maioria dos nossos escritores [que] são indivíduos desarmoniosos, pouco sabedores de sua própria língua e tradições" [great majority of our writers (who) are unharmonious individuals, scarcely knowledgeable of their own language and traditions] (*Empalhador* 25). Similarly he praises the "equilíbrio de ritmos" [equilibrium of rhythms] in Oneida Alvarenga's *Menina Boba*

(*Empalhador* 61), Gabriela Mistral's linguistic achievements "no seu magistral poema do milho, onde a linguagem mais pura de Castela se equilibra perfeitamente em suas necessidades americanas" [in her magisterial poem about maize, where the purest language of Castile equilibrates itself perfectly in its American necessities] (*Empalhador* 219), and even Disney's accomplishments in a review of the 1940 film *Fantasia:* "Agora nem a música prevalece sôbre o cinema, nem êste sôbre ela. O equilíbrio é conseguido" [The music does not prevail over the cinema, nor the latter over the former. Equilibrium is achieved] (*Baile* 72–73).[14] Glossing the influence of Keyserling's concept of the Sein in *Macunaíma,* Lopez refers to Mário's second preface for that text: "Ele [o Sein] é que / estabelece / faz da arte e da vida um sistema de vasos comunicantes, equilibrando o líquido que agora não turtuveio em chamar de lágrima" [It is (the Sein) that / establishes / makes of art and life a system of communicating vessels, equilibrating the liquid that I do not hesitate now to call tears] (qtd. in *Ramais* 112). Equilibration here balances art and life, or Huidobro's "Mundo subjetivo" and "Mundo objetivo," to emotionally powerful results.

In a 1944 letter to his great friend Carlos Drummond de Andrade, Mário's description of his process of editing and correction invokes the lexicon of equilibrium while echoing his discourse in "Prefácio" and *Escrava:* "Tudo está em conservar o equilíbrio da liberdade. Eu quando escrevo quase nunca 'surge' a correção imediata, pra não prejudicar a corrente do que está vindo, em geral deixo a correção pra depois. Neste depois, sim, insisto em buscar a correção, mas espero que ela 'surja' pra decidir pelo melhor" [The key is to conserve the equilibrium of liberty. When I write, correction hardly ever "surges" immediately, so that it does not impede the flow of what's coming, in general I leave correction for a later time. At that later time is when I do insist on searching for correction, but I wait for it to "surge" in order to decide for the best] (*Lição* 233; qtd. in Kiefer 29–30).[15] The presence in this citation, a year before Mário's death, of key terms from "Prefácio" and *Escrava* already glossed in this analysis—such as *equilíbrio*, *prejudicar*, and *surge/surja*—indicates the durability of Mário's basic poetics tenets.

Conclusion

A Poetics of Equilibrium
and the Avant-Garde Paradox

> Creo que todos los poetas de todos los tiempos han
> afirmado lo mismo: el deseo es un testimonio de
> nuestra condición desgarrada; asimismo, es una
> tentativa por recobrar nuestra mitad perdida. Y el
> amor, como la imagen poética, es un instante de
> reconciliación de los contrarios.
>
> Octavio Paz
El arco y la lira

From Aristotle to Bloom, the history of poetics presents dominant discursive functions in both *description* and *prescription*.
While a poetics necessarily reflects, to some extent, the norms
that are already accepted or in the process of formalization at
the time, it also endeavors, in the very act of explicating these
norms, to promote them as a timeless, universal interpretation
of poetry that can guide writers of the present and future. Poetic history is therefore a history of dialogue, as each poetics
alternately denies or expands (or both) the arguments of the
previous ones. The descriptive nature of poetics, related to the
poetry of the moment, perhaps receives more attention, hence
Mário's query: "Onde nunca jamais se viu uma estética
preceder as obras de arte que ela justificará?" (OI 246); a poetics is inevitably derivative. Yet there exists, complementarily,
the idealized outlook that sanctifies, to varying degrees of intent, the poetics as a theory of Poetry (not just the poetry of a
period or movement) destined to provide a lasting model, even
if that model serves only as a point of departure for differing
poetics. The "intra-poetic relationships" that articulate Bloom's
The Anxiety of Influence can thus be expanded into intra-*poetics* relationships. The degree of difference resides in the fact

that a poetics, essentially a broad act of meta-poetry, encompasses more than the aim of most individual poems, though those poems may themselves be expressions or examples of a certain poetics.

I identify five processes that comprise these functions of description and prescription in poetics: (1) differentiation, (2) exemplification, (3) establishment, (4) idealization, and (5) prophecy. The first two processes pertain strictly to the function of description, while the last two adhere to the function of prescription. The middle process, establishment, acts within both functions and links the other four processes. By way of conclusion, I incorporate here the above system to comparatively analyze—in a brief recapitulation—the main thematic and formal characteristics of Huidobro's and Mário's poetics, and to contrast the temporal concerns of the avant-garde, as expressed by some of its most important theorists, with the universal sense of poetry in equilibrium.

• Poetics: Description

Differentiation, the first process of description, revokes previous poetic ideals, thereby setting the stage for the establishment of new ones. In *The Theory of the Avant-Garde,* Renato Poggioli shows that, even in this act of rupture, an avant-garde poetics can be surprisingly traditional: "Like any artistic tradition, however antitraditional it may be, the avant-garde also has its conventions [that], in a conscious or unconscious way, are directly and rigidly determined by an inverse relation to traditional conventions" (56). For example, both Huidobro and Mário condemn traditional mimesis—"non serviam" (715), "fotografia colorida" (PC 65). Both poets, after having begun their published careers with poetry collections imitating the previous styles of Hispanic *modernismo* and Brazilian *parnasianismo* (*Ecos del Alma* and *Há uma Gota de Sangue em Cada Poema,* respectively), reverse themselves and finally renounce their predecessors. Mário censures restrictive rhymes and rhythms ("um leito de Procusto" [PC 66]) and is joined by Huidobro in rebuking the limitation of poetic themes ("EL GRAN PELIGRO DEL POEMA ES LO POÉTICO" [752]) as unfeasible in the increasingly industrialized and interconnected modern world.

The act of differentiation consists not only of the abolishment of traditional prosodic norms but also of the rejection of other contemporary poetics. In the vanguard contest for originality, such differentiation assumes a special intensity for both authors. To prove himself in Paris and assert his original ideas, Huidobro reacts strongly against the surrealists by balancing out their exaltation of the unconscious—"Yo también proclamo el inconsciente, pero el inconsciente de los hombres conscientes" (748)—and by denouncing a period in his own artistic past in which he experimented with the unconscious. Both he and Mário distance themselves from Marinetti by debunking the futurist's claims of originality, though this act reflects a greater personal struggle in the case of Mário; his public need to overcome the *futurista* misnomer that had been attributed to him developed into an intense dislike for Marinetti, whose São Paulo lecture Mário refused to attend because, as Mário said, it was going to be an "espetáculo de vaias mais ou menos preparadas" [a spectacle of more-or-less prepared boos] and their meeting would be an agitated "discussão" [argument] (qtd. in Martins 78). Furthermore, both Huidobro and Mário react against an ignorant and conservative bourgeoisie—specifically, against that group's association of vanguard art with lunacy ("La poesía de los locos" [744], "NÃO SOMOS LOUCOS" [OI 245]); against that group's generalization that the only goal of the avant-garde is to idolize machines ("Nada de máquinas ni de moderno en sí" [752], "não é porque pense com elas escrever moderno, mas porque sendo meu livro moderno, elas têm nele sua razão de ser" [PC 74]); and against their hoary equivalence of art with truth ("diferencia entre la verdad de la vida y la verdad del arte" [720], Christ's "Verdade" compared to Mário's "minha verdade" [OI 201].

Like differentiation, the didactic process of exemplification involves both the past and the present; the poets seek to appropriate past authority as much as to identify contemporary talent (including, at times, themselves). Though an appraisal of the past seems contradictory to the avant-garde, Poggioli shows that it is not impossible:

> In the rare moments when avant-garde art seeks to justify itself by the authority or arbitration of history, in any one of the partial and infrequent fits of humanism or traditionalism

that now and again afflict it, even it deigns to look for its
own patent of nobility in the chronicles of the past and to
trace for itself a family tree of more or less authentic ances-
tors, more or less distant precursors. (70)

The creation of a universal poetics is just such a "rare moment"
when a vanguard writer may embrace select, reduced examples
of traditional authority. For example, both Huidobro and Mário
find support in Goethe's evaluations of the role of reason in
producing non-mimetic art; both refer to classical sources such
as Plato and Aristotle, to modern philosophers and scientists,
and to several generations of French poets. Yet while Huidobro
berates his contemporaries Cocteau and Soupault in an act of
differentiation, Mário cites the same two poets in an act of exemplification. Clearly Mário's initial bias toward the unconscious allows his greater affinity with the French surrealists. In
general, Mário gives more examples and cites many more poets, including other Brazilian writers and Huidobro; again, the
nature of *Escrava* as a formal and illustrative treatise, and
Mário's physical remove from the aesthetic turf wars in Paris,
are decisive circumstances. Huidobro, though quick to exemplify with and differentiate from French artists, cites only two
Spanish poets (Larrea and Diego). Moreover, due as much to
the perceived psychological ramifications of being an egotistical foreigner in France as to his numerous personal vendettas,
Huidobro does not cite any of his fellow Chilean or Latin
American writers, except the mythified "viejo poeta indígena
de Sudamérica" (719), which would seem to appoint Huidobro
as the sole South American heir of the Aymaran's generative
poetic powers.

Arising naturally from exemplification, the central process
of establishment in poetics links the functional elements of description and prescription because it entails the authors' expression of their main ideas, necessarily pertaining to what poetry
is now *and* to what it should be in the future. These ideas can
be expressed in any or all of the following stylistic modes: expository, pseudoscientific or allegorical. Thus the main idea of
equilibrium, or the development of and insistence on both conscious and unconscious roles in poetic creation, is presented in
the straightforward, expository mode—for example—by
Huidobro's pairs of opposites in "La poesía," "La creación

pura," "El creacionismo," and "Total," and by Mário's development of Dermée's *pensar/pesar* analogy; in the pseudoscientific mode by Mário's formulae and Huidobro's box flow chart, among other examples; and in the allegorical mode by the slave/master and gender distinctions in the parables, in addition to the graphic balance of "Aviso a los turistas" as allegory, and the unconscious/conscious dialectic of the Dom Lirismo allegory.

However, although both poets undeniably solidify the message of their poetics in the concept of equilibrium, their points of difference stand out as degrees of separation. The main difference resides in Huidobro's desire for totality in all aspects of poetic creation, as compared to Mário's penchant for precisely delineating the elements of conscious and unconscious processes. For example, Mário states clearly that inspiration, as the lyric impulse, arises in the unconscious and later undergoes conscious modification. Huidobro, in contrast, declares that inspiration derives from the state of "delirio," which is the same as the "superconsciencia"—an exalted state of conscious and unconscious forces in tandem. In the same vein, whereas the ultimate goal of Huidobro's mystique appears as union with the godhead in "Las siete palabras del poeta" (a union, therefore, with supreme creativity that is tantamount to an assimilation of the semiotic force), Mário never advocates such an extreme but rather opts to speak only of a telegraphic contact with the unconscious or the semiotic: "O que realmente existe é o subconsciente enviando à inteligéncia telegramas e mais telegramas" (OI 209).

The act of establishment includes not only the *matter* of the poetics—the main principles, but also the *discourse*—the techniques by which the poets express and communicate those principles. These literary techniques, it must be noted, are not necessarily the same as the poetic principles, because the poetics are prose texts, thus displaying different generic flexibilities; the techniques therefore connect more to the way in which the poetic principles (or goals) are described than to the principles themselves. In this way, the stylistic modes noted above (expository, pseudoscientific, allegorical) present themes in a variety of contexts. The poets' use of allegory, which has tended to articulate their main themes and thus the main points of this study, provides the best example. Allegory in general, and specifically the parable genre, unites a mysterious brevity—in which everything is symbolic—with a didactic form and message; the genre suits the mystical and illustrative purposes of a poetics ideally. In the expository mode, both poets expand generic limitations with the anti-mystique "Manifiesto tal vez," the parodic "Dedicatória," and the mock manifesto of "Prefácio" in order to undermine, lightheartedly, the presumptuousness of traditional ideas about poetic themes, conventions, and schools. Similarly, the pseudoscientific mode, as much in Mário's equations as in Huidobro's appropriation of mechanics, electronics, and evolution, can be noted as a technique to establish legitimacy and, as Russell notes in *Poets, Prophets and Revolutionaries,* to evoke the discovery of the unknown and to express the desire for certainty of outcome regarding artistic theories (27). The fact that technological and urban imagery acquires great importance in avant-garde *poetry* is of course a related phenomenon, but the *poetics* references meet a didactic, meta-aesthetic aim as much as a popularizing, aesthetic one.

Having declared this, it must still be recognized that the images used to expound the principles of establishment are almost always very closely related to the principles themselves. It is not surprising that Huidobro's tree and cross images appear in his poetics as much as in his poetry *(Adán, Poemas Articos, Altazor),* in both contexts emphasizing the poet's oracular mystique. Mário develops an opposing view of the poet as a voice of the people; the men-in-the-street motif (always as opposed to the bourgeoisie), present in his poetics, is endorsed also in his poetry *(Paulicéia,* "Carnaval Carioca," *Remate de males).* Thus the ivory tower, while losing out to the streetcar in Mário's poetics, becomes the archetype of the tree and the cross in Huidobro's. An integral part of Huidobro's technique, then, is this very construction of a cosmic mythos, which differs substantially from Mário's more personable and quotidian style. In poetics as much as in poetry, Huidobro must create the striking image, the alternate universe, whereas Mário is more interested in reconciling the psychological interpretation of simultaneous sensory phenomena with the artist's social concerns.

• Poetics: Prescription

The prescriptive function of poetics continues in idealization, which is the acclamation of the current generation of poets as the model for the future. For example, Huidobro distinguishes the *creacionistas* (more a theoretical than an actual generation) as the first to completely separate art from nature—they are "los primeros poetas que han aportado al arte el poema inventado en todas sus partes por el autor" (729). Mário makes the same claim for the *modernistas* regarding the important distinction between artistic beauty and natural beauty: "somente agora é que [o Belo artístico] se liberta da geminação obrigatoria a que o sujeitou a humana estultície" [only now has artistic Beauty freed itself from the obligatory pairing to which human imbecility has subjected it] (OI 207). In addition, Mário seeks the unconditional justification of his generation, in spite of its flaws (such as exaggeration)—the artists are "poetas sinceros que, sem mentiras nem métricas, refletem a eloquéncia vertiginosa da nossa vida" [sincere poets who, without lies nor meters, reflect the vertiginous eloquence of our life] (OI 223).

Idealization also seeks the paradigmatic universalization of the stated poetic conventions through identification with the absolute, Poetry. To wit, Huidobro's declaration: "La poesía creacionista adquiere proporciones internacionales, pasa a ser la Poesía, y se hace accesible a todos los pueblos y razas" (736). Mário's allegorization of Poetry displays a universalizing agenda as early as the beginning of his treatise in "Parábola" and in his equations, while in other sections of the text he attempts to show that a distinctly modern (and thus "recently discovered") poetic trait is universal because it has existed always, for example: "E mesmo na literatura de lingua portuguesa trechos em que grandes poetas observando o que se passava no eu interior procuraram embora atemorizados realizar a simultaneidade" [And even in Portuguese-language literature there are passages in which great poets, observing what was happening in the inner "I" attempted, although frightened, to achieve simultaneity] (OI 290). The same goal is met by association of poetry with Art as a universal.

Whereas idealization aims to preserve the accomplishments and beliefs of the current generation as universally prescriptive models, prophecy presents a step beyond in that it offers outright, though vague, predictions regarding the future state of poetry. Within the avant-garde, such predictions inevitably involve sacrifice, as Russell explains:

> Caught between the opposing impulses of negation and creation and between a denial of the present and a desire for the future, each avant-garde writer recognizes to some extent that he or she is trapped within the present that is to be negated and that, consequently, the writer must be sacrificed to the future that will follow from that sacrifice. (38)

The writer is willing to sacrifice because he or she presumes the capacity of foretelling the future as positively affected by the sacrifice. For Huidobro and Mário, this process begins in self-comparison with Christ. Huidobro assumes this messianic and sacrificial role very seriously, the most overt instance being "Las siete palabras del poeta"; Mário only facetiously likens himself to Muhammad first in "Prefácio" and then to Christ in "Parábola," though he later emerges as a Christ-figure, in the hallucination of endnote Q, through the images of suffering before a crowd of mocking strangers whom he nonetheless loves unconditionally.[1]

For Huidobro, the romanticist concept of the poet as seer, besides stimulating his egocentrism, animates his entire mythos of the poet's exclusive access to a central and eternal prophetic vision, giving life to supposedly clairvoyant statements such as "Hay signos en el cielo" (739). He often records his faith in the future in the manifestos' concluding statements such as "El viento vuelve mi flauta hacia el porvenir" (740) and "Lo esperamos con los oídos abiertos como los brazos del amor" (756), referring to the "total" poet who will someday lead. Though Mário also has great confidence in the future, his vision is not so much mysterious as propagandistic in his closing images of the new pilgrimage to Ararat: "Mas lá seguimos todos irmanados por um mesmo ideal de aventura e sinceridade, escoteiros da nova Poesia" [But there we go on, made as brothers by a sole ideal of adventure and sincerity, scouts of the new Poetry] (OI 274). Mário denies Marinetti the position of leadership in this pilgrimage: "Marinetti que muitos imaginam o cruciferário da procissão, vai atrasadote, preocupado em *sustentar* seu futurismo" [Marinetti, whom many imagine to be the cross-bearer of the procession, comes along behind, concerned with *sustaining* his futurism] (OI 274); significantly, the guiding position is associated with the cross ("cruciferário") and thus with the figure of leader, martyr, savior, and prophet.

The mechanics of prophecy as process expose the fragility of the poets' predictions. Huidobro fights to maintain a firm line by constantly quoting himself on previous occasions, thus limiting any perceived change of perspective in his message, but at the same time always pushing his predictions further into the future. In spite of his apparent consistency, he can change directions on a whim, as with his sudden abandonment of pseudoscientific discourse in "Necesidad de una estética poética compuesta por los poetas." Perhaps most telling is the debilitation of the initial revolution in "Non serviam," which becomes only the call for such a revolution in later manifestos. Mário, in contrast, is more honest about his changing ideas over time, for example in his open reworking of the polyphonics theory as "simultaneidade" and in his increased appreciation for the role of intelligence in "Postfácio"; in fact these changing ideas, in reaction to articles in *L'Esprit Nouveau* and other sources, spur the writing of both "Prefácio" and "Postfácio" and become a leitmotif in Mário's profoundly reflective self-portrait of an aesthetics in evolution.

Just as each poetics universalizes its view of poetry, this schematic review of the two authors' poetics as function and process has attempted to relate the texts to a general definition of poetics. This definition, however, must now be considered within the particular context of the avant-garde sensibility to time and imminence. Specifically, the right to develop and change ideas, in the light of the prophetic role of the vanguard artist, leads to an essential avant-garde contradiction in originality and continuity. How can the avant-garde's initial, fleeting goals of newness, originality, and the expression of the modern moment be extended into a movement in and of itself? The question ultimately becomes one of finding a way to move on, of surpassing one's previously innovative works, although ideally the high value placed on individual expression would allow constant renewal.

The establishment of a poetics offers a solution: it characterizes the avant-garde in the very proclamation of the modern moment and yet, simultaneously, dissolves it into the universal of Poetry. This moves a step beyond the whims of the fashion-dictated vanguard movements, because a poetics not only describes but also prescribes. In Huidobro's and Mário's poetics, the prescription is equilibrium. Specifically, a poetics of equilibrium moves beyond the initially destructive phase of the avant-garde, in which so many other manifestos, proclamations, and even artists and movements stagnate, by endorsing a plan for new creation in the artist's balance of conscious self with collective unconscious. Since a poetics presents ideals, equilibrium becomes the prescriptive goal of future poetry, thereby universalizing (which is not the same as institutionalizing) the avant-garde dialectic of destruction and creation.

• Equilibrium

Universalization, through the idea of equilibrium, recognizes essentially the inevitably temporal element of the avant-garde; in one sense it betrays the avant-garde because it views it as no longer unique or as ultimately destined to expire, but universalization also attempts to transcend time with a lasting construct of meaning. Equilibrium thus stabilizes the avant-garde within artistic tradition. In *The Concept of the Avant-Garde,* John Weightman offers an interpretation of vanguard stability:

> *Avant-garde* artists and thinkers sense the problem of finding values in flux and they are trying—often perhaps neurotically—to espouse what they think is the movement of history by anticipating the crest of the next wave *(la nouvelle vague),* or alternatively they may be trying to escape from the dilemma of perpetual movement by finding some substitute for eternity, *i.e.* some God-substitute. Quite often, I think, they are trying to do both things at once, and this is why so many *avant-gardes* have both a progressive and a non-progressive aspect. (24)

Equilibrium is exactly that "escape from the dilemma of perpetual movement" in that it stabilizes, balances, and thus annuls the equal and opposite "progressive" and "non-progressive" temporal aspects. The divine substitute that Weightman indicates is likewise fulfilled in equilibrium, since the concept often leads to association with supernatural creative powers; in Huidobro's case, equilibrium corresponds to the poet's orientation in the *aleph,* often depicted by the sacred symbols of the cross, the Tree of Knowledge, and the New Jerusalem, while in Mário's case the harmony of poetic composition connotes the spiritual insight of Christ's Truth and the initial, divine creation of Eden. Furthermore, equilibrium tempers avant-garde exaggeration. Russell emphasizes the avant-garde tendency to be "dominated by a single and narrow principle, such as the primacy of the subconscious (surrealism), technology (Italian futurism), [etc.]" (37). The balance of opposing factors, or the totality of factors, implied in the concept of equilibrium surpasses such fragmentation, working toward the reconciliation of the various idées fixes defining modernity.

What validity is there to the belief that such a seemingly reactionary stance within the avant-garde depends on factors in Latin American society? One could argue that a remove from the wars and decadence of Europe, or perhaps a more idealistic confidence in the possibility of societal renewal in Brazil or Chile, fomented a heterogeneous approach to assimilating the European vanguard tenets and a consequent hodgepodge of contradictions needing to be resolved. Certainly Videla de Rivero's affirmation regarding Latin American syncretism, and the relevance of Oswald de Andrade's *antropofagia* theory (in which foreign influences are digested to be assimilated and expressed in an altered way) among other factors, would seem to support such a view. Unruh highlights the immediacy of the exotic in the New World:

> But in Latin America, the vanguardist encounter between Western society and its imagined "others" affirmed a historical specificity and cultural proximity that the European avant-gardes could not claim [even] though many Latin Americans might have had relatively little personal contact with the non-Western cultures present within their own and even though most vanguardist writers participated little in those cultures [. . .] (140)

This underlying autochthonous link supports a specifically Latin American need for balance in the avant-garde, in this case an equilibrium of non-Western and Western cultural influences. The ease with which Huidobro can claim to have studied with an Aymaran guru and Mário can famously call himself a "tupi tangendo um alaúde" [a Tupi strumming a lute] (in *Paulicéia*'s "O trovador," PC 83) while critically engaging with the leading European artists of their time, is a conceit unavailable to those same European artists. It is a defense mechanism, a display of nationalist pride, a clever legitimation, and a defining aspect of the Latin American avant-garde.

Yet the unifying trait of *cosmopolitismo,* in all of its ramifications—the facilitation of transatlantic communications and travel, an international urban identity—coupled with the specific instances of European travel by writers like Huidobro, combine to suggest, once again, the universal appeal of equilibrium. In fact, the spirit of equilibrium (if not the letter) probably arose in Europe among some of the moderate surrealists.[2] Russell notes that surrealism as a philosophy

> balanced, in differing proportions, oppositions between passivity and activism, aesthetic determinism and freedom, irrationality and rationality, and psychic reception and projection. All of the surrealist techniques sought to provoke the "surrealist state of mind," a mental condition in which each opposition would be reconciled. (141)

In spite of such a desired reconciliation, it was easy to associate surrealism exclusively with the unconscious (because the surrealists denied any conscious role whatsoever in automatic writing), as Huidobro did in his interpretation of Breton's manifesto and other surrealist acts. Yet if automatic writing, as an extreme technique, proved to be just another flash in the pan, then the more moderate position—not so much that the unconscious should dominate but rather that its importance should be enhanced to match that of conscious thought—successfully influenced posterior aesthetics perhaps more than any other avant-garde movement.

In Latin America, further study is needed to explore the related and specific aesthetic contexts in the works of other theorists, for example Maples Arce's bombastic lexicon of equilibrium in the *estridentista* manifesto "Actual No. 1" ("La verdad estética, es tan sólo un estado de emoción incoercible desenrollado en un plano extrabasal de equivalencia integralista") and Borges's use of synthesis as defining concept in the *ultraísta* documents ("El ultraísmo no es quizás otra cosa que la espléndida síntesis de la literatura antigua, que la última piedra redondeando su milenaria fábrica") (qtd. in Verani 88, 250). This small list of instances of equilibrium in Europe and Latin America does not pretend to be exhaustive, but in any case the most important of these variations on equilibrium is that of the moderate surrealists. Through a more conscious cultivation of the unconscious, surrealism as poetics became, as Paz noted, a way of life much more than just an aesthetic movement.

Avant-garde expression in early twentieth-century Latin America encompassed an immensely diverse spectrum as far as the adoption of European ideas, reactions against them, and the promotion of national social agendas implicitly or explicitly related to new aesthetic interpretations. Of those writers who addressed the creation of a new poetics, Huidobro and Mário are two of the most important by virtue of their extensive theoretical texts. Huidobro achieves a greater portrayal of the reconciliation of conscious and unconscious processes through the creation and varied description of his mythical, alternative poetic world, itself the embodiment of *creacionismo*. His "hilos eléctricos entre las palabras" (716) illuminate and then detonate images born of unexpected connections. Mário maintains an equilibrium of these creatively essential, but separate, conscious and unconscious processes in the thematic and structural organization of his texts and in the central paradox of the individual and the collectivity in simultaneity. His harmonic and polyphonic images, in contrast to Huidobro's, "não se ligam" (PC 68) but rather construct a mosaic of equipollent entities. Both authors stand out as eventually more conservative avant-garde leaders whose ability for aesthetic compromise provided a solid legacy in the act of universalizing avant-garde poetry through the poetics of equilibrium.

Appendix
English Translations

The following are English translations for the longer Portuguese quotations. They are keyed to the text by the numbers in brackets. All translations are mine.

Introduction
A Desire for Equilibrium in Avant-Garde Poetics: The Parables "Non serviam" and "Parabola d'*A escrava que não é Isaura*"

1   And after centuries and centuries . . .
     An ingenious vagabond born October 20, 1854 happened to pass
     by the mountain.

Chapter Four
"Prefácio Interessantíssimo" as Mock Manifesto

2   Reader:

     Hallucinationism is founded.

                                    *

     This preface, though interesting, is useless.

3   And excuse me for being so far behind the contemporary artistic
     movements. I am outmoded, I confess. No one can liberate him-
     self, all at once, from the grandmother-theories that he imbibed;
     and the author of this book would be a hypocrite if he pretended to
     represent a modern orientation that he still does not understand
     well.

4   Some facts. Not all of them. And no conclusions. For whomever
     accepts me both are useless. The curious will take pleasure in

finding out my conclusions, juxtaposing work and facts. For whomever rejects me, it's a lost cause to explain that which, before reading, he has already not accepted.

5   When I feel the lyric impulse I write without thinking all that my unconscious is shouting to me. I think later: not only to correct, but also to justify what I wrote. Hence the reason for this Very Interesting Preface.

6   "This Koran is no more than a confusion of mixed-up, incoherent dreams. It is not inspiration received from God, but rather created by the author. Muhammad is not a prophet, he's a man who writes verses. Let him present some sign that reveals his destiny, like the ancient prophets." Maybe they will say of me what they said of the creator of Allah. The whole difference between the two of us: Muhammad presented himself as a prophet; I judged that it would be more convenient to present myself as a lunatic.

7   I was vain. I tried to come out of obscurity. Now I have pride. It wouldn't weigh on me to go back into obscurity. I thought that my ideas (which aren't even mine) would be disputed: they disputed my intentions. I won't be quiet any longer. They would ridicule my silence as much as they would this cry.

8   Forgive me for giving some worth to my book. There is no father who, being a father, would abandon his deformed, drowning son in order to save the neighbor's handsome heir. The wet nurse of the story was a huge perverted ham.

9   Inspiration is fleeting, violent. Any little imp will perturb it or even silence it. Art, which added to Lyricism yields Poetry, does not consist of impairing the crazed course of the lyric state to warn it of the rocks and wire fences along the path. Let it trip, fall down, and get hurt. Art is weeding out of the poem, later, fastidious repetitions, romantic sentimentalities, and useless or inexpressive details.

10   Artistic beauty: arbitrary, conventional, transient—a question of fashion. Natural beauty: immutable, objective, natural—it has the eternity that nature will have. Art doesn't consist of reproducing nature, nor is that its goal. All the great artists, whether consciously (Raphael of the Madonna paintings, Rodin of the Balzac statue, Beethoven in his *Pastoral Symphony,* Machado de Assis with his novel *The Posthumous Memoirs of Bras Cubas*) or unconsciously (the vast majority), were deformers of nature. From this I infer that artistic beauty will be all the more artistic, all the more subjective,

the more it is distanced from natural beauty. Let others infer whatever they want. It matters little to me.

11 Our senses are fragile. Perception of exterior things is weak, impaired by a thousand pretenses that derive from our physical and moral defects: diseases, prejudices, indispositions, antipathies, ignorance, heredity, circumstances of time and place, etc.

12 There is the order of the schoolchildren who leave their classes hand-in-hand, two-by-two. There is an order for the high school students, who come down the stairs four steps at a time, graciously bumping into each other. There is an order, even higher, in the unfettered fury of the elements.

13 Marinetti was great when he rediscovered the suggestive, associative, symbolic, universal, and musical power of the word in liberty. But: as old as Adam. Marinetti was wrong: he made it into a system. It's only a very powerful auxiliary. I use words in freedom. I feel like my cup is too big for me, and yet I still drink from the cups of others.

14 Oral harmony is not realized, like musical harmony, by the senses, because words don't mesh into each other like sounds do, rather they become entangled, they become incomprehensible. The realization of poetic harmony is carried out by intelligence. Comprehension of the temporal arts is never immediate, only mediated. In temporal art we coordinate consecutive acts of memory, which we assimilate in a final entirety. This entirety, the result of successive states of consciousness, gives the final, complete comprehension of the finished music, poetry, or dance.

15 However: if you by chance have experienced some powerful, unforeseen event in your life (you have, naturally), recall the disordered tumult of the many ideas that in that moment rioted within your brain. Those ideas, reduced to the telegraphic minimum of words, did not follow upon themselves, because they did not form part of any phrase, they had no reply, solution, continuity. They were vibrating, resounding, piling up, superimposing themselves. Without connection, without apparent agreement—although born of the same event—they formed, by their rapid succession, true simultaneities, true harmonies accompanying the broad and vibrant melody of the event.

16 Ribot said somewhere that inspiration is a coded telegram transmitted by unconscious activity to the conscious activity that

translates it. The conscious activity can be shared by the poet and the reader. That's the way of the poet who does not despoil and coldly fragment the lyric moment; and good-naturedly concedes to the reader the glory of collaborating in the poems.

17   When one of the poems from this book was published, many people said to me, "I didn't understand it." There were some people, however, who confessed: "I understood it, but I didn't feel it." My friends . . . I perceived more than once that they felt, but they didn't understand. Evidently my book is good.

18   A well-known writer said of my friends and me that we were either geniuses or idiots. I think he's right. We feel, my friends and I, the longing of the lighthouse. If we were so much of a flock as to have a collective school, it would certainly be called "Lighthouseism." Our desire: to illuminate. The extreme left wing where we have placed ourselves permits no middle term. If geniuses: we will indicate the route to follow; idiots: shipwrecks to avoid.

19   I will always find, too, some man or woman who will sway to the liberating cadence of my verses. In that moment: a new Amphion, dark and bespectacled, I will make the very rocks come together to form walls by the magic of my song. And within those walls we will hide our tribe.

20   And the poetic school "hallucinationism" is ended.

*

Next book I'll found another one.

*

And I don't want any disciples. In art: school =
imbecility of many for the vanity of one.

*

I could have quoted Gorch Fock and avoided the
Very Interesting Preface. "Every song of
freedom is born in jail."

Chapter Five
At the Dock and on the Street: The Loss of Purity and Solidarity in Mário's Poetics

21 Dom Lirismo, upon disembarking from the El Dorado of the Unconscious at the dock in the land of the Conscious, is inspected by the medic, Intelligence, who cleans him of his eccentricities and any and all disease that could spread confusion, obscurity in the little progressive land. Dom Lirismo suffers one more customs inspection, discovered by Freud, who called it Censure. I am a smuggler! And I'm against the mandatory vaccination law.

22 It seems that I am all instinct . . . It's not true. There is in my book, and it does not bother me, a pronounced intellectualist tendency. What do you expect? I manage to smuggle my silks without paying duties. But it is psychologically impossible to free myself of the injections and tonics.

23 You will easily perceive that if in my poetry grammar is sometimes despised, it suffers no grave insults in this very interesting preface. Preface: arduous march of my higher self. Verses: landscape of my deeper self.

24 Could it be possible to force a surge in perfection for the arts? To skip evolution so that contemporary works gain serenity, clarity, humanity? Do we write for others or for ourselves? For all the others or for just a few others? Should one write for the future or for the present? What is the artist's obligation?

25 Of these two roads, on one there is the moral obligation that torments us (me), on the other there is the valor to achieve aesthetically the contemporary state, which it would be ungrateful, almost wicked, to spoil, mask, in the name of a future terrain that does not belong to us.

26 Pains and sorrows! Doubts and struggles. I feel exhausted. Did my heart stop? Just an automobile, out there . . . It is afternoon, more serene. E si vedono comparire delle immagini. There are some boys who whistle in my ears, booing, barking, and crowing . . . Dogs claw my garments on the terrible street, they bite my feet, they scrape my flesh . . . I am stripped. Nude. In front of those who scoff me. Stripped, too, of the illusion with which I intended to love oceanic humanity. But the human waves beat against my chest that is like a dock of love. They gnaw me. They gnaw me. A faraway,

penetrating pain . . . But the sea salt spurs me on. I raise myself up one more time. And in the face of the evil, unconscious, universal laughter, I have the proud joy of being a sad man. And I keep on going. No one approaches me. They yell from a distance: —"Lunatic! Lunatic!" I turn around. I respond: —"Lunatics! Lunatics!" It's hilarious. And I end up finding in everything a profound humor: in humanity, in me, in fatigue, in inquietude, and in that celebrated freedom.

27 The streetcar begins the journey, / no one on the seat, / I am alone, without. // Then a man gets on, / sits down on the seat, / I go now a companion. // The streetcar is full, / Once again, however, / I am no longer anybody.

28 That nonexistence of exterior manifestation from those around me, the despicable deference, the absolute lack of hope for the city boy, word of honor, is detestable. It punishes. Oh ye men who live in the backlands, why do ye treat me this way! I want to be like ye, I love and respect ye!

29 The second time the creature leapt out of the water, I could no longer control my emotion. Word of honor: I was scared. I felt like crying, my companions weren't saying anything anymore, they had abandoned me! Oh what a disgraceful being!

30 I had two bundles in hand. One for the Conservatory, the other for the Post Office, and they created in me some kind of decision. My ash-colored clothes were blotted out by the foggy afternoon and a quasi-sensation of nudity bothered me. Fortunately the gentle winds came, whipped up from the turbulent plains, and they caressed me, they carried me away to other animal worlds where the living is good.

31 There I was, drinking coffee, the victim. It was the much more logical happiness of first freeing myself of the bundles so that I could then better enjoy the drink, the rustics. And, from the other side of the scene, still and always springtime, Ariel, Chico Antônio, Nosso Senhor, ultimately the whole disequilibrium against life.

Chapter Six
Balancing the Equations: Mário's Struggle to Define Aesthetic Simultaneity

32 When we analyze with care the *matter* of his poems and the stylistic *technique* created to express it, the force of accommodation

achieved by the poet becomes clear: to harmonize the *fragmented and multiform vision of reality* (demanded by the historic moment and by aesthetic renovation) with his *organizing intelligence* (demanded by his nature).

33 Need for expression + need for communication + need for action + need for pleasure = Fine Arts.

34 Man receives sensation through his senses. According to the degree of receptivity and productive sensitivity, he feels, without the smallest parcel of intelligence entering into the process, the NEED TO EXPRESS the received sensation by means of gesture.

35 Of the arts thus born the one that utilizes articulated voices is called poetry.
(That's my conjecture. Those who know will see that although I systematize audaciously I do not remove myself from the most recent conjectures, made by psychologists and aesthetes, regarding the origin of the fine arts.)

36 Pure lyricism + Criticism + Word = Poetry

37 ([. .] In the end, intelligence creates on top of pure lyricism in prose whereas in *modernista* poetry pure lyricism is graphed out with a minimum of any development that intelligence could practice upon it. This is at least the tendency, though it is not always followed.)

38 I gave you a recipe . . . I didn't mention the proportions of the ingredients. It should be: a maximum of lyricism and a maximum of criticism to acquire the maximum expression. This is why Dermée wrote: "The poet is an ardent soul lead by a cool head."

39 Maximum lyricism + Maximum criticism = Maximum expression

40 Now: observing the evolution of poetry through the ages what does one see? The continuous growth of the Guarisancar of tulles, nainsooks, lace, silk stockings, etc., from the initial parable. It was intelligence, romanticized by the concern for beauty, that brought us to the two existing meters and other crochets, filets, and frivolities. Worse still: intelligence, weighing things and facts from nature and life, chose just a few that became the *poetic subjects*.

41 The poet's intelligence—which no longer dwells in an ivory tower—receives the telegram in the streetcar, when the poor thing is going to the department, to the College of Philosophy, to the

movies. Virgin, synthetic, energetic, the telegram gives him strong commotions, divinatory exaltations, sublimations, poetry.

42   The Horaces + Othello + Radio antenna + Electric cables = 4 subjects. Result: richness, fullness, plethora.

43   Luis Aranha drank in the universe. He killed czars in Russia, he loved in Japan, he enjoyed Paris, he robbed in the United States, by simultaneity, without leaving S. Paulo, only because at the time he was doing his geographic gymnastics, he fell gravely ill and became delirious. Thus was born the admirable "Gyrating Poem."

44   —Down with rhetoric!
      —With much pleasure. But let's conserve eloquence, legitimate daughter of life.

45   [. . .] two results—one new, originating from the progress of experimental psychology; the other old, originating from inevitable reality:
      1.°: respect for the freedom of the unconscious.
As a consequence: destruction of the poetic subject.
      2.°: the poet reintegrated into his life and times.
Thus: renovation of the sacred fury.

46   But that is not yet art.
      It is missing the maximum of criticism of which I spoke and that Migot calls "analytical intention."

47   Intelligence forms ideas based on sensation. And as it exteriorizes them in words it acts as one who compares and weighs. Intelligence weighs sensation not with kilos but with words. I can even use, metaphorically, the verb *to weigh* (Dermée) for the act of thinking since intelligence, linking subject and predicate in order to recognize their equipolence, weighs their respective values.

48   Our eyes see a dog.
      Sensation.
      Intelligence weighs the sensation and concludes that it corresponds exactly to the universal term *dog*, pertaining to that bulky collection of weights that is the dictionary.
      The pointer of our faculty of reason moved to the vertical position.
      The weight is correct.

49　The poet begins with a complete sensation, he dissociates it through analysis and chooses the elements with which he will build another whole, I won't say more homogenous, I won't say more perfect than nature's but

OF ANOTHER PERFECTION,
OF ANOTHER HOMOGENEITY.
Nature exists fatally, *without its own will*. The poet creates by intelligence, *by his own will*.

50　We are really primitives. And like all primitives, realists and stylists. The sincere realization of the affective material and of the unconscious is our realism. By means of our deforming and synthetic imagination we are stylists. The problem is combining these contradictory tendencies in an equilibrated whole.

51　The difference is that analogy is subconscious while periphrasis is an exaggerated, forced, and pretentious intellectualism.
　　It is imperative to not return to Rambouillet!
　　It is imperative to not repeat Góngora [!]
　　IT IS IMPERATIVE TO AVOID MALLARMÉ!

52　*The poet does not photograph the unconscious.*
　　It is inspiration that is unconscious, not creation. There can be no force of will without attention.

53　But the Parnassian magistrate reads us and gets angry because he doesn't find in our poems intellectual logic, development, seriation of planes, and other assorted Idola Theatri.
　　But he's searching the poem for something that doesn't exist there!

54　But, screaming like Pharisees, they demand of us a total aesthetic of 400 pages in quarto . . .
　　That is what's really nonsense.
　　Where was it ever seen that an aesthetic preceded the works of art that it will justify?

55　Undeniable: the effect of image association is effusive, magnificent, and mainly natural, psychological but . . .
　　look out for the serpent among the flowers:
　　The poet becomes so dexterous in its manipulation that he substitutes sensitivity, the lyricism produced by sensations, for an artless, very amusing game of images, born of a single, initial

inspiration. It is the law of least effort, it is a constant schism that can lead to ruin.

56   Contemporary life makes us simultaneous inhabitants of all the lands of the universe.
    Ease of transportation allows us to slap our soles on the pavement in Tokyo, New York, Paris, and Rome in the same April.
    Through the newspaper we are omnipresent.
    Languages shuffle themselves.
    Peoples mix themselves.

57   Contemporary man is a multiplied being.
    . . . three races are fused in my flesh . . .
    Three?

58   I was educated in a French academy. I palpitate with enthusiasm, with love for the renovation of the Italian musical arts. I acknowledge and study Huidobro and Unamuno. The United States fills me with enthusiasm as if it were my own homeland. With [the aviator] Gago Coutinho's adventure I was Portuguese. I was Russian during the Congress of Genoa. German in the Congress of Versailles. But I didn't vote for anybody in the last Brazilian election.

59   There is no stroll, no crossing of the street in which this division is not, more or less, a psychological state. To achieve it in the apparently heedless polytonal polyphony of received sensations is to construct the simultaneous poem. Could there be impressionism in that? No, because we do not later abandon criticism and the search for equilibrium, inevitable dignifiers of the work of art.

60   Sudden unobstructed view of a landscape: one does not perceive

        first a tree,
        then another tree,
        then another tree,
        then a horse,
        then a man,
        then a cloud,
        then a creek, etc.,

but rather all of this simultaneously.

61   It is that the poet, choosing with discretion (criticism, will for analysis to obtain eurythmics, and Art) with discretion some few poor values did not worry himself with their relative poverty of

expression but rather with the richness of the final total complex sensation.

62 And it is bedecked with the steel of indifference,

>   the linens of serenity,
>   the plushes of love,
>   the uproarious satins of enthusiasm, that

we depart to the east, destination Ararat.

63 This book, guys, no longer represents My whole Truth from head to toe [. . .] But the change isn't really that significant, either. The matrix is still the same. [. . .] But in the end the hair is thinning out, the mouth is fixed in less juvenile lines and shall we suppose that My Truth has lost a tooth in the sparring? Naturally. She has sparred quite a bit. So these are the changes: less hair and fewer teeth, more muscles and certainly much more serenity.

64 It's that we poets, too, distinguish ourselves by the same dominant characteristic of the human species, stupidity. Isn't it true that we have the conviction that Truths exist on this Earth, yet each one of us sees things his own way and re-creates them in a subjective, individual reality!

65 The sentimental justifications were insufficient because it is in intelligence that reason and consciousness dwell. [. . .] All of these ratiocinations provoked a total revision of values, from which came the new renaissance of intelligence.

66 She was a servant ordered only to administer the alleviating little remedies of the didactic-technical-poetic pharmacopea ohoh! when her part should have been, if not superiority and priority, then dominion, orientation, and the last word. In contemporary discourse, guys, it is once again intelligence that intones the "I have spoken."

Notes

Preface
The Latin American Avant-Garde: Context for Vicente Huidobro's and Mário de Andrade's Poetics

1. Although critics do not agree on the duration of the avant-garde period in Latin America, a generally accepted range lasts from 1914 to 1938. Schwartz enumerates the following views on the duration of the Latin American avant-garde: 1916–35 (Verani), 1916–39 (Schopf), 1919–29 (Osorio), 1905–? (Szabolscsi), 1914–38 (Schwartz) (28–32). Teles maintains that Brazil's case is distinct, having begun in 1922 (with precursors as early as 1917) and ended only recently, albeit in an extended final phase (*Vanguarda* 14). Throughout the text I will mean Latin America to encompass Spanish America (the Spanish-speaking nations of the Americas) and Brazil.

2. The Brazilian vanguard movement known as *modernismo* had nothing to do with Hispanic *modernismo,* which roughly corresponded to the *parnasianismo* period in Brazil. These two latter periods were direct precursors of the avant-garde; they were the styles against which the new artists reacted.

3. For the sake of clarity, the avant-garde can be designated as a period, while the various "ismos" can be called movements that make up the avant-garde period, in Latin America as in the rest of the world.

4. I shall follow convention in referring to Mário de Andrade by his first name.

5. The purpose here is not to reproduce biographies but rather to give a brief and schematic account of relevant highlights. Biographical information on both authors is abundant; my main sources for these paragraphs are Concha, Cornejo, all of de Costa's work, Teitelboim, Lopez ("Uma Cronologia para Mário de Andrade"), and Alves.

6. Regarding the protagonists, Pizarro observes that "La fuerza antiheroica de este Cid magnificado, amado y a veces ridiculizado tiernamente, llevado en todo caso a lo cotidiano, es la misma que guía al perezoso y sensual «héroe» Macunaíma" (67).

7. Unless noted otherwise, all translations are mine.

Introduction
A Desire for Equilibrium in Avant-Garde Poetics: The Parables "Non serviam" and "Parabola d'*A escrava que não é Isaura*"

1. Huidobro's close friend Juan Larrea, and Jaime Concha among others (see Concha 46), insist that "Non serviam" was written later than 1914. This is only one of many discrepancies in Huidobro's chronology; a complete discussion of Huidobro's chronological inconsistencies may be found in de Costa and in Bajarlía.

2. Goic points out that Huidobro posits this confrontation against Nature, and not against realism as his European contemporaries generally did (60); the more abstract and symbolic Nature presents a greater creative license, especially within the parable format.

3. Huidobro mentions Alomar's text in *Pasando y pasando* (1914); Larrea comments on the way in which Huidobro uses the text to disparage Marinetti. Larrea also insinuates that Huidobro may have learned about Alomar's ideas through Darío's *Dilucidaciones* and *El canto errante*. See also Camurati (34–64) regarding Huidobro's reception of Alomar's and Vasseur's ideas.

4. The title is a ludic allusion to Bernardo Guimarães's well-known 1875 novel, *A Escrava Isaura*, about a slave who flees her licentious master to find true love in the arms of an idealistic youth.

5. Huidobro does mention Lucifer's insurrection in the manifesto "La creación pura": "El Hombre sacude su yugo, se rebela contra la naturaleza como antaño se rebelara Lucifer contra Dios, a pesar de que esta rebelión sólo es aparente [. . .]" (720). Again the context relates to a new, parallel creation more than to a world in opposition; the poet's rebelliousness undeniably links him to Lucifer (Altazor as a fallen angel), but Huidobro stresses the creative result of the revolution and consequently the poet's Adam-like nature.

6. Mário uses the word *subconsciência* in the unspecialized sense; in psychoanalytic terms, this force is really the "unconscious." Either the word *unconscious* or at times Jung's term, the *collective unconscious*, will be used throughout this study except when quoting Mário.

7. The parable text does not mention Noah or the flood, but Poetry survives intact undoubtedly because of her strategic location atop Mount Ararat.

8. See Jung, *Mysterium Coniunctionis*, ch. 5, "Adam and Eve," esp. pp. 388–90.

9. The following discussion is based on Todorov's lecture "Living Together Alone," presented at the University of Virginia on Oct. 12, 1994. Some of the material for this lecture appears in his *On Human Diversity: Nationalism, Racism, and Exoticism in French Thought;* see esp. pp. 178–84.

10. It is interesting to note that several critics, including Bary, Concha, and Paz, see Huidobro as an aerial or ethereal poet, especially in two of his best-known works, *Altazor* and *Temblor de cielo* (in contrast to, for example, Vallejo as a terrestrial poet). Such a preference on Huidobro's part could be interpreted as a manifestation of the desire for independence from the Earth Mother.

11. Furthermore, Adam's unilateral creation of Poetry may be seen to reflect male homosexual fantasies of reproduction. The presentation is similar in verses from the "Rito do Irmão Pequeno" section of Mário's *Livro Azul:* "Meu irmão é tão bonito como o pássaro amarelo, / Ele acaba de nascer do escuro da noite vasta!" [My brother is as beautiful as the yellow bird, / He has just been born from the darkness of the vast night!]

(PC 331) and "E quando a terra for terra, / Só nós dois, e mais ninguém, / De mim nascerão os brancos, / De você, a escuridão" [And when the earth will be the earth, /Just the two of us, and no one else, / From me will be born the whites, / From you the darkness] (PC 335). However, Poetry's decidedly feminine essence in "Parábola" alters the dynamics of the male-male relationship in "Rito do Irmão Pequeno."

12. Unruh highlights Huidobro's strategic move here to the first-person plural from his "overuse" of the first-person singular (37).

Part One
Poetry as Orientation of the Creative Self: Vicente Huidobro

1. Besides the attention drawn by the centennial of Huidobro's birth (1993) and as a measure of popularity, his works showed an appearance rate of 79 percent on the reading lists of graduate programs in Hispanic literature in U.S. universities in the mid-1990s (surpassed by Neruda, Vallejo, and Paz in the twentieth-century Spanish American poets category). With a 54 percent appearance rate on the graduate reading lists, *Altazor* (erroneously classified as a nineteenth-century work) was the most frequently listed poetic title of the twentieth century (without counting brief poems, which did not appear on the list as works) among all the book-length poetic titles by Spanish American and Spanish writers (see Brown and Johnson).

2. Ivan A. Schulman's article, inspired by "Non serviam," and the quotes from manifestos in Saúl Yurkievich's analysis "Arte poética" in *Fundadores* (68–71) exemplify this tendency.

3. Recent interest in Huidobro's poetics is evident in the 1999 translation from the French of his 1925 *Manifestes,* as *Manifestos Manifest* published in Green Integer's small-format portable series of "Essays, Manifestos, Statements, Speeches, Maxims, Epistles, Diaristic Notes, Narratives, Natural Histories, Poems, Plays, Performances, Ramblings, Revelations and all such ephemera as may appear necessary to bring society into a slight tremolo of confusion and fright at least" (n. pag.). Because it is a translation of *Manifestes,* it does not include "Non serviam," "La poesía," "La creación pura," and "Total." Nor does it include any introduction, preface, foreword, afterword, etc., other than the blurb on the back cover, which offers a brief biography of Huidobro and categorization of the texts.

4. Unless specified, all information regarding the publishing histories of the manifestos derives from Nicholas Hey's bibliographic guide.

5. See Navarrete Orta (141–44) for further information on the elusive chronology of the manifestos.

6. It is not clear who translated the manifestos originally published in French for Montes's *Obras completas.* Huidobro may have translated them into Spanish himself, or he may have written them in Spanish originally and then translated them, with or without help, into French. The only acknowledged translator in Hey's bibliographic guide is Angel Cruchaga Santa María, who translated "Les sept paroles du poète" into Spanish for *La Nación* in 1926.

7. My categorization differs from those found on the back cover of the 1999 *Manifestes* English translation: "*Manifestos Manifest* contains autobiographical reassessments of his writing, such as 'Manifestos Manifest' and 'Creationism,' more typically manifesto-like statements such as 'Futurism and Machinism' and 'Manifesto Mayhaps,' and comically inspired poetic prose pieces such as 'The Poetry of Madmen,' 'Tourist Advisory,' and 'The Seven Oaths of the Poet.' Through all these one cannot but hear the voice of this great poet, declaiming, exploring, proselytizing, remembering, and discovering." As I will show in my analysis, I disagree with the consideration of "Manifesto Mayhaps" as a more typical manifesto, and also the use of the "comically inspired" epithet for the three texts lumped under it.

Chapter One
Poetic Engineering: Creating the Poetic Realm in Huidobro's Early Manifestos

1. Navarrete Orta clarifies that the first printed version of this text appeared as the prologue to the first edition of *Temblor de cielo* in 1931 (144).

2. The udders also suggest Audumla, the life-giving cosmic cow of the Icelandic Eddas, which in the context of the perhaps incestuous "tabú del cielo," relates poetry through the collective unconscious to the initial mythological creation of the world.

3. An earlier manuscript of this manifesto, catalogued as MS 090 (02349) in the archives at the Fundación Vicente Huidobro, ends without the extensive imagery: "Toda poesía válida tiende al último límite de la imaginación. / Y hay además ese balanceo de mar entre dos estrellas. / Y hay que la Poesía es un desafío a la Razón porque ella es la única razón posible." The image of balance, noticeably, is already present, but Huidobro's later inclusion of the tree, throat, and tongue imagery in the final version enriches the manifesto by linking it more closely to such imagery in his poetry.

4. Gutiérrez Mouat utilizes the Fiat Lux phrase to characterize the poetic voice's usurpation of divine power in *Temblor de cielo:* "Por mi garganta la tiniebla vuelve a la luz" (108).

5. Mário read this manifesto in *L'Esprit Nouveau* and incorporated some of its ideas in *A escrava que não é Isaura*. This influence will be discussed in Chapter 4.

6. For a detailed comparison of Huidobro's chart with the traditional conceptualization of the workings of a machine, see Hahn, "Del reino mecánico" 725.

7. Perdigó has shown Saint-Pol Roux's importance to Huidobro as a precursor who embraced the poet figure as a "son of the secret gnostic doctrines, and an equivalent of God" (128).

8. Unruh stresses that in fact "the very distancing quality in modern art that Ortega called dehumanization turns the public toward, not away from, lived experience" (22).

9. Huidobro continues the manifesto text by repeating that these ideas were his before arriving in Paris. He then quotes an aphorism he had delivered in Madrid in 1921: "El Arte es una cosa y la Naturaleza otra. Yo amo mucho el Arte y mucho la Naturaleza. Y si aceptáis las representaciones que un hombre hace de la Naturaleza, ello prueba que no amáis ni la Naturaleza ni el Arte" (739). In summing up, he reaffirms that the *creacionistas* are the first to totally differentiate art and nature by presenting the integrally invented poem to the world.

10. A fertility spirit of the Pueblo people, Kokopelli is portrayed as a hunchbacked flautist.

11. Unruh compares these pejorative "charlatanes de feria" to the poets parodied by Maese López in Huidobro's 1934 satirical play *En la luna* (196, 277).

12. The idea retains a certain popular following in Magnetic Poetry®, a box of magnetized words for creating compositions on the refrigerator door.

13. See discussion on p. 2.

14. Even so the lunatics have their place; Huidobro would prefer "el libro de un loco" over anything by Edmond Rostand, yet would prefer Eluard over both (747).

Chapter Two
Orientation and Trajectory in "Aviso a los turistas" and "Manifiesto tal vez"

1. The multitude of visual perspectives here shares creationism's relationship to cubism, examined with reference to Huidobro's poems in Susana Benko's book-length study and a chapter of Camurati's analysis (79–119).

2. Harold Bloom portrays this artistic anxiety in reference to the Kabbalah, which he designates "a psychology of belatedness" (*Kabbalah* 43). The Kabbalah was an object of Huidobro's assiduous study; as noted, in *Vientos contrarios* he emphasizes his many hours of devotion to "la Astrología, a la Alquimia, a la Cábala antigua y al ocultismo en general" (794). In so doing he follows a poetic affinity of many generations. The critical interpretation that Bloom gives to the Kabbalah has little to do with the magical inspiration that Huidobro and other poets sought; nonetheless, the characteristic interpenetration or influence among several creative elements stands out in both cases.

3. In his article "Decir sin decir," Octavio Paz reproduces a photomontage from Huidobro's era that, thanks to a camera trick, shows

"Huidobro hablando consigo mismo" (13). Paz notes here (and he is not the only one to affirm it) that the great mythic double of Huidobro is Altazor (12). Without a doubt, Altazor is a double (Adam and El Cid are others) of his creator, among those who appear in Huidobro's poetic and narrative works. The identity of the double in "Aviso a los turistas" is more introspective.

4. A discrepancy, due probably to a translation error, exists between the original version in French, "Avis aux touristes" (reproduced in *Vicente Huidobro: The Careers of a Poet* by de Costa 80) and the Spanish version "Aviso a los turistas" (751 in the first volume of the Montes edition). The ordinal sequence of the passenger cars' tourist classes is inverted, from "les wagons de troisième, de seconde et même de première classe" to "los vagones de primera, de segunda e incluso de tercera clase." The French version, with its surprising emphasis on the first class, makes more sense given the pejorative cast of the vendors in the manifesto.

5. Reference is probably made to the North Pole, although the proximity of Huidobro's country of origin to Antarctica suggests a potential bipolarity. Huidobro's works are full of references to the polar regions (especially the North Pole), which became a kind of obsessive orientation in his writing.

6. Among the vanguard texts that propose a demythification of poetic theme one must include Huidobro's rival Neruda's "Sobre una poesía sin pureza," although his poetry "penetrada por el sudor y el humo, oliente a orina y a azucena, salpicada por las diversas profesiones que se ejercen dentro y fuera de la ley" (485) implies a human solidarity distant from the still oracular poetry of Huidobro. Additionally, Neruda welcomes "la melancolía, el gastado sentimentalismo" as "lo poético elemental e imprescindible" (486); in contrast, sentimentalism is too distasteful for Huidobro.

7. Huidobro's use of the term *camino* in reference to the surrealists in "Manifiesto de manifiestos" is noteworthy here: "Debemos darles crédito, aunque no aceptemos su camino y no creamos en la exactitud de su teoría" (727).

8. For Eduardo Mitre the general sense of the throat as symbol in Huidobo's works "cifra ese equilibrio de lucidez apasionada en que debe generarse el poema" (24).

9. Sucre describes the impossibility of achieving poetic creation: "El absoluto de la poesía reside en una imposibilidad que, sin embargo, se vuelve una continua posibilidad: el poema nunca está *hecho* sino perpetuamente *haciéndose* (¿y, por ello mismo, *deshaciéndose?*). La poesía está ligada a la búsqueda de lo que no se podrá encontrar" (229; original emphasis). In my opinion, each image of the poem is fixed as such while simultaneously suggesting other images (the primordial elements of all vanguard poetry). The poem "que no se podrá encontrar" illustrates the search for new images and expression.

Chapter Three
Dimensions of the Poet God: Huidobro's Final Manifestos

1. As another example of Huidobro's divine affectations, Larrea quotes personal correspondence from Huidobro in which the latter calls himself "San Vicente Huidobro" and "este gran Santo-El Angel del Apocalipsis" (273).

2. This comparison to great poets of the past contradicts Huidobro's recurring claim that the true poet has yet to be born. The inconsistency seems to be either an oversight or an exaggeration for rhetorical effect.

3. "Interrogación a Vicente Huidobro," *Tierra* 1.4 (1937): 110–14. This interview and those following are compiled in Huidobro, *Textos inéditos y dispersos,* ed. José Alberto de la Fuente A. (Santiago: Universitaria, 1993), 63.

4. Huidobro, *Textos* 61.

5. "La poesía contemporánea empieza en mí," *La Nación,* 28 May 1939, Huidobro, *Textos* 65.

6. "La Colina del Desencantado," *Zig-Zag,* 26 Sept. 1946, Huidobro, *Textos* 79–80.

Part Two
Poetry as Contraband from the Unconscious: Mário de Andrade

1. The chronology of this period in Mário's production is heavily documented; see Lopez's "Cronologia geral"; Martins (48–85); and Roig (69–76).

Chapter Four
"Prefácio Interessantíssimo" as Mock Manifesto

1. In Diléa Zanotto Manfio's edition of the *Poesias Completas,* from which I cite, the paragraphs/text sections of "Prefácio" are numbered.

2. The term *mestre* must again be stressed. The poetic predecessors, like the master Mário in the dedicatory poem, have outlived their utility in Mário's apprenticeship at this moment of rebellion.

3. Mário nurtured a special fondness for the succinct clarity of equations. He would later write feverishly in his preparatory notes for *Macunaíma,* "Amar Verbo Intranzivo + Clan do Jaboti = Macunaíma" (qtd. in Lopez, "Vontade/Variante," in her edition of Mário's *Macunaíma* xxv).

4. Lopez identifies French Symbolist poet and art theorist Gustave Kahn (1859–1936) as an important source for Mário's harmonics theory (*Mariodeandradiando* 21).

5. The embrace of a collective soul in Mário's aesthetics is complemented by his insistence that his own soul was collective, and that ideally a soul should have room for many different ones; this is the heart of "simultaneidade" as it applies to Mário's personal and racial identification. The following references from Mário's writings, cited by Pacheco (124), are found in Brito (224, 1958 ed.): "Não me pus a reler essas obras parnasianas com a alma vária, pueril e fantástica, correspondente ao meu tempo, mas fui buscar, dentre as minhas muitas almas, aquela que construi para entender a geração parnasiana" [I didn't set myself to re-reading those Parnassian works with the restless, puerile, and fantasizing soul that corresponds to my time, but rather I went in search of, among my many souls, that one that I constructed to understand the Parnassian generation] and "Só a visão estreita, a escravização ignóbil dos que se ilharam numa escola permite a ignorância infecunda dos que têm um alma só, paupérrima e impiedosa" [Only the narrow vision, the ignoble slavery of those who isolated themselves in a school permits the infertile ignorance of those who have only one soul, extremely poor and impious].

Chapter Five
At the Dock and on the Street: The Loss of Purity and Solidarity in Mário's Poetics

1. Both loci focalize what Schelling terms Mário's "grande cuidado em definir com maior precisão possível os limites que lhe eram impostos pela sua posição enquanto intelectual da elite, e em evitar o rousseauísmo ingênuo em que, segundo ele, caíra o líder do Movimento Antropofágico, Oswald de Andrade" [great care in defining with the greatest possible precision the limits imposed on him by his position as an intellectual of the elite, and in avoiding the ingenuous Rousseauism into which, according to him, had fallen the leader of the Anthropophagy Movement, Oswald de Andrade] (124).

2. In *Ramais e Caminho* Lopez clarifies that Mário's interest in folklore began some years after writing "Prefácio." Nonetheless, Eldorado is and was a widely known legend, and the essential elements are present in Mário's allegory. Lopez herself establishes precedent for Mário's knowledge of the legend when she mentions Poe's "Eldorado" as a reference for Mário's 1918 "A Divina Preguiça" [Divine Sloth]; Eldorado is "o repouso sem fim, 'ócio gigantesco,' com que nossos indígenas caracterizavam a vida eterna" [the endless repose, "gigantic leisure," with which our indigenous peoples characterized eternal life] (111).

3. The Jungian model of the collective unconscious provides a means of full recuperation of lost symbols or other forms of expression, while the Kristevan model of the Unconscious, following Freud, maintains notions of irrecoverable loss. The difference of degree traces both of Mário's dominant tensions in this poetics: the fight against an inevitable loss of expression, and the quest to unite with a collective identity in order to regain or renew shared meaning.

4. The motif of purifying water appears also in Mário's *Macunaíma* and in *Balança, Trombeta e Battleship.* Lopez makes a fruitful comparison of the motif in those two texts in her edition of the latter (67).

5. Compare Mário's use of the term in a February 1926 article from *O Jornal,* "Música Brasileira": "o desequilíbrio da nossa cultura, provocado pela importação das civilizações exóticas européias, pouco afeiçoáveis aos nossos ideais étnicos, aos nossos modos de ser" [the imbalance of our culture, provoked by the importation of exotic European civilizations, barely adaptable to our ethnic ideals, to our lifestyles] (qtd. in Lopez, *Ramais e Caminho* 226).

Chapter Six
Balancing the Equations: Mário's Struggle to Define Aesthetic Simultaneity

1. For a discussion of chronology and futurism, see Martins (77–80).

2. Huidobro's "La creación pura" is revealed, at the beginning of the second part of *Escrava,* as one of Mário's sources.

3. Grembecki further suggests that, of Mário's two biggest sources from *L'Esprit Nouveau,* Dermée has more strength in matters of lyricism or sensibility, whereas Huidobro's influence is greater in issues of critical thinking/intelligence (69–70). Huidobro's influence does not have to be proved, since Mário mentions him directly (in "Segunda Parte") along with Dermée; however, even in "Primeira Parte," Huidobro's box flow chart, as much as Dermée's equation, seems to have affected Mário's overall presentation and not just his ideas related to the poet's conscious role. Suárez and Tomlins fail to acknowledge Huidobro's role in their otherwise accurate presentation of Mário's aesthetic influences in *Escrava;* the authors mistakenly attribute to Dermée the flow chart from "La création pure" that outlines the interplay between the objective and subjective worlds, a key conceptualization that Mário did recognize as Huidobro's (47).

4. In general these comments also establish links to the harlequin figure of *Paulicéia* (the importance of this figure as a simultaneous identity, illustrated by Haberly) and the shape-shifting protagonist of *Macunaíma.*

5. California is an island of unimaginable wealth in gold and jewels in an early-sixteenth-century Spanish novel; Spanish explorers applied the name to the western peninsula of New Spain, which they thought was an island. Mário's use of the name here recalls his reference to El Dorado in "Prefácio"; the submerged treasure of the unconscious is recovered in the wealth of new images that *modernista* poetry, acknowledging the creative role of the unconscious, now presents.

6. Although they do not appear in the body of the text, the following headings for "Segunda Parte" are printed in the table of contents in the

Martins's *Obra Imatura* edition: "Enumeração dos Novos Princípios" [Enumeration of the New Principles], "Verso-livre e Rima-livre" [Free Verse and Free Rhyme], "Vitória do Dicionário" [Victory of the Dictionary], "Analogia e Paráfrase" [Analogy and Periphrasis], "Substituição da Ordem Intelectual pela Ordem Subconsciente" [Substitution of the Intellectual Order for the Unconscious Order], "Associação de Imagens" [Image Association], "Rapidez e Síntese" [Speed and Synthesis], "Poesia Pampsíquica" [Panpsychic Poetry], "Simultaneidade ou Polifonismo" [Simultaneity or Polyphonics], and "A Música da Poesia" [The Music of Poetry] (n. pag.). These headings offer a more complete breakdown of the contents than Mário's six principles, which are complemented here by other topics. It is uncertain whether Mário himself composed or even authorized these headings. In any case, Mário's organization of six principles in the body of the text (like Bloom's *The Anxiety of Influence*) may reflect an instance of Aristotle's influence; the latter's *Poetics* analyzes six elements, similarly organized into two groups.

7. These ideas resemble Jean Piaget's observations about equilibrium as a function of learning. Upon encountering a new situation or complex sensation, one is thrown off balance and must adapt (to restore balance) by evaluating and assimilating the initial situation; intelligence is therefore accommodation, or one's ability to adapt to the environment. See *The Equilibration of Cognitive Structures: The Central Problem of Intellectual Development*.

8. For example, Huidobro: "Es preciso hacer notar esta diferencia entre la verdad de la vida y la verdad del arte; una que existe antes del artista, y otra que le es posterior, que es producida por éste" (720) and "la tendencia natural del arte a separarse más y más de la realidad preexistente para buscar su propia verdad, dejando atrás todo lo superfluo y todo lo que puede impedir su realización perfecta" (719).

9. The latter ideas are summed up famously in Oswald de Andrade's English-language pun on Shakespeare: "Tupy, or not tupy that is the question."

10. The author elaborates in endnote F: "Mallarmé tinha o que chamaremos sensações por analogia. Nada de novo. Poetas de todas as épocas as tiveram. Mas Mallarmé, percebida a analogia inicial, abandonava a sensação, o lirismo, preocupando-se unicamente com a analogia criada. Contava-a e o que é pior desenvolvia-a intelectualmente obtendo assim enigmas que são joias de factura mas desprovidos muitas vezes de lirismo e sentimento" [Mallarmé had what we can call sensations by analogy. Nothing new. Poets of all eras had them. But Mallarmé, once he perceived the initial analogy, would abandon sensation, lyricism, preoccupying himself only with the created analogy. He would calculate it and, what's worse, develop it intellectually obtaining in this way enigmas that are jewels of craftsmanship but are often deprived of lyricism and sentiment] (OI 282).

11. Mário notes that this substitution process is not unanimous among his contemporaries; the degree to which Góngora, for example, can be evaluated within the framework of the "associação de imagens" is a significant point of accommodation regarding Spain's vanguard poets, who revitalized Góngora's work and in fact took their name, the Generation of 1927, from the 300th anniversary observance of his death.

12. "Desequilíbrio" is Mário's critical evaluation of an exaggerated interruption of associations in Blaise Cendrars's "Prose du Transsibérien" in endnote I (OI 286).

13. It is worth noting again that the primacy for Mário of the "comoção" as the register of artistic sensation hearkens back to his emblematic first verse of "Inspiração" in *Paulicéia:* "São Paulo! comoção de minha vida . . ." [São Paulo! commotion of my life] (PC 83).

14. Perhaps the most curious example of Mário's love for balance is his naming of the character Balança in *Balança, Trombeta e Battleship.* In her edition notes, Lopez forms a "quadro das oposições" between Balança and Trombeta (66).

15. Kiefer's *Mercúrio veste amarelo* provides a great service to scholars of Mário's work by synthesizing and analyzing some of the overriding themes of his poetics as presented in his correspondence. The organization of citations from Mário's letters—parts I and II are "Os Elementos Inconscientes da Arte Poética" and "Os Elementos Conscientes da Arte Poética," respectively—acknowledges Mário's central dichotomy. The development of many of Mário's key themes—for example, the difference between poetry and lyricism, or the importance of artisan-like technical skills—appears unchanged in his letters a decade or more after the composition of "Prefácio" and *Escrava.* Most importantly for the purposes of this study, Kiefer's citations prove that in his final years Mário's descriptions of the predominantly unconscious act of poetic creation followed by the conscious task of correcting, polishing, etc., continue to promote his poetics of equilibrium.

Conclusion
A Poetics of Equilibrium and the Avant-Garde Paradox

1. In *Mariodeandradiando,* Lopez provides a detailed background of Mário's Catholic inclinations and readings about Jesus (4–8).

2. Also in Europe one can note the title of a Russian vanguard magazine, *Vesy (The Balance)* (Poggioli 23).

Works Cited

L'Abatte, Maria de Lourdes Patrini. "Apenas um Prefácio . . ." *Múltiplo Mário: Ensaios*. Ed. Maria Ignez Novais Ayala and Eduardo de Assis Duarte. João Pessoa: UFPB; Natal: UFRN, 1997. 53–62.

Alfani, María Rosaria. "El efecto cine en *Manifestes y Ecuatorial* de V. Huidobro." *Discurso Literario* 4 (1987): 475–83.

Alves, Henrique L. *Mário de Andrade*. São Paulo: Do Escritor, 1975.

Ambrozio, Leonilda. "Mário de Andrade e Vicente Huidobro: Identidades." *Letras* [Curitiba] 31 (1982): 103–13.

Andrade, Mário de. *Aspectos da Literatura Brasileira*. São Paulo: Martins, 1972.

———. *O Baile das Quatro Artes*. São Paulo: Martins, 1975.

———. *Balança, Trombeta e Battleship, ou o Descobrimento da Alma*. Ed. Telê Porto Ancona Lopez. São Paulo: Instituto Moreira Salles–Instituto de Estudos Brasileiros, 1994.

———. *O Empalhador de Passarinho*. São Paulo: Martins, 1972.

———. *Entrevistas e Depoimentos*. Ed. Telê Porto Ancona Lopez. São Paulo: T.A. Queiroz, 1983.

———. *A Lição do Amigo. Cartas de Mário de Andrade*. Ed. Carlos Drummond de Andrade. Rio de Janeiro: José Olympio, 1982.

———. *Macunaíma*. Ed. Telê Porto Ancona Lopez. Coleção Arquivos. Florianópolis: UFSC, 1988.

———. *Obra Imatura*. São Paulo: Martins, 1972.

———. *Poesias Completas*. Ed. Diléa Zanotto Manfio. Belo Horizonte: Itatiaia, 1987.

———. *Táxi e Crônicas no Diario Nacional*. Ed. Telê Porto Ancona Lopez. São Paulo: Duas Cidades / Secretaria de Cultura, Ciência e Tecnologia, 1976.

Andrade, Oswald de. "O Meu Poeta Futurista." *Jornal do Comércio* [São Paulo] 27 May 1921.

Antelo, Raul. *Na Ilha de Marapatá. Mário de Andrade Lê os Hispano-americanos*. São Paulo: Hucitec, 1989.

Bajarlía, Juan-Jacobo. *La polémica Reverdy-Huidobro: origen del ultraísmo*. Buenos Aires: Devenir, 1964.

Bary, David. *Huidobro o la vocación poética*. Granada: Universidad de Granada, 1963.

———. *Nuevos estudios sobre Huidobro y Larrea*. Valencia: Pre-Textos, 1984.

Benko, Susana. *Vicente Huidobro y el cubismo*. Caracas: Banco Provincial, 1993.

Bloom, Harold. *The Anxiety of Influence: A Theory of Poetry*. New York: Oxford UP, 1973.

———. *Kabbalah and Criticism*. New York: Continuum, 1983.

Borges, Jorge Luis. "Al margen de la moderna lírica." *Grecia* 39 (1920): 15–17. Reproduced in Verani 249–50.

Brito, Mário da Silva. *História do Modernismo Brasileiro*. Vol. 1: *Antecedentes da Semana de Arte Moderna*. Rio de Janeiro: Civilização Brasileira, 1964.

Brotherston, Gordon. *Latin American Poetry: Origins and Presence*. Cambridge: Cambridge UP, 1975.

Brown, Joan L., and Crista Johnson. "Required Reading: The Canon in Spanish and Spanish American Literature." *Hispania* 81 (1998): 1–19.

Calinescu, Matei. *Five Faces of Modernity*. Durham: Duke UP, 1987.

Campbell, Joseph. *The Hero with a Thousand Faces*. Bollingen Series 17. Princeton: Princeton UP, 1973.

Campos, Haroldo de. *A Arte no Horizonte do Provável*. São Paulo: Perspectiva, 1969.

Camurati, Mireya. *Poesía y poética de Vicente Huidobro*. Buenos Aires: García Cambeiro, 1980.

Castillo, Jorge Luis. "La estética de la modernidad en los manifiestos de las vanguardias latinoamericanas." *La Torre* 29 (1994): 149–69.

Coelho, Nelly Novaes. *Mário de Andrade para a Jovem Geração*. Coleção Escritores de Hoje. São Paulo: Saraiva, 1970.

Concha, Jaime. *Vicente Huidobro*. Madrid: Jucar, 1980.

Le Corbusier (Charles Edouard Jeanneret). "Le sentimente déborde." *L'Esprit Nouveau* 19 (Dec. 1923): 223.

Cornejo, Paulina. "Cronología huidobriana." Pizarro, *Sobre Huidobro* 93–104.

Costa, René de. *En pos de Huidobro: siete ensayos de aproximación*. Santiago: Editorial Universitaria, 1980.

———. *Vicente Huidobro: The Careers of a Poet*. London: Oxford UP, 1984.

———, ed. *Vicente Huidobro y el creacionismo*. Madrid: Taurus, 1975.

Darío, Rubén. *Prosas profanas*. Buenos Aires, 1896.

Derrida, Jacques. *Dissemination*. Trans. Barbara Johnson. Chicago: U of Chicago P, 1981.

dos Santos, Matildes Demetrio. "A Correspondência de Mário e a 'Felicidade' no Credo Modernista." *Revista do Instituto de Estudos Brasileiros* 36 (1994): 95–107.

Earle, Peter G. "Los manifiestos de Huidobro." *Revista Iberoamericana* 45 (1979): 165–74.

Eliade, Mircea. *Images et symboles*. Paris: Gallimard, 1952.

Feres, Nites Therezinha. *Leituras em Francês de Mário de Andrade*. São Paulo: Instituto de Estudos Brasileiros, 1969.

Forster, Merlin H., and K. David Jackson. *Vanguardism in Latin American Literature: An Annotated Bibliographical Guide*. Westport, CT: Greenwood, 1990.

Fuente, José Alberto de la. "Vicente Huidobro: Compromiso social y revolución poética." *Literatura y Lingüística* 4 (1990–91): 57–72.

Gilbert, Sandra M., and Susan Gubar. *The Madwoman in the Attic: The Woman Writer and the Nineteenth-Century Literary Imagination*. New Haven: Yale UP, 1979.

Goic, Cedomil. *La poesía de Vicente Huidobro*. Santiago: Nueva Universidad, 1974.

González, Mike, and David Treece. *The Gathering of Voices: The Twentieth-Century Poetry of Latin America*. London: Verso, 1992.

Grembecki, Maria Helena. *Mário de Andrade e "L'Esprit Nouveau."* São Paulo: Instituto de Estudos Brasileiros, 1969.

Grünfeld, Mihai G. *Antología de la poesía latinoamericana de vanguardia (1916–1935)*. Madrid: Hiperión, 1995.

Gutiérrez Mouat, Ricardo. *El espacio de la crítica*. Madrid: Orígenes, 1989.

Haberly, David T. *Three Sad Races: Racial Identity and National Consciousness in Brazilian Literature*. New York: U of Cambridge, 1983.

Hahn, Oscar. "Vicente Huidobro: del reino mecánico al Apocalipsis." *Revista Iberoamericana* 168–69 (1994): 723–30.

———. "Vicente Huidobro o la voluntad inaugural." *Revista Iberoamericana* 106–07 (1979): 19–27.

Hart, Thomas R. "The Literary Criticism of Mário de Andrade." *The Disciplines of Criticism: Essays in Literary Theory, Interpretation, and History*. Ed. Peter Demetz, Thomas Greene, and Lowry Nelson, Jr. New Haven: Yale UP, 1968. 265–88.

Hegel, Georg Wilhelm Friedrich. *Phenomenology of Spirit*. Trans. A. V. Miller. London: Oxford UP, 1977.

Hemming, John. *The Search for El Dorado*. New York: Dutton, 1979.

Hey, Nicholas. "Guía bibliográfica de la obra de Vicente Huidobro." Huidobro, *Obras completas* 2: 723–65.

Huidobro, Vicente. *Manifestos Manifest*. Trans. Gilbert Alter-Gilbert. Los Angeles: Green Integer, 1999.

———. MS 090 (02349). Fundación Vicente Huidobro. Santiago, Chile.

———. *Obras completas*. Ed. Hugo Montes. Vol. 1. Santiago: Andrés Bello, 1976.

———. *Textos inéditos y dispersos*. Ed. José Alberto de la Fuente A. Santiago: Editorial Universitaria, 1993.

Jackson, K. David. "An Enormous Laugh: The Comic Spirit in Brazilian Modernist Literature." Pao and Hernández-Rodríguez 49–75.

Jung, Carl Gustav. *Alchemical Studies*. Trans. R. F. C. Hull. Princeton: Princeton UP, 1967.

———. *Mysterium Coniunctionis*. Trans. R. F. C. Hull. Princeton: Princeton UP, 1963.

Kiefer, Charles. *Mercúrio Veste Amarelo: A Poética nas Cartas de Mário de Andrade*. Porto Alegre: Mercado Aberto, 1994.

Kris, Ernst. *Psychoanalytic Explorations in Art*. Madison: International UP, 1952.

Kristeva, Julia. *Revolution in Poetic Language*. Trans. Margaret Waller. Ed. Toril Moi. New York: Columbia UP, 1984.

Lacan, Jacques, and the *école freudienne*. *Feminine Sexuality*. Ed. Juliet Mitchell and Jacqueline Rose. Trans. Jacqueline Rose. New York: Norton, 1982.

Larrea, Juan. "Vicente Huidobro en vanguardia." *Revista Ibero-americana* 45 (1979): 213–73.

Lima, Luiz Costa. *Lira e Antilira*. Rio de Janeiro: Civilização Brasileira, 1968.

Lopez, Telê Porto Ancona. "Cronologia Geral da Obra de Mário de Andrade." *Revista do Instituto de Estudos Brasileiros* 7 (1969): 139–72.

———. *Mário de Andrade: Ramais e Caminho*. São Paulo: Livraria Duas Cidades, 1972.

———. *Mariodeandradiando*. São Paulo: Hucitec, 1996.

———. "Uma Cronologia para Mário de Andrade." Andrade, *Entrevistas e Depoimentos* 5–11.

————. "Vontade/Variante." Andrade, *Macunaíma* xxv–lii.

Maples Arce, Manuel. "Actual No. 1." Xalapa: placard text, 1921. Reproduced in Verani 83–89.

Martins, Wilson. *O Modernismo (1916–1945)*. A Literatura Brasileira 6. São Paulo: Cultrix, 1969.

Mitre, Eduardo. *Huidobro, hambre de espacio y sed de cielo*. Caracas: Monte Avila, 1980.

Naud, José Santiago. "Huidobro e o Brasil." *Homenagem a Vicente Huidobro*. Brasília: Instituto Cultural Brasil Chile, 1988. 27–32.

Navarrete Orta, Luis. *Poesía y poética en Vicente Huidobro (1912–1931)*. Caracas: Fondo Editorial de Humanidades y Educación, 1988.

Neruda, Pablo. "Sobre una poesía sin pureza." Reproduced in Schwartz 485–86.

Nist, John. *The Modernist Movement in Brazil*. Austin: U of Texas P, 1967.

Oliver, Kelly. *Reading Kristeva: Unraveling the Double-Bind*. Bloomington: Indiana UP, 1993.

Ortega y Gasset, José. *La deshumanización del arte y otros ensayos de estética*. 1925. Madrid: Espasa-Calpe, 1987.

Osorio, Nelson, ed. *Manifestos, proclamas y polémicas de la vanguardia literaria hispanoamericana*. Caracas: Biblioteca Ayacucho, 1988.

Pacheco, João. *Poesia e Prosa de Mário de Andrade*. São Paulo: Martins, 1970.

Pao, María T., and Rafael Hernández-Rodríguez, eds. *¡Agítese bien! A New Look at the Hispanic Avant-Gardes*. Newark: Juan de la Cuesta, 2002.

"Parable." *Merriam-Webster's Encyclopedia of Literature*. 1995. 855–56.

Paz, Octavio. *El arco y la lira*. 3rd ed. Mexico City: Fondo de Cultura Económica, 1986.

————. "Decir sin decir." *Vuelta* 107.9 (1985): 12–13.

————. *Los hijos del limo*. Barcelona: Seix Barral, 1985.

————. *Las peras del olmo*. Barcelona: Seix Barral, 1974.

Perdigó, Luisa Marina. *The Origins of Vicente Huidobro's "Creacionismo" (1911–1916) and Its Evolution (1917–1947)*. Pittsburgh: Mellen UP, 1994.

Pestino, Joseph F. "Mário de Andrade and André Breton: Strange Bedfellows." *Tinta* 1.4 (1984): 15–20.

Piaget, Jean. *The Equilibration of Cognitive Structures: The Central Problem of Intellectual Development*. Trans. Terrance Brown and Kishore Julian Thampy. Chicago: U of Chicago P, c1985.

Pizarro, Ana. *Sobre Huidobro y las vanguardias*. Santiago: Editorial de la Universidad de Santiago de Chile, 1994.

Poggioli, Renato. *The Theory of the Avant-Garde*. Cambridge: Harvard UP, 1968.

Quiroga, José. "Vicente Huidobro: The Poetics of the Invisible Texts." *Hispania* 75.3 (1992): 516–26.

Raynal, Maurice. *Peinture moderne*. Geneva: Skira, 1953.

Recht, Paul. "Science et esthétique: Équilibre." *L'Esprit Nouveau* 4 (Jan. 1921): 483–85.

Rivero-Potter, Alicia. *Autor/Lector: Huidobro, Borges, Fuentes, Sarduy*. Latin American Literature and Culture. Detroit: Wayne State UP, 1991.

Roig, Adrien. *Modernismo e Realismo. Mário de Andrade, Manuel Bandeira e Raul Pompeia*. Rio de Janeiro: Presença, 1981.

Russell, Charles. *Poets, Prophets, and Revolutionaries: The Literary Avant-Garde from Rimbaud through Postmodernism*. New York: Oxford UP, 1985.

Rutter, Frank Paul. "Vicente Huidobro: The Emergent Years (1916–1925)." Diss. U of Virginia, 1976.

Schaya, Leo. *The Universal Meaning of the Kabbalah*. Trans. Nancy Pearson. Baltimore: Penguin, 1973.

Schelling, Vivian. *A Presença do Povo na Cultura Brasileira*. Trans. Federico Carotti. Campinas: UNICAMP, 1991.

Schopf, Federico. *Del vanguardismo a la antipoesía*. Rome: Bulzoni, 1986.

Schulman, Ivan A. "'Non serviam': Huidobro y los orígenes de la modernidad." *Revista Iberoamericana* 45 (1979): 9–17.

Schwartz, Jorge. *Las vanguardias latinoamericanas: textos programáticos y críticos*. Madrid: Cátedra, 1991.

Schwarz, Roberto. "O Psicologismo na Poética de Mário de Andrade." *A Sereia e o Desconfiado: Ensaios Críticos*. Rio de Janeiro: Civilização Brasileira, 1965. 1–11.

Suárez, José I., and Jack E. Tomlins. *Mário de Andrade: The Creative Works*. Lewisburg, PA: Bucknell UP, 2000.

Sucre, Guillermo. *La máscara, la transparencia: ensayos sobre poesía hispanoamericana*. Mexico City: Fondo de Cultura Económica, 1985.

Szabolscsi, Miklós. "La 'vanguardia' literaria y artística como fenómeno internacional." *Casa de las Américas* 74 (1972): 4–17.

Teitelboim, Volodia. *Huidobro, la marcha infinita*. Santiago: Sudamericana, 1996.

Teles, Gilberto Mendonça. *A Escrituração da Escrita. Teoria e Prática do Texto Literário*. Petrópolis: Vozes, 1996.

———. *Vanguarda Européia e Modernismo Brasileiro: Apresentação dos Principais Poemas, Manifestos, Prefácios e Conferências Vanguardistas, de 1857 até Hoje*. Petrópolis: Vozes, 1972.

Todorov, Tzvetan. "Living Together Alone." University of Virginia. 12 Oct. 1994.

———. *On Human Diversity: Nationalism, Racism, and Exoticism in French Thought*. Trans. Catherine Porter. Cambridge: Harvard UP, 1993.

Unruh, Vicky. *Latin American Vanguards: The Art of Contentious Encounters*. Berkeley: U of California P, 1994.

Verani, Hugo J. *Las vanguardias literarias en Hispanoamérica (Manifiestos, proclamas y otros escritos)*. Mexico City: Fondo de Cultura Económica, 1995.

Videla de Rivero, Gloria. *Direcciones del vanguardismo hispanoamericano. Estudios sobre poesía de vanguardia en la década del veinte: documentos*. Instituto Internacional de Literatura Iberoamericana. Pittsburgh: U of Pittsburgh, 1994.

Weightman, John. *The Concept of the Avant-Garde: Explorations in Modernism*. London: Alcove, 1973.

Wentzlaff-Eggebert, Harald. *Las literaturas hispánicas de vanguardia: orientación bibliográfica*. Bibliotheca Ibero-Americana. Frankfurt: Vervuert, 1991.

Yurkievich, Saúl. *Fundadores de la nueva poesía latinoamericana: Vallejo, Huidobro, Borges, Girondo, Neruda, Paz*. Barcelona: Barral, 1978.

Works Consulted

Amaral, Aracy. *Artes Plásticas na Semana de 22*. São Paulo: Perspectiva, 1970.

Aullón de Haro, Pedro. "La transcendencia de la poesía y el pensamiento poético de Vicente Huidobro." *Revista de Occidente* 86–87 (1988): 41–58.

Bandeira, Manuel. "Mário de Andrade e a Questão da Língua." *Itinerário de Pasárgada*. Rio de Janeiro: São José, 1957. 127–42.

Berriel, Carlos E. O., ed. *Mário de Andrade/Hoje*. São Paulo: Ensaio, 1990.

Bürger, Peter. *Theory of the Avant-Garde*. Trans. Michael Shaw. Minneapolis: U of Minnesota P, 1984.

Camara, Cristiana Yamada. *Mário na Lopes Chaves*. São Paulo: Memorial da América Latina, 1996.

Cano Ballesta, Juan. *Literatura y tecnología: las letras españolas ante la revolución industrial (1900–1933)*. Madrid: Orígenes, 1981.

Caracciolo Trejo, E. *La poesía de Vicente Huidobro y la vanguardia*. Madrid: Gredos, 1974.

Castillo Peralta, Tito, ed. "Homenaje a Vicente Huidobro (1893–1948)." *Atenea* 467 (1993): 7–159.

Castro, Moacir Werneck de. *Mário de Andrade: Exílio no Rio*. Rio de Janeiro: Rocco, 1989.

Dassin, Joan. *Política e Poesia de Mário de Andrade*. Trans. Antonio Dimas. São Paulo: Livraria Duas Cidades, 1978.

Faria, Maria Alice de Oliveira. "Mário de Andrade e os Contemporâneos no Início da Década de Vinte." *Revista de Letras* [São Paulo] 23 (1983): 11–22.

Fraser, Howard M. *In the Presence of Mystery: Modernist Fiction and the Occult*. Chapel Hill: Department of Romance Languages, U of North Carolina, 1992.

Friedrich, Hugo. *Estructura de la Lírica Moderna*. Trans. Juan Petit. Barcelona: Seix Barral, 1959.

Gilman, Richard. "The Idea of the Avant-Garde." *Partisan Review* 39.3 (1972): 382–96.

Guelfi, Maria Lúcia Fernandes. *Estética e Ideologia na Década de Vinte*. São Paulo: Instituto de Estudos Brasileiros, 1987.

Hahn, Oscar. "*Altazor*, el canon de la vanguardia y el recuerdo de otras vidas más altas." *Hispamérica* 59 (1991): 11–21.

Hahn, Oscar. "Los desfases de Vicente Huidobro." *Hispanic Poetry Review* 1.1 (1999): 3–15.

Huidobro, Vicente. *Altazor*. Ed. René de Costa. Madrid: Cátedra, 1988.

———. *Obras completas*. Ed. Braulio Arenas. Santiago: Zig-Zag, 1964.

Inojosa, Joaquim. *Os Andrades e Outros Aspectos do Modernismo*. Rio de Janeiro: Civilização Brasileira, 1975.

Keyserling, Count Hermann. *La vida íntima: ensayos proximistas*. Santiago: Zig-Zag, 1933?

Knoll, Víctor. *Paciente Arlequinada. Uma leitura da Obra Poética de Mário de Andrade*. São Paulo: Hucitec, 1983.

Lihn, Enrique. "El lugar de Huidobro." Costa, *Vicente Huidobro y el creacionismo* 363–83.

Madrid, Alberto. "Vicente Huidobro: Hacer poesía y hacer el discurso de la poesía." *Cuadernos Hispanoamericanos* 12 (1993): 9–23.

Mitre, Eduardo. "La imagen en Vicente Huidobro." *Revista Iberoamericana* 94 (1976): 79–85.

Monteiro, Adolfo Casais. *Figuras e Problemas da Literatura Brasileira Contemporânea*. São Paulo: Instituto de Estudos Brasileiros, 1972.

Montes, Hugo. "Rasgos clásicos del creacionismo." *Revista Chilena de Literatura* 22 (1983): 129–37.

Moscoso de Cordero, María Eugenia. *La metáfora en "Altazor."* Cuenca: Universidade de Cuenca, 1987.

Müller-Bergh, Klaus. Rev. of *Direcciones del vanguardismo hispanoamericano. Estudios sobre poesía de vanguardia en la década del veinte: documentos,* by Gloria Videla de Rivero. *Hispanic Review* 61 (1993): 451–54.

Navarrete Orta, Luis. *El proyecto estético-ideológico de Vicente Huidobro*. Santiago: Ateneo, 1993.

Peregrino Junior, João. *O Movimento Modernista*. Rio de Janeiro: Ministério da Educação e Cultura, 1954.

Pizarro, Ana. "América Latina: Vanguardia y modernidad periférica." *Hispamérica* 59 (1991): 23–35.

———, ed. *La literatura latinoamericana como proceso*. Buenos Aires: Association pour l'étude socio-culturelle des Arts, des Littératures de l'Amérique Latine, 1985.

———, ed. *Modernidad, Postmodernidad y Vanguardias: situando a Huidobro*. Santiago: Fundación Vicente Huidobro, 1993.

Rodríguez Monegal, Emir. *Mário de Andrade / Borges: Um Diálogo dos Anos 20.* São Paulo: Perspectiva, 1978.

Ross, Waldo. "Vicente Huidobro—Las personificaciones generan la conciencia creadora del poeta." *Problemática de la literatura hispano-americana.* Berlin: Colloquium Verlag, 1976. 35–47.

Ruzza, Maria Lidia Neghme. "Vanguarda e Modernidade na Obra Poética de Vicente Huidobro (desde *Canciones de la noche, 1913* até *Altazor, 1931*)." Diss. Universidade de São Paulo, 1991.

Schelling, Vivian. "Mário de Andrade: A Primitive Intellectual." *Bulletin of Hispanic Studies* 65.1 (1988): 73–86.

Sefamí, Jacobo. Rev. of *Las vanguardias latinoamericanas: textos programáticos y críticos,* by Jorge Schwartz. *Revista Chilena de Literatura* 40 (1992): 159–60.

Shattuck, Roger. *The Banquet Years: The Origins of the Avant-Garde in France (1885 to World War I).* Vintage Books. New York: Knopf, 1968.

Szmulewicz, Efraín. *Vicente Huidobro: Biografía emotiva.* Santiago: Universitaria, 1978.

Wood, Cecil. *The Creacionismo of Vicente Huidobro.* Frederickton: York, 1978.

Yúdice, George. *Vicente Huidobro y la motivación del lenguaje.* Buenos Aires: Galerna, 1978.

Zonana, Víctor Gustavo. *Metáfora y simbolización en "Altazor."* Mendoza: Universidade Nacional de Cuyo, 1994.

Index

About the Author

Bruce Dean Willis, University of Tulsa, focuses his research on Latin American poetry, poetics, and performance. He has published articles and chapters on poets Vicente Huidobro, Mário de Andrade, Pablo Neruda, Manuel Bandeira, and José Carlos Limeira. He edited *Essays on Hispanic and Luso-Brazilian Literature and Film in Memory of Dr. Howard M. Fraser.* Presently he is working on a study of representations of the body in early-twentieth-century Brazilian literature.